The Road Taken

The Road Taken

✦

An Anthology

edited by Cyndy Muscatel

iUniverse, Inc.

New York Bloomington Shanghai

The Road Taken
An Anthology

iUniverse books may be ordered through booksellers or by contacting:

iUniverse
1663 Liberty Drive
Bloomington, IN 47403
www.iuniverse.com
1-800-Authors (1-800-288-4677)

ISBN: 978-0-595-49916-8 (pbk)
ISBN: 978-0-595-61304-5 (ebk)

Printed in the United States of America

From her students:

Dedicated to
Cyndy Muscatel, teacher, mentor, friend.
We are forever grateful.

Contents

Poetry

Essays And Memoirs

Writing Aerobics

Dolores Carruthers

Judy Cohn

Phyllis Costello

Shirley Gibson

Gitta Gorman

Else Jacobs

Eleanor Johnson

Anita Knight

Carol Mann

Cheryl McFadden

Mary Burton Olson, M.D.

Ralph Spencer

Judy Cohn

Virginia Cummings

Shirley Gibson

Bill Hinthorn

Anita Knight

Carol Mann

Cheryl McFadden

Mary Burton Olson, M.D.

Dawn Huntley Spitz

Acknowledgements

We would like to acknowledge Seniors Making Art for funding, and Mizell Senior Center for a class facility.

Special acknowledgement goes to Gitta Gorman for her outstanding photography.

This book would not have been published without the leadership and untiring work of Carol Mann and Eric Spitz, as well as Dolores Carruthers and Kay Virgiel.

Special thanks also to Phyllis Costello, Virginia Cummings, Martin S. Goldberg, Alan Rosenbluth, Dawn Spitz, Tony Manne and John Craig.

Two roads diverged in a wood, and I,
I took the one less traveled by,
And that has made all the difference.

—*Robert Frost*

Foreword

At the beginning of the new millennium, I started teaching a Creative Writing Class at the Mizell Senior Center in Palm Springs, California. Our sponsor was Seniors Making Art, a Seattle based organization that promotes artistic creativity in senior citizens.

Open to all ages, the class population now starts at sixty and moves up. Don't let stereotypes about chronological age blind you—our group is vibrant, creative and energetic.

If you came into our class on a Wednesday morning and looked around, you'd think we were just an ordinary group. But each of us has been touched by great loves and great losses. Some are war heroes. Some are war widows. Some of us have experienced the loves of our lives and some, the bitterness of betrayal. Some have faced the greatest grief—the loss of a child. Our class is made up of lawyers, doctors, engineers, business people, volunteers, pharmacists, actors, art docents, teachers—you name it. Although our professions differ, we all share a creative spirit, a desire to express ourselves through the written word, and an ability to look closely at the world. Oh, and did I mention, we have the guts and tenacity to keep on learning? Many are now contest winners and published authors.

I originally thought the class would be an introductory one, which would spur people to write on their own. Now it would be more proper to call our two hours a Masters Workshop. We warm up each Wednesday morning with what we call Writing Aerobics. In the last section of the book, you can find samples of these stream of consciousness, muse inspired works that exercise our writing muscles. I give the students a phrase and they take off for about 10 minutes of non-stop writing. It's always a kick to see how people diverge from the original road onto one of their own.

Each week we study a different aspect of the craft of fiction or creative non-fiction writing. We've focused on the importance of plot and character in order to develop a good story that will engage the reader. We know our main protagonist must have a problem, a CONFLICT, that has high stakes attached to it so the reader will care. In today's fast moving world, readers want to be at the scene. As authors, we don't tell what's happening in a story—we've learned to use a cinematic approach. We *show* what's happening to our characters, real or fictional, through dialogue and action. In class, we study psychology and create charts to build multi-dimensional characters. We practice using the five senses to create depth in our stories.

We strive to be professional and current. We've become adept computer users. We keep up with the changing world of publishing as well as the new Internet resource sites. We've learned fragments can be effective and that it is now perfectly correct to end a sentence with a preposition. We also learned 'hunk' is out and 'hottie' is in. Which reminds me, there is one thing that hasn't changed. Sex is always in.

And we write, write, write. We write from the heart and let the words flow. Plenty of time after to polish our work. We finish the first draft and then change to editors. We've learned to eliminate the chaff—to write clear sentences that develop characterization and promote story.

Through this process, each of the 26 writers has developed his or her own authentic style—their unique voice. The learning curve in publishing this book was steep, but we not only survived, we thrived. On the following pages, you will see the results of our endeavors.—*Cyndy Muscatel*

Short Stories

A Midnight Visitor

Dolores Carruthers

Announcing its presence by whirling through the countryside, the midnight visitor howled against the walls of the house. Startled by its unholy roar, I woke wide eyed, listening. The nearest railroad was 20 miles away so I knew it couldn't be the devil's train coming to visit. I lay there uncertain if I should wake my sleeping husband or greet the visitor alone.

The latter won and I eased out of bed, wrapped myself in hastily garbed courage, and walked to the bedroom windows. The trees lining the backyard looked like black dancing sticks against the moonlit sky. Looking down on the deck, I could see our new, summer screen house still standing but badly injured, its metal frame twisted into contorted shapes. The hurricane, too impatient to wait for its fast moving winds to rip off its canvas roof, had collapsed it with a powerful gust.

As I listened to the howling wind, looking at the results of its destructive nature, I stood silent. If I didn't move, perhaps, I could escape its awareness. I scanned the darkened neighborhood around us. Nothing stirred, not a flicker of light or life. Was I the only one who had heard the roaring, who was witnessing its power?

Trembling from facing an aroused nature, I felt like a lonely bystander at the scene of a crime not yet visited by rescuers. Finally I turned, and went back to bed. What else could I do when the midnight visitor had woken only me? I posed no threat to its ravaging journey.

Aced

Judy Cohn

The morning dew had not yet evaporated as Ken maneuvered the SUV along the rutted, gravelly path.

"Take it easy, Ken, I'm going to lose my breakfast on this bitch of a road."

"Hold on, Mike, we'll be there in a minute."

Ken almost hit the sign pointing to the golf club. He turned right and pulled into a large patch of broken macadam that masqueraded for a parking lot. He and his two buddies, Dan and Mike, emerged from the car a bit shaken, but still looking like models for a *Golf Digest* fashion ad. They kicked away beer cans along the weedy path as they approached a large building.

"Holy shit. What the hell kind of golf course is this? Do they call this broken down barn a clubhouse?"

Dan gave his friend a surprised look. "Oh come on, Mike, it's probably the maintenance shack."

"Mike might be right, Dan. I don't see any other buildings around." Ken was always the practical one. "Let's see if anyone's inside."

They pushed open the splintered wooden door and were greeted by two men dressed in khaki pants and green jackets.

"Good morning y'all. I'm Phil, the manager, and Ted here is my assistant. You must be the Maloney threesome. Welcome to Emerald Green Golf Club."

"Thanks. I'm Ken Maloney and these are my two friends, Mike Bartlett and Dan Parks. This is the last day of a wonderful golfing trip. We've played some beautiful courses in Alabama and now we're here."

Ken shot Mike a glance, hoping he wouldn't open his mouth. Their plane didn't leave till midnight and it was too nice a day not to play golf, even on a lousy course. They paid for their round, and asked where they would find the carts.

They were ready to go when Ted called to them. "Are you guys betting men?"

"What do you mean?" Ken asked.

"Well, we all have a little deal here. It's called the hole in one pot. If you each put in $50.00 and you get a hole in one, you win the pot. It's up to $5,000 now. Interested?"

"Mike, Dan, what do you say? I'm game."

"I'm in." Mike put a $50.00 bill on the counter.

"Me, too." Dan counted out two 20's and a 10.

"Great." Ted smiled as he collected the money. "Just one other thing."

Enough of this, Ken thought. Let's get to the tee.

"Since there's only three of you, we have a fellow who would like to make it a foursome."

"Is he a good golfer?"

"Absolutely. He's got a very low handicap. You'll like him. He's been playing here for a few days so he can help you around the course."

Ian was waiting for them when they got to the tee. The men shook hands. Ken was the first to comment on his accent.

"Are you from England, Ian?"

"No, New Zealand."

"First trip?"

"I was here soon after 9/11. I was the number one finalist in an essay contest about that tragic day and I won the trip."

"So you're a writer."

"Only as a hobby. I'm a greensman at a country club near Auckland. It's a great job except when I get hit by golf balls."

"Wow man, does that happen often?" Mike had hit his drive and now joined the conversation.

"I've been hit a few times, but it's okay. I've collected a lot of money," Ian said.

They moved quickly through the front nine. Ian was helpful by showing them the lay of the fairways, but Ken found it annoying when he would tell them it was essential to hit a bump and run shot, or to use a lob wedge over the bunker. They were good golfers. They didn't need his advice about that. Ian seemed to like the word essential and used it often. When they finished the ninth hole, Mike told him it was essential that they make a pit stop before moving on.

The twelfth hole was a long par three. Ken landed just short of the green, Ian was way to the right, Dan's ball landed on the green, but far from the cup. They had all used five irons. Mike decided to use his new hybrid club, which was equivalent to a four iron. The ball landed on the front of the green, and rolled,

rolled, rolled into the cup. They all jumped up and down, yelling congratulations and high fiving Mike.

"That certainly was a sparkler."

"A what, Ian?" Mike looked at him quizzically.

"That's what my pals and I back home call a hole in one."

"Well here we call it a freakin' Ace. I win that pot they have there in the clubhouse plus all the perks you get for acing the hole. And you, my faithful buds, will share in the purse. Maybe I'll even cut you in a little bit, Ian."

The thirteenth tee was littered with debris. Dan picked up two paper plates and some Styrofoam cups. It was obvious that the rabbits, geese, and ducks were dining well on the garbage. Ken looked down to take his practice swing.

"Geeze, guys, we need a pooper scooper here. Oops, I'm sorry Mike. You're up first. How could I forget."

"It's okay, Ken, go ahead."

Ken hit, then Dan.

When Mike got up to the tee he realized Ian was missing. "Hey, you guys, our new best friend isn't here. Must be in the woods taking a pee."

He took his stance, swung the club, and sliced the ball right. They heard a clunk and a loud yowl.

"Oh my God, that wasn't a tree you hit, Mike, that was Ian."

They rushed over and found Ian slumped next to a large tree. He was totally out of it. Ken, a fitness expert, felt his pulse and declared that he was okay, just winded. Not wanting to move him, they decided to leave him there while they finished their round. They knew a complete eighteen holes had to be played in order to get credit for the hole in one. They didn't want to deny Mike his victory and that $5,000 pot was waiting to be claimed.

Ken wrote a note telling Ian they would be back. He rummaged through his bag, found a safety pin, attached the note to Ian's shirt, and off they went. They played the rest of the game with little conversation. Mike text-messaged his wife about the hole in one, but didn't mention his other ace. Every so often he'd ask the others if they thought Ian would be okay. Not to worry, they told him. He'd be fine.

As they finished the eighteenth hole, they marveled at the fact that they were the only ones on the course that entire morning. They drove back to thirteen with Mike leading the way. He jumped out of his cart before the others reached the spot under the tree where they'd left Ian.

"What the hell is going on? The guy isn't here," he yelled to his friends. "He must have come to and walked back in. Guess he didn't trust us to come back for him. At least he's okay. That guy said he made money every time he was hit. I'm going in to collect, not pay out."

The three decided they wouldn't tell Phil and Ted about the incident with Ian. If they were asked, they'd say he left early to go-back to his hotel. They put their clubs into the SUV, and returned the carts, making sure they took the scorecard. The two green jackets were at a table drinking beer when they got back to the clubhouse.

Mike waved the scorecard as he approached Phil and Ted.

"I aced the twelfth hole. We're here to collect our five thou."

"Great." Phil took the card from Mike and looked it over. "Looks like you did it. Where are all the signatures? I only see two."

"Yeah. I signed and Dan attested. That's all I need."

"Not here. You were playing in a foursome. We need the other player's signature."

"What are you nuts? That's not the USGA rule."

"Maybe not, but it's our rule. Ken here can sign and you just need to get Ian. Otherwise you don't get your money. Rules are rules."

"He left early. We don't know where he is." Mike reached out and was ready to grab Phil by the collar when Ken and Dan pulled him back.

"Whoa y'all. We just might have to get the sheriff here," Phil said.

Ken and Dan had moved to a corner. Mike joined them, lowering his voice so Phil and Ted couldn't hear. "What should we do?"

Ken knew those two jerks wouldn't hesitate to call the sheriff. "We should high tail it out of here. If they find out about Ian we'll really be in trouble."

"What about our 50 bucks?" Dan asked.

"Forget it. Let's just leave as fast as we can."

They ran to the parking lot, jumped into the car, and pulled away. They were discussing what had become of their new pal when Dan, sitting in the back seat heard some noise. He turned to look out the window.

"I don't believe it. Look at the front of that shithole clubhouse."

Ken looked in his rearview mirror and Mike turned around to see Phil and Ted standing by the door with Ian next to them. All three were laughing as they waved goodbye.

Mike had all he could do to control himself. "I'll bet those two old farts were bullshitting us all the time," he said.

"And how about that jerk, Ian. He was obviously in on it," Dan said. "What do you think, Ken?"

"We'll just never know guys, we'll just never know."

An Artist's Work

Eric H. Spitz

The wind howled. Raging water rushed over levees and poured into the streets and lawns of New Orleans. Only 200 yards from the southeast levee, the Rouge Nursing Home took on water rapidly. The bus driver yelled at the patients gathering their possessions to hurry.

"Thelma, come on, come on." An elderly lady pounded on Thelma's door. It was locked.

Thelma sat at her easel and continued painting what she could see outside her window. Her right hand drooped uselessly on her lap. The water was now gushing across the boulevard that fronted the home and had flooded the basement. Her shoes were soaked and she trembled from the cold that numbed her legs.

She rose painfully and limped to her spaniel who whimpered at her feet. With a great effort, she pushed open her window with her good arm and lifted the dog outside.

"Take care of him, please," Thelma yelled to the bus driver who was helping patients to board. He picked up the dog, and Thelma struggled to close the window.

She sat down at her easel again and picked up her brush.

◆   ◆   ◆

Thelma Watts had been a successful artist, well-known in Louisiana for her landscapes and portraits of fishermen plying their trade in open waters. Never married, she was attractive in a masculine way—hair cut short, trim figure, a strong profile, firm chin and dominant blue eyes. She always wore slacks and a sweater, which hid her femininity and scared off potential suitors.

After graduating from LSU where she majored in art, she took a small apartment near the bayou. She spent the day sketching and painting the fishermen. She sold every painting although she dreaded parting with even one. Men did not interest her, only her work.

Her reputation as a creative, imaginative artist spread throughout the state, but she ignored most calls from agents and galleries that wanted to promote her works. Her only companion was a Labrador Retriever who followed her to the docks and market and sat patiently by her side the many hours she worked. After fifteen years, the dog died. Thelma took the loss stoically and hung his portrait conspicuously near her easel. She soon found another dog. A fisherman had died—his Springer Spaniel homeless.

The years passed. Thelma continued painting. Her only contact with humanity was her weekly trips to the market, the dog always at her side.

In her eighties, she began to have trouble negotiating the steps that led down to the docks, even with the cane she was forced to use. Her neighbors saw her fall a few times, approached her, and tried to talk her into moving into a care facility. She refused.

One morning, a neighbor found her sprawled on the pathway, face down, her dog standing over her whining. They called 911. She was taken to the hospital.

"You can't live alone anymore," she was told. "You must go to a facility that can help you take care of yourself." She had suffered a stroke, which paralyzed her right side.

"I'll never go to a nursing home," she said calmly.

"You can't use your arm, Thelma. I'm afraid your painting days are over."

"I'll use the left one."

"If you refuse, we'll have to get a court order."

Forced to acquiesce, she moved to the Rouge Nursing Home.

◆　　　◆　　　◆

The cold water was covering her thighs as she painted the last of the hurricane's devastations—the dismembered docks, the throngs of people running away from the onrushing water, dogs and cats trying to swim somewhere.

Her easel began to float away from her. She grabbed her painting with her good hand, and limped over to the sofa. With a great effort, she climbed onto it and lifted her work to the top of her bookcase.

Some days later, she was found drowned in her room. Her last painting depicting the storm was sold for twenty thousand dollars. In her will, she left the proceeds to the local animal shelter.

Anything You Can Do

Judy Cohn

Jane McCann was happy that she'd decided to leave for the airport an hour earlier than planned. Traffic was light, and they'd arrived in plenty of time to eat before boarding the plane.

"What do you want for breakfast, Blueberry?"

"Scrambled eggs, Mama, with lots of bacon. I need energy for our plane trip."

Jane laughed. "You're not flying the plane, Blueberry."

"I know, Mama, but I need energy to see everything."

Blueberry and her mother finished eating, walked to the gate, and waited for section six to be announced. "I'm going to call Dad on my cell phone. I want to say goodbye one more time."

"Okay, but let's not be too long."

Once on the plane, with seat belts firmly in place, Blueberry took out her book and began to read. She moved her mouth silently as her fingers whisked through the pages. Before long she turned to her mother.

"I just finished, *Charlotte's Web.*"

"That's the fourth time you've read it."

"I know. Once each year since I was seven, and always before we visit Grandma and Grandpa. It's my favorite story. I can just picture Fern and Wilbur, and I love Charlotte. She's so kind. Maybe one of her children lives in Grandma and Grandpa's barn."

Jane leaned over and gave her daughter a hug. "Why don't you look out the window, Blueberry? We're flying above the clouds." She reached into her bag, pulled out some cotton balls and handed them to her daughter.

Blueberry grasped the balls and twirled them in her hands.

"The clouds look like puffs of cotton. They look like a bed of puffs all over the sky," Jane said. "It's so beautiful."

Two flight attendants were pushing the beverage cart down the aisle. One of them stopped at Row 10 and looked over at the young girl sitting in the window seat.

"Hello, young lady. Can I get you anything?"

"I'll have a coke, please."

The flight attendant poured the soda, and handed the cup and the can to Blueberry.

"Thank you so much," Blueberry said.

"You're welcome. You are so cute and very polite. What's your name?"

"Elizabeth McCann, but everybody calls me Blueberry."

"Blueberry? How did you get that name?"

"When I was little I liked to eat blueberries. I would stuff so many into my mouth that they'd squish all over and the juice would dribble down my chin. My teeth and tongue turned bright blue. Mama said I ate so many that I'd turn into a blueberry. So that's how I got my name."

"What are you going to do in Colorado?"

"We're going to see my Grandma and Grandpa. They live on a ranch with horses and cows. Grandma calls it a mini ranch, but it sure seems big to me. It takes me a long time to run around it."

"Sounds like you'll have a great time. See you later, Blueberry."

Susie and Bob Blake, Blueberry's grandparents, were at the arrival gate. After lots of hugs and kisses, they all climbed into the truck for the half hour trip to Ridgway, chattering all the way.

They arrived at the ranch, unloaded the car, and carried the suitcases into the house. They hadn't been there a minute when the phone rang. It was the Blakes' friend, Evelyn, who lived on a neighboring ranch. One of her horses was missing and she was frantic. Bob offered to go over there and see what he could do.

After he left and they were unpacked, Blueberry was ready to explore.

"I want to go outside and walk around the ranch, Grandma."

"Are you sure you can manage that?"

"Of course. I can do anything, can't I, Mama?"

"Okay, but make sure you take your phone. We wouldn't want you getting lost."

"I won't. I know my way around here. I'll be fine."

Once out the door, Blueberry began the long walk along the dirt path that led to the front gate. Her right arm swung beside her while her left hand clutched the split rail fence that lined the path. Reaching the gate, she was momentarily startled to hear the clip clop of a horse's hooves along the paved road.

I shouldn't be surprised. This is horse country. Then she heard the crack of a whip and a man's voice yelling, "Get a move on you stupid animal."

The clip clop became faster, but not for long. She heard the horse whinny, then came a loud scream, and a plop as the rider fell to the ground. The horse took off. From the sound of his hooves, Blueberry knew he was going in the opposite direction. The man lay on the ground, moaning in pain.

Blueberry pulled her cell phone from her pocket, pressed it four times for the Blake's number. "Grandma, you and Mama come out to the road real quick! I found the man who stole Evelyn's horse. I think he's hurt really bad," she said.

Susie and Jane arrived at the gate in the pick up truck. Jane grabbed her daughter and hugged her tight, while Susie called 911. Then Jane stepped back and looked directly at her eleven-year-old.

"Blueberry, how could you tell what happened?"

"You mean because I'm blind, Mama? I may not be able to see, but I sure can hear."

Jane laughed and hugged Blueberry again. "Elizabeth Blueberry McCann you're absolutely right. You certainly can do anything."

Baggage

Carol Mann

Dull green paint clung to the walls of the waiting room like swamp moss. Somewhere in the background, an air conditioner labored, unable to handle the humid summer heat. Its sound grated like a jackhammer. I closed my eyes, wishing the night had never happened. Everything seemed unreal.

I kept asking myself—why? What possibly could be God's scheme? Why did He take my husband in a senseless car accident? In my wildest nightmare, I never saw myself a widow at twenty-two.

Memories collided into each other. Falling in love. High school graduation. Marrying young. The cramped apartment. Our first fight. A new puppy.

Settling down was hard, but we did it. Andy found a job with the water department. I finished cosmetology school. We almost had enough money for a down payment on a small condo. Now, suddenly, I had nothing.

I rubbed my eyes, aware my throat scratched like a dry pen on paper.

The waiting room door opened. Deanne Walker carried two steaming cups of coffee from the vending machine in the hall.

"All the soft drinks were gone." She sat beside me and held out a cup. "Lila, honey, we've been down here almost forty-five minutes. What an awful night. My Brad is still in surgery." Her voice softened, almost a whisper. "And you have to go through this."

"Thank you." Coffee. I needed a jolt, something to replace the numbness. I brushed at my cheeks, wondering if the tears would every stop.

We sat in silence, each taking a sip, each looking at the brown vinyl floor or the windows with tired Venetian blinds. Two dusty fluorescent fixtures hung from the ceiling, the lighting dim and washed out like I felt. Deanne insisted I have something.

I felt my anger jutting into the space between us. Did she feel it? I resented her, my best friend. Her good luck, my bad. I tried to push it aside.

Was it God? Was it a lottery? Was it fate? On a clear summer evening after a baseball game, Andy and Brad swerved off the road at high speed, through a fence, and into a tree. To be taken so young wasn't fair.

I'd never again feel Andy's skin against mine or watch him pat on after-shave or wash his work clothes. I'd never smell his special hamburgers cooking on our grill, a favorite thing to do on a Sunday afternoon.

Dark, bitter thoughts pushed into my sadness. Like the coffee, they were difficult to swallow.

I remembered the moment my world changed. The call from the Sheriff's Department came at 2:30 AM, jarring my fitful sleep. Andy should have been home from the game around midnight. Would I ever forget that unexpected voice?

"Mrs. Connery?"

A woman. Why wasn't it Andy with some explanation? Why was I hearing a woman's voice? "This is the Inyo County Sheriff's Office. We regret to inform you that your husband has been in an accident. He is at County Hospital."

"What!" Panic had slid over me like cold, black silk. "Is he—?"

"The officers were told by the paramedics it's serious. Shall we send a car?"

"No—no. I can get there myself."

I hung up, feeling light-headed. Every piece of clothing I touched tangled in my fingers. Jeans, T-shirt, sandals, ponytail in a thick blue elastic band. As I rushed to dress, the phone rang again. Nerves pounded in the back of my head. It was Deanne.

"Did they call you?" She plunged on. "Brad and Andy have been rushed to County Hospital. We can go together. I'll pick you up in twenty minutes."

When we arrived at the hospital, I learned the worst from the trauma room doctor. Andy died on the operating table. Brad, still in surgery, was expected to live, in serious but stable condition. Paperwork. Insurance. After, an intern brought us to the basement waiting room.

I wanted to scream—why was it my husband? I dabbed at my eyes with a damp handkerchief.

"I don't know what I'm going to do."

Deanne studied her coarse, reddened hands—waitress's hands. When she looked at me, I could see the kindness in her eyes, but it grated, sandpaper against my hurt.

"You're strong, Lila. It won't be easy, but you'll push on. I know you. You've done it before." Pale lipstick surrounded her half-smile. "Remember when you broke your ankle two days before the senior prom? You made it, crutches and all. Even did our hair."

I felt her gentle touch on my wrist. I slapped it away. "Easy for you. Your husband is in surgery. Mine is on a slab. But you're damned right. I can push on, and I know it."

The surprise on Deanne's face flashed away. "Brad could have died, too. I'm your best friend. What should I feel? Anger? Pity? I feel sad for you. I don't know why it was your husband and not mine. I don't know why it had to be either one of them!"

She whirled around and walked over by a window.

I couldn't stop myself. "Brad was the one driving, the one who likes his hopped up Mustang, the one who likes his beer."

"That was mean, Lila."

"Well, mean it is. Just ask me. I have a dead husband to prove it."

The silence hung between us, laden with unspoken words, unhealthy like the air of the closed room.

"I didn't deserve that," she muttered.

Before I could dump more resentment, a man in green scrubs entered. "Mrs. Connery?" He looked at Deanne and then at me, his eyebrows raised, questioning.

I nodded. "I'm Mrs. Connery."

"I'm Dr. Stanton. We're ready."

"Do you want me to go with you?" Deanne waited.

"No." I walked to the door.

Dr. Stanton took my arm. Our footsteps echoed in the drab hall. By a heavy door, he paused, his hand on the gray metal knob. I read a small tarnished plaque. Hospital Morgue.

Inside, I stood by the gurney. The outline of Andy's body beneath a white sheet made my knees want to buckle. I'd never told him the words he wanted to hear—words I couldn't say—something I couldn't discuss. Tell him now, I thought, and hope he hears.

I glanced at Dr. Stanton. I'll ask him to leave for a moment so he won't think I'm crazy, talking to a dead man. Then I can say it. *Andy—I forgive you.*

"There's no easy way to do this, Mrs. Connery. Are you ready?"

The doctor's voice prodded me. I took a deep breath. He lifted the cloth.

"Oh, God." My hand went to my mouth. My voice sounded like it would strangle me, like it was someone else's.

The doctor folded his hands. He looked at the floor.

My skin prickled. "That's not my husband."

"I beg your pardon?" Dr. Stanton read the toe tag. "It says——."

"That's not Andy," I whispered.

Dr. Stanton looked nonplussed. "Are you s——?"

"Of course, I'm sure. It's Brad Walker. Brad and Andy were in the car together."

He stepped to a wall phone by the door and punched a number. Heavy weight dropped from my shoulders. I lifted my head. We had a second chance.

The doctor attempted to muffle his voice. "The accident victims brought in this morning. The deceased is Brad Walker. Who the hell is handling the paperwork up there?"

I hugged myself, to keep the good news close. I'd be a better wife, a better lover, a better friend. My bargains with God spilled like diamonds from a jeweler's pouch.

The doctor nodded and hung up. "Your husband should be out of surgery soon."

"Thank you——." Part of me wanted to fly. Part of me wanted to collapse. "How is he?"

"You'll have to talk to the surgeon. It shouldn't be too much longer."

I said a prayer.

I thought of Deanne, waiting alone. Dr. Stanton took my elbow, ushering me out of the room, away from the smell of chemicals and death.

"Is that Mrs. Walker with you?"

"Yes."

He shook his head. "I'm sorry this happened, Mrs. Connery."

"Please let me tell her about Brad," I said.

"I'll wait in the hall." He opened the door to the waiting room.

Deanne stood. She stepped toward me, but stopped, hesitant. I put my hands out. We cradled each other in a hug.

"Oh, Lila, honey."

"Let's sit down."

We perched on the uncomfortable chairs. I didn't know where to look.

Deanne cocked her head. "What's the matter?"

"The man in the morgue——."

"Yes. Go on."

"It isn't Andy."

"I don't understand."

"Andy isn't dead."

"What do you mean?"

"They made a mistake."

"Well, who is it? Do they know?"

"Deanne, it's Brad."

She stiffened. "Well, there's just no end to your spite, is there? What kind of bad joke is this?"

"Someone made a mistake in the paperwork. Andy is in surgery. Brad is—." I stopped.

Deanne stared at me. I nodded. I watched her body fold into itself. She rocked forward and back, sobbing.

I wrapped my arms around her. "I'm so sorry, so, so, sorry."

What had I been thinking? I had no idea of Andy's condition. Deanne was a widow. We needed our friendship. There wasn't room for baggage, not now.

"Can you forgive my stupid words? I wish I could take them back."

"It's all right, Lila."

"Dr. Stanton is in the hall. Are you ready? Do you want to wait a few minutes?"

Deanne bit her lip. She dug in her purse and pulled out a tissue. "I'm ready. Please come with me."

I helped her stand. She seemed so frail.

On our way to the door, Deanne paused. "Will you call the bowling alley? Tell them what happened?"

"Please don't worry. I'll take care of it."

"Lila, I can't lose my job now. Ruthie Hanson can cover for me." Deanne walked into the hall.

Ruthie Hanson. The name stopped me cold.

Oh, Deanne. It was Ruthie who told me about your one-nighter last winter—with Andy—after too many bowling alley beers.

I never told you I knew.

Bonnie Madison

Cheryl French

It was two-thirty in the morning on a dreary Sunday morning. Bonnie Madison closed the piano keyboard and sat transfixed by the yellow overhead lights that blinded her tonight from everything but herself.

The San Francisco Jazz Lounge was silent now, except for the sound of Harry Jamison sweeping the well-worn floors and the rattling of cable cars moving across the tracks.

"Aren't you ready to go home yet?" Harry called from across the room.

"In a minute. Just need to finish a few things."

Finish a few things, she thought to herself. Like how I got to be seventy-years-old and still don't know where I'm headed. Like how the years passed by so quickly, without me noticing. The past? What happened to the past? What happened to that Bonnie Madison, the girl that couldn't miss? That blue-eyed, angel faced, dream of a girl, with the glorious voice. Bonnie sat back and remembered.

Jack Kerouac had met me once at a party at the Artist's Hut in Hollywood. Or, should I say, I met him. We were introduced and I thought he was the coolest and hippist man I had ever seen. He told me I was hot and that my jazzy rendition of "I'm A Fool To Want You" was the best he had ever heard this side of Billie Holiday. Those were the days. The 50's. Man, what a time! Black jazz joints alive with sultry sounds and oh, so cool musicians jamming and grooving 'til all hours of the night. Stand-up headliners, like Mort Saul and Lenny Bruce, entertainers with names like Miles Davis, Duke Ellington, Eartha Kitt, Mel Torme. I played Michael's Pub in New York with Mel a few times, what a dream. His voice was incredible. Oh, I sang with the best. George Shearing accompanying me on the piano; Sarah Vaughn and I harmonizing together until late at night in that cozy little club in the Village.

What was that saying my old friend Jack Keroac liked to quote? Oh, yeah, he always said, "You can't go home again". Anyway, that's what Thomas Wolfe said, so I guess it's probably true. Home. Where life was simpler. I wanted to go home so many times.

My name was Bonnie Baker back in 1948. Nice and simple. The two story farm house seemed old, even then. It sat in the middle of an Iowa cornfield, a quiet solitary place, hidden by oak trees and soothed by gentle breezes on warm summer nights. I always wished I could grow tall like those cornstalks, but alas, God saw to it that I would only reach five-feet-one. I had wanted to be a blonde, like those Hollywood movie stars, but again, nature saw to crown me a brunette. I dreamed of Hollywood and the Bright Lights of New York. And like so many girls, I "wanted to make it there".

I got my chance when I saw an ad in the *Iowaian*—a newspaper for open auditions for a USO Show. They were looking for a wholesome type girl with a jazzy voice, and I thought I might fit the bill. No harm in trying.

Mom and Dad begged me not to go.

"Just marry a nice boy from around here," Mom said. "He'll take good care of you and you won't have to worry about taking care of yourself."

But neither Mom or Dad could stop me. No one could have stopped me. I went off to Sioux City with my sheet music and a dream. The dream came true, or so I thought, as I won that contest and many more like it. I moved to New York and hung out in the Village. The town was really swinging with Clubs like Eddie Carroll's Swinging Affair. I played them all, with the best of the jazz musicians of the day. We smoked dope and drank and did all the crazy things we were supposed to do. But I got tired. Boy, did I get tired of it all. And lonely. Everybody was really lonely. But nobody wanted you to show it. Very uncool to be lonely. But I knew. And I tried to keep going and going and going.

I finally couldn't keep up anymore. My voice started to go. And I had to go. Go someplace peaceful and serene. No more all night jam sessions. No more trying to get just one more gig. No more burning the midnight oil with the best of the best. I was Bonnie Madison. The girl with the steamy, sultry voice. I could keep up with the best of them, Sarah, Billie and the rest. But I was tired, man I was tired. Ready to give up…. or was I?

Joe Higgins met me one night in L.A.. There was something special about him that I had never seen before in a man. Something in his eyes. A kindness and sweetness that I had forgotten existed. The world I had lived in the past twenty years had been filled with a different kind of man. Not a Joe Higgins kind of man. No, sir. So, I took a chance. Gave him a chance.

He didn't disappoint me. My only disappointment was with myself. But I had achieved what I had wanted, hadn't I? I was given the chance to grab the spotlight and I had taken it. Now it was over. Time passes. We hardly notice it until we look back.

"Bonnie, your husband's here." Harry's voice woke her from her faded dream.
"Be right there."
Bonnie Madison packed up her sheet music, grabbed her coat off the coat rack and raced out to the familiar white Chevrolet parked at the curb. She eyed the handsome, gray-haired man behind the wheel. As she climbed in beside him he put his arms around her, kissed her tenderly and said in a low and gentle voice, "Let's go home, baby."

Confessions of the Hot Flash Queen

Cyndy Muscatel

So I woke up drenched in sweat, with this pounding headache and a mouth as dry as a used postage stamp. I stumbled to the bathroom for an Extra Strength Tylenol and got a flash of ancient déjà vu. I'd felt like this after drinking bourbon in the back seat of my date's car thirty years ago. But this was no college hangover. No, honey, ready or not, this was Head-On-Menopause.

At the sink, I soaked a washcloth with cold water. I studied my face in the mirror as I wiped it. "Still freckles on white after all these years," I said. "Not too many lines—mostly around the eyes." Smile lines, that's what they were. The one vertical line between my eyebrows had my ex-husband's name written all over it.

Something liquid hit my head. I looked up and took a drop in the eye. Water. As in rain. It was raining again. My roof couldn't take it, and neither could I.

I charged down the hall to my guest room. When I pushed open the door, my worst fears were not denied. The ceiling was weeping right above the crib where my grandson slept on Tuesdays and Thursdays. I shook my fist at the ceiling, at the rain, at my ex-husband Dan, and for good measure, the banker who was hassling me about the loan for a new roof. It might have been immature, but it made me feel better. It was either anger or tears, and I'd learned the hard way that crying got you nowhere.

Back in bed, it took me a while to fall asleep. I had an appointment with the loan officer in the afternoon after work. Pierson had been putting me off for no good reason. For me, it was now a matter of triage. I needed that roof, and I needed it now.

Naturally, I woke up late. I threw on a sweatshirt, a pair of jeans, and some Keds. In the kitchen, I poured myself a bowl of organic oatmeal clusters. I ate the cereal without milk. My lactose intolerance level was on high alert. I was even off my three-a-day cappuccino habit. Milk, with or without a moustache, was killing my gut. Maybe that was menopause, too?

21

On the way to work, I had a serious hot flash. Heat flooded my neck and shot upwards. I didn't know I had so many sweat glands on my face. Although it was raining, I rolled down the car window. This was Seattle, so rain reigns. But it was June—enough already!

I decided to stop at Expresso-Mio. One cappuccino wasn't going to do me in. The only problem was that five other brainiacs were ahead of me in the drive-thru. By the time I got my drink, it was me foaming, forget the milk.

I walked into Shear Ecstasy at 9:15. I worked there four days a week doing people's hair. I loved it. Just the smells of shampoos and permanent solution made me happy.

"Hey, Connie, you're barely late," the receptionist called as I passed her desk.

"Yeah, yeah," I said.

I nodded at Susie, my first client of the day. "Be right with you."

"Don't worry. I have plenty of time. Allison's in pre-school all morning."

Susie talked in a voice that was a cross between a Stepford Wife and Marilyn Monroe singing, "Happy Birthday, Mr. President". She was one of those forty-somethings who'd decided to retire from Corporate America and have a child to bring meaning to her old age. She was leafing through *Ladies' Home Journal*. Did people still read that?

I put my purse away and slurped up the remainder of my cappuccino.

"I just want a trim," Susie said as I led her back from the shampoo bowl.

Susie's hair was halfway down her back. I'd been trying to get her to cut it for a year.

"You know, even the movie stars are getting shorter hair cuts," I said. "I'm not talking Britney Spears and buzz cuts, here. But Paris Hilton actually has a bob. It's only the extensions that give her the longer look."

Susie looked up from her chamomile tea. "I'm no Paris Hilton," she said.

"Hey, no offense intended. You are definitely nothing like Paris Hilton. I don't even know why I mentioned her name."

Sweat broke out on my forehead. I grabbed the magazine out of her hand and started fanning myself. "It must be these hot flashes. I'm sweating so much I'm getting dehydrated, and I can't think straight. For all I know, Paris Hilton had her hair cut before she went to jail. Her mother or her nanny, or whoever it is who takes care of her, probably said it would be hard to condition in her isolation cell, and she better have it cut to avoid split ends. So afterwards, she's just kept it short."

I handed the magazine back to Susie. She looked a little apprehensive. Or were the granny glasses making her eyes look round with fear?

"Maybe I should come back another day," she said.

"How come?"

"You seem a little … a little …"

"Round the bend?" I suggested. "Estrogen deprived? Cuckoo?"

She clutched her purse tighter and nodded.

"Don't worry." I patted her shoulder. "It's really just caffeine deficit. Let me get a cup of coffee, and I'll be my old self."

"Well, if you're sure."

"Not to worry," I said.

Java fortified, I combed out the wet strands of Susie's hair, smoothing it before I began to cut. Doing this never failed to soothe me. I felt the same about freshly sharpened scissors cutting precisely through strands of hair. It was kind of like vacuuming—orderly, and you saw the results right away.

"How come you're smiling?" Susie asked.

"No reason. Just thinking about how much I love my job."

For a moment, the only sound in the salon was loud jazz coming through the speakers. I cut off an inch more of Susie's hair. It definitely needed it.

"I see you've decided to go gray like me," she said.

My eyes met hers in the mirror. "Why would you say that?"

"Gee, did I say something wrong? It's just that you have so much gray showing I figured you were letting your hair go natural."

Not in this lifetime, sister! I moved closer to the mirror and tilted my head. Sure enough, there was a fuzzy white caterpillar of gray visible along my part. "Jesus Frango Christ," I muttered. When had that happened? Why hadn't I noticed it? When was the last time I'd had Faye color it?

By lunchtime, I was in a funk. Susie had been gone three hours, her hair four inches shorter than when she came in. I think she said she liked it—that she thought the shorter length would help her night sweats.

I'd had three other clients come in. The last was a teenage boy. His mother had written him an excuse to get out of school so the top third of his black hair could be bleached white blond. It looked funky, but rather skunk-like, too. Hey, I was just there to serve.

Faye, my best buddy who worked on the other side of the salon, had brought me a burrito from next door for lunch. I bit into it and looked at the leftover bleach in the bowl. If I bleached my hair the same as the teenage punker's, my gray wouldn't show so fast.

What did I have to lose? Didn't blondes have more fun? Maybe if I were blond, I'd find a man. Not waiting to assess if I really wanted a man in my life, or if I could stand any more *F-U-N*, I applied the bleach.

Have I mentioned I'm a redhead and have the pale complexion, freckles, and green eyes that go with the syndrome? Gwen Stefani looked swell as a platinum blonde. Me? Not so good. When I was finished, I looked in the mirror. I was white on white, barely visible. It was like Harry Potter's Invisibility Cloak had dropped over my head.

Only after I'd blown dry my hair did I hear the shriek. From the corner of my eye, I saw Faye running across the salon toward me. Of course, everyone turned to look at her. Did she always have to make a scene?

"Oh, my God. What did you do?" she asked.

"Went blonde?" A quaver ran up and down my tonsils. "Went a little crazy?"

"Oh, my God," Faye repeated. "Why?"

"Why? That's like asking why NASA sends shuttles out into space." I shook my head. "I don't know why. I tried a little at first, and when I liked it, I mixed up a batch and bleached the whole darn thing."

Faye crossed her arms over her chest. "You look like a middle-aged punker. Next thing I know, you'll have your nose pierced. Then how will you go to Grandparent's Day at Connor's pre-school?"

Faye is a good friend. The only problem is that even though she's younger than I am, sometimes she acts like she's my mother. She stood looking at me, hands on her hips. I had this feeling I was soon going to be put in time-out.

"You fried the ends of your hair," she yelled.

Such outrage over nothing, I thought. Then I peered closer at the mirror. My hair did look like I'd been struck by white lightning.

"I'll have to cut it," I said. "Damn, and it's just grown out to one length."

Faye tapped her toe. "Don't you have that appointment with the loan guy at the bank this afternoon?"

"Oh, my God, you're right. With that prissy Matthew Pierson."

I dropped my head into my hands. Even the faint smells of hair bleach and coffee failed to soothe me. "I am so screwed."

"Hey, it's not the end of the world," Faye said. "Get a grip."

I lifted my head and looked at her. "You don't understand. The roof is so bad. It's leaking in so many places I can't keep up with it anymore."

"I can't understand why Dan won't pay for it. He can so afford it."

I shook my head. I was determined that I wouldn't call my ex. Dr. Dan had reduced our life together to a cliché when he'd left me for "a younger woman". At least she hadn't been his nurse. The flip side, as his accountant, Brandy knew how to hide assets like a military camouflage expert. The result was they lived in luxury, and I didn't have enough money to fix the roof.

"Dan may be able to afford it, but I can't afford to ask him," I said.

Faye put her arm around me. "Okay, but just don't take no for an answer from the loan guy."

Just don't take no for an answer, I repeated silently as I waited to see Pierson later that afternoon.

I'd run home, taken a quick shower, and changed into a suit. I'd made it to the bank on time, but now I sat cooling my sling-backed heels. I leafed through my folder for a third time. Every objection Pierson had brought up, I'd taken care of. I felt calm. I felt energized ... I felt a little too warm.

"Mrs. Bailey?"

I heard my name called, and I jumped. It was Ichabod Crane, the loan officer from hell.

"Hello, Mr. Pierson." I stood up, my voice dripping hypocrisy. "How are you?"

"Fine." He smiled at me for the first time in our short history. I hadn't realized he had a space between his two front teeth.

"I barely recognized you. You look so different," he said.

I managed a smile. My heart was beating hard—not a good sign. It meant either a heart attack or a hot flash was imminent. In this case, maybe both.

"I really like your hair," Pierson said.

My hair was cut short, real short. By the time Faye had cut off all the split ends, I was channeling Mia Farrow when she was married to Frank Sinatra—sort of that neurotic, scarecrow look. Why did Pierson like it? I shuddered to think.

He held my chair for me, also another first.

Still smiling, he went around his desk and sat down. "I'd really like to give you loan approval today. But there are still a couple sticking points."

"Really?" I crossed my arms. I'd been through this routine with Pierson twice before. What more could have cropped up? "And those are?"

"It's that pesky matter of you having such a new credit rating. You only established it two years ago."

"We've gone through that, Mr. Pierson. That's when I got divorced. I cleared that 'pesky' little matter up with the bank manager. You were supposed to take care of the forms."

He opened up a folder on his desk. "Oh? Perhaps I forgot."

When he started leafing through the papers in the folder, I realized he hadn't taken the time to prepare for our meeting. My estrogen-deprived body began to heat from the core. I'd had enough of this little pipsqueak.

I stood and put my hands on the edge of his desk. "Listen closely, Mr. Pierson. I'm not leaving here today without that loan. I have taken care of every objection you had. This meeting should just be a formality."

"Please sit down, Mrs. Bailey. Just let me look through the file a minute," Pierson said.

I felt my face flush. "You should have done your homework before I got here. Maybe because I'm a woman and I only need a small loan you thought I wasn't important enough."

Pierson swallowed, sending his Adam's apple into a bobbing frenzy. "Now, Mrs. Bailey ..."

"And maybe it's because I'm older, too. That would be two strikes against you. Sexism and ageism."

"Strikes? Sexism? Ageism?" Pierson stuttered the words.

I sat back and smiled at him. "Two good reasons to sue you and the bank for discrimination."

It was amazing how fast Pierson could get the paperwork done once I pointed out his politically incorrect actions—including his skuzzy compliment on my hair.

I ran my fingers through it as I drove home, the loan approval safely on the seat next to me. My platinum white locks were après-hot flash damp again, but who cared? Maybe I could add a little gel and spike it. Maybe even do a faux Mohawk?

Hey, it's all about going with the flow.

Dead Cat Bounce

Ralph Spencer

People say I am very level headed, not known for taking risks, firmly grounded with my feet planted in good conservative New England soil. This has almost been true with one exception.

I attended the annual meeting of the American Historical Society, which met on the Big Island in Hawaii. On the second day of the conference, I gave a paper on my best selling biography *Bill Clinton: Entitlement and Power*. The conference ran for another three days. I decided to sneak away and pursue my real passion—a game of golf. I had brought my clubs along hoping to be able to work in a game. I called the magnificent Pirates Cove Golf and Country Club and booked a 10:12 tee time.

I drove my rental car to the club early so that I'd have time to hit some warm up shots on the practice tee. The man swinging a club next to me was tall—maybe six foot two or three—and powerfully built. He was totally in control of his swing from take off to delivery of the shot.

"Have you played this course before?" I asked.

"Nope, my first time on it. How about you?"

"My first time, too. What's your tee time?"

"10:12."

"Looks like we'll be together."

Also warming up were an elderly couple, both obviously with huge handicaps. They pounded away with the inexperience of true beginners. The woman overheard us talking. "We're also scheduled to play at 10:12," she said.

I inwardly groaned and guessed the big man did, too. Five hours looking for balls in the rough, trees, and rocks and watching these two good people butcher a magnificent golf course was not something I wanted.

The big man held out his hand. "Since we'll be together, we should introduce ourselves. My name is Mike Brennan—from New York."

"I'm Randall Jackson from just outside Boston."

"It looks like we're lots better than this couple," Mike said quietly.

27

"So it does."

"I wonder if the starter would let us go off first—get out of their way and let them putter along as they are able."

"Worth a try," I said.

We approached the starter and pled our case for going off just ahead of the elderly couple. "This is most irregular," the starter said. "But I'll see what we can do. We're not overly busy this morning."

"Thanks," I said.

As we sat in our golf cart waiting for our turn, Mike said, "Do you want to make this game more interesting?"

"How?"

"Let's play it as a skins game. You know, whoever wins the hole gets the prize for that hole. If you shoot one better than me, you get the prize. If I shoot one better than you, I get the prize. If we shoot the same score then the prize is carried over to the next hole."

"Sounds interesting." My latent competitiveness surged to the forefront. "What's the prize?"

"Let's say, $25.00 on the first hole. $100.00 on the second and then we'll discuss what should be next."

"Brennan and Jackson," the starter called.

"You can have the honors," Mike offered.

I set my ball on the tee, then shifted my feet from side to side. After a brief moment to compose myself, I took the first shot of the game of my life—a soaring drive down the right side of the fairway, nearly three hundred yards long. It landed in a good position for my approach to the green.

Mike stepped forward and took two precise practice swings, then stepped up to his ball. Becoming very still, he began his back swing. He drew his club far back and then very high. But the results were amazing. His shot flew about as far as mine but was pushed off into the low rough.

As we made our way up the fairway, Mike looked over at me. "What do you do for a living?"

"I'm Full Professor of American History at Harvard in Cambridge. What about you?"

"I'm a day trader," Mike said. "I live on the computer virtually every day buying and selling stocks on line."

"I've never traded in stocks—only mutual funds where someone else does the trading."

"Lots of people do that, but I deal in hundreds of thousands of dollars every day. I get a giant adrenalin kick out of taking risks, buying what others aren't, and then sitting with my finger on the mouse ready to click the instant I can turn a profit."

"You must be very rich to do something like that. I'd be afraid I'd lose everything."

"Well, it's a challenge for me to be the one in charge of my own fate."

We arrived at our balls. Mike hit his second shot. I noticed again how very precise and disciplined he was; always doing the same preparation—two swings, then carefully setting up, then taking the club back slowly and very high. His shot was good, but came up a few yards short of the green. My second shot, a six iron, was right on the money, landing 11 feet from the hole—a good chance for me to Birdie.

We drove our cart up to the green and got out. Mike chipped on and was a few feet away from the hole—an easy par. I scrunched down and sized up the green—the break and the grain—and stood over my putt. I struck it firmly and it rolled toward the hole. It wasn't a sensational putt, but it got the job done. It held its line and dropped in. I won the first skin—$25.

As we drove over to the second tee, Mike looked at me again. "I've seen you somewhere before. I know it. Maybe on TV or something?"

"Well, yes, you might have." I blushed just a little. "I'm a regular on the CNN Sunday night panel show, "Political Perspectives."

"Yeah, that's it. I knew I had seen you before. You're good—challenging the biases of those other panelists."

"It's fun," I said. "That's where I get my adrenalin kick."

It was time to tee up for the second hole, a par five 547 yards. I still had the honors.

"$100 on this hole," Mike reminded me.

Again our tee shots were above average for distance and accuracy. As we rode in the cart toward them I asked, "What is your specialty in this day trading business?"

Mike grinned. "I'm probably one of America's best 'dead cat bounce' experts." 'What's that?"

"A dead cat bounce refers to a stock that is about to die. It means that like a dead cat doesn't bounce when you drop it, so a stock that is dead won't bounce back up. It's going down the tubes, so to speak. I figure out which stocks are about to become dead cats and use that knowledge to make a killing on the stock market. I sucker someone into promising to buy the stock at an inflated price on the date just before I analyze it will die. Then on that date as the stock price plummets, I buy enough to cover my sales. The differential between what the sucker has to pay and what I had to pay to buy the stock makes one huge profit. It's pretty complicated, but it's a real blast doing it every day."

Our second and third shots were routine and as a result we both parred the hole—the $100 was a carry over skin.

As we were waiting for the foursome ahead of us to clear the green on the third hole, a par three 212 yards, Mike said, "You and I are about equal. We both have talent and experience. I'd like to make the game more challenging by putting something real on the line. Why don't we play the third for $500 and then double that every hole until the 9th and we'll talk again."

I gulped. I'd never played for stakes like that in my life. The little tournaments in my home course in Newton, Massachusetts, were petty compared to what Mike proposed. But I didn't want to be considered a wimp and so amazingly out of my mouth came these words, "You're on. Let's do it." From that moment, the game became serious business. I'd never concentrated so hard and focused on my game as I did there at Pirates Cove.

To describe 18 holes of golf shot-by-shot is like watching paint dry or grass grow. Suffice it to say, both of us were playing golf as if our lives depended on it. After the 9th hole, the hole worth $32,000, Mike had won $15,100 and I had won $16,525. We halved the 9th and it was carried over to the 10th.

We swung our golf cart by the snack bar. Each of us bought a sandwich and a Gatorade before heading to the 10th tee. Chewing on his ham and cheese sandwich, Mike smiled. "This is great fun! You are good and you are winning—but not by much."

"I guess so," I admitted. "I've never played a skins game before, let alone one where the purse was so big."

"Want to change it for the back nine?"

"What have you got in mind?" I was almost afraid to ask.

"Let's put up something that belongs to each of us. Do you own any time shares?"

"Yes, I've got a week in southern Spain."

"Great. I've got a week here in Hawaii—actually I'm staying in my unit now. It's magnificent—two bedrooms overlooking the ocean. Let's play the 10th hole for our time-shares—if I win the hole I get the carry over plus your time-share. If you win the hole you get the $32,000 plus my time share."

I hesitated a moment. But then I thought I had come this far I might as well trust my golf game and agreed.

With that we got out of the cart and walked up to the 10th tee to begin the last nine holes.

We agreed that for the 11th hole we would play for his air miles and my AMEX points. On the 12th hole we decided to make the prize for winning his season box seats to the New York Giants NFL games and my box seats for the Boston Red Sox home games. When we arrived at the 13th, we came up with his art collection and my collection of rare first edition books. On the 14th we opted to risk our golf club memberships. He belonged to an exclusive club on Long Island near Manhasset and I belonged to the Newton Golf and Country Club just outside of Boston.

The stakes were going up rapidly, but I couldn't turn back. To do that would be to forfeit all that had been won. For the 15th hole we struggled to name a prize. I asked him, "What kind of car do you drive?"

"I have a classic Jaguar. What about you?"

"I have a new Cadillac Escalade."

"Sounds like this might be about equal. Let's put our cars up for the winner of this hole."

I nodded.

Hawaii is noted for its changeable weather. We had begun in glorious warm sunshine, but by now it was afternoon. As often happens, storm clouds began to gather in the sky and move toward us. The bright sunshine was disappearing rapidly as the clouds swirled overhead. But the threat of rain wasn't going to stop this contest. We were now out for "blood," as they say.

As you might expect, by the sixteenth hole we were very tense and barely speaking to each other because the stakes were immense. We were running out of things that we could offer as a prize. I thought about all that was on the line—how I'd lost my rare book collection because my putt rimmed out, how I was going to have to sell something valuable to pay the $32,000 he had won when he beat me on the 10th hole. But then I was going to be able to fly all over the world on his air miles and driving around in a classic Jaguar wouldn't be too shabby either.

"We need something big," he said.

"You make a lot of money." I was thinking ahead about how I might pay him. "I'll take 6 months of your earnings on the stock market. In exchange, I'll put up my entire Full Professor's salary plus my royalties from my best selling book."

He paused. "That's a go with me, but I better win this hole."

"That was exactly what I was thinking."

As we teed off, the rain began to fall, but neither of us considered stopping. The hole was halved, the prize carried over to the 17th. There was only one thing we hadn't put on the line—that was our homes. He lived in a nine-room condo overlooking Central Park in Manhattan. I owned a large historic New England early 1800's white clapboard listed on the historical registry for its importance and significance. We agreed—the prize for the 17th was our homes.

By now the rain was coming down much harder and there were sounds of thunder coming ever closer. Again we played adequate golf—both of us Bogied the hole.

As we'd been going along, we had written down everything that was offered as prizes, keeping track of who had won which skin.

With the thunder and lightening ever increasing, I felt we ought to stop even though I dared not say anything for fear that he would think that I had chickened out. So I kept my mouth shut tight, determined to win the 18th hole regardless of what the prize was.

Mike grinned at me. "This has been quite a match. I can honestly say it's the most exciting golf I've ever played. There is only one thing left for us to do."

"What's that?" I innocently asked the high-risk day trader.

"We'll play the 18th for the whole kettle of fish—all or nothing. The winner of the 18th hole gets everything on this list."

I couldn't believe my ears. Dare I risk putting the rest of my life into the winning of one hole of golf? Did I have the conviction that I was better than Mike, good enough to beat this arrogant, passionate, confident golfer? My stomach was full of butterflies, but with the courage born of confidence (or was it just male bravado?) I said with far more steadiness than I felt, "That sounds good to me. I can't wait to take everything you own."

"Let's make this legal. Why don't we both sign this paper stating what we've decided so there's no weaseling out after the game is over," he suggested.

And so sitting in our golf cart with the rain coming down and thunder booming all around, we signed the agreement—the winner of the 18th hole would get everything we had played for from the first hole.

The 18th hole was a long par four dogleg right winding around the rocky cliffs of the Pacific Ocean. The green was guarded on the left by a large bunker that was located in front and high above the left side of the green. Given the lousy weather, Mike hit a tremendous drive down the left side of the fairway. I thought about cutting the corner and going over the rocks and the Pacific to a small landing area just short of the green. On a good day, and if the stakes hadn't been so immense, I know I would have tried. But instead I decided to play more conservatively and laid up 225 yards in the middle of the fairway.

Mike's second shot landed on top of the grassy rim of the large sand bunker, 90 yards from the green. My second shot wasn't pretty. It went slicing toward the dreaded rocks. When I got to my ball I knew that I wasn't going to be on the green with my next shot. I did my best with rain beating down, my club handle wet, and my glasses water spattered. My shot came up short of the green.

Mike went toward his ball. He climbed up the hill to the top grassy knoll above the sand trap. As I had seen all day, he stood and took his two practice swings. Then he placed his feet carefully making sure they were correctly positioned. He drew his chipping wedge back very slowly to the high point above his head.

And then the totally unexpected happened! A bolt of lightening flashed from the sky hitting Mike's raised club and shooting mega-volts of electricity down its shaft and into his body. Mike dropped in a heap to the ground.

Before going over to him, I chipped onto the green and two putted for a Bogie. Then I went to him. He was dead, of course. I took the piece of paper we had both signed before teeing off for the 18th and wrote: "I, Randall Jackson, won the 18th hole due to the fact that Mike Brennan was forced to withdraw and did not complete the round."

I left the 18th green, got into the cart, drove to the clubhouse to report the accident. I smiled to myself. I had just become a very wealthy man—a Jaguar, a condo in New York, hundreds of thousands of dollars, etc., etc. Not a bad result from a single game of golf.

As I took my clubs off the electric golf cart and began carrying them to my car, I paused a moment to think about Mike and what he had said. He was right. "Dead cats don't bounce!"

Death Sentence Postscript

Martin S. Goldberg

The cards fate dealt me for my first sixty-three years were a winning hand. Year sixty-three began a descent into a bottomless hole. Stress, from my duties as a judge trying some criminal cases that required imposition of the death penalty, had taken its toll. The stress led me to my family doctor who prescribed medication to relieve the symptoms.

By year sixty-five, life had become a nightmare. My wife Anne discovered her family's legacy—a legacy that transformed her from a vibrant woman into a mindless mass of clay.

The mass breathed, but not much more. It lay motionless, bent in a fetal position, encumbered with diapers and fed through tubes. After forty years of marriage, she had lost all sense of life.

As I watched the relentless progression of Alzheimer's in my wife, the intense emotional pain I experienced was unbearable. I prayed, "Please make her better." When she continued downhill, I changed my prayer. "Dear God, if Anne can't get better, please don't let her get worse."

Recently, I had noticed recurring memory lapses in myself, and a diminished sense of perception. Our family doctor mapped my future with his diagnosis. He said, "Bill, it hurts to tell you this. Your problem is early stage Alzheimer's."

I returned home determined to act before it was too late. Anne couldn't be saved, nor could I prevent my descent into nothingness. To resolve this, I was going to end Anne's life and leave with her. I wouldn't let it take me to the final stages nor permit it to progress any further in her.

I didn't have much time left to carry out our death sentence. Before it happened, a question had to be answered. Should I take our only son with us? Or should his life be spared only to endure a descent into a black hole from which there was no return?

I was a father wracked with uncertainty—either choice posed a quandary. What should I do? Could I gamble with his life and hope medical science would find a cure? In the alternative, should he be spared from the inevitable family curse and depart this life now?

The plans for ending Anne's existence and mine are complete. During the night, I will carry her frail body out to our garage and place her in the front seat of our car. I'll lock the garage, take my place behind the wheel, start the engine, and hold her in my arms as we slip into eternity. There will be a tape in the dash playing the melodies we danced to so long ago. I'll leave this note.

Dear Son,

After intense soul searching about your future, I have altered my plan to take you with us. I hope you will forgive me for this decision. I'm sentencing you to life with a prayer as we depart. I pray for the riddle of Alzheimer's to be solved in time to spare you from our family curse.

With much love, I am,

Your devoted father

Post Script:

Several days following the discovery of Judge Williams and his wife's bodies in their garage, their son Jack found an unopened letter in the mailbox. The letter had been deposited on the day they died.

The letter read:

"Dear Bill,

I have some good news. I want you to discontinue taking the medication I prescribed for your stress. I learned it has a side effect that impairs memory and cognition. It can imitate Alzheimer's. You can rest easy. I'm satisfied you don't have Alzheimer's."

Sincerely,

Cal Rosen, MD

Detective Roscoe's Unusual Case

Shirley Gibson

The body lay face down in the peonies.

As detective Roscoe took a look around, he noticed the grandeur of the mansion. The lawn was perfectly manicured. Rows of petunias and marigolds lined the blacktop driveway. As he'd driven up, he'd seen the pool and tennis court near the three-car garage.

"You are Mrs. Wilson, and you live here?" the detective asked the woman who'd come to the door.

"Yes, I live here with my husband, Robert."

"How long have you lived here?"

"It will be twenty years the thirty-first of March." She pointed to the body. "Is he dead?"

"Yes, ma'am."

"What happened?" Mr. Wilson asked.

"We'll know the cause of death from the coroner's reports. It looks like he was attempting a burglary and had a heart attack."

"Well, he sure made a mess of my flower beds. You know, Jose just planted them last week and tomorrow my garden club is coming over for lunch. How am I going to have time to replant them so it will look presentable?"

"Mrs. Wilson, a man died in your flower bed. Aren't you a little bit curious as to what he wanted?"

"Oh, he was probably after my husband's antique collection of rare stamps and other rare collections. We have had burglary attempts in the past and installed a unique burglar alarm. You see, when you enter the property nothing happens so they think we don't have an alarm. When they try the window, a projector inside projects a ghost onto the window. Then you hear an eerie voice say, 'I am going to get you' as water squirts them in the face from around the window sill. We thought this would scare the burglars away."

The detective shook his head. "That could have been the cause of his death."

"We didn't mean to kill anyone," Clara said, shaken.

"No sir, we aren't killers, but a man must protect his family and valuables," Robert added.

One week later the detective made a house call to the Wilson's.

The detective opened his notes. "The man's name is Thomas Brown. He was fifty-six. He had a son that needed surgery and the insurance company dropped him because of too many hospital bills. His son will die without the surgery. He lost his job because he was spending too much time in the hospital. With no job and no income, he was desperate. He also suffered from a weak heart. He leaves his wife Joan, and son Mathew behind."

The Wilsons sat there for a moment. Then Clara got up and asked her husband to accompany her to the kitchen. When she came out she was carrying a silver tray with a tea pot, creamer, and sugar bowl. There were oatmeal and chocolate cookies neatly arranged on a silver tray.

"How do you take your tea?" Clara asked.

She poured, and then picked up her own cup. "Bob and I had a talk and we decided that we want to pay for the boy's surgery as we feel responsible for his father's death."

The surgery went well. They met Rose, the boy's mother, and learned that she was being evicted for not paying her rent. Rose was somewhat plain looking, with long brown hair and green eyes. She looked like her clothes were from the Goodwill store. Clara couldn't resist taking Rose to her favorite salon.

Clara wore designer clothes and her gray hair was neatly done. Her makeup was flawless next to her blue eyes. You could tell she was a beauty in her younger days. Tom was distinguished with his gray hair, wearing a tweed blazer with navy pants. He was a member of many clubs in town. They had more money than they could ever spend.

They made arrangements for Rose and Jacob to come live at their mansion because it was too big for just the two of them. They found that Rose and Mathew brought new life to the dull stuffy house.

Clara felt years younger just having Rose and Mathew there.

Escape From Vienna

Eric H. Spitz

The overnight express to Prague was due at midnight at the main terminal in Vienna. There were very few people in the waiting room when Gertrude and Richard Stein arrived. Richard wore two suits. Gertrude was able to bring only a fraction of her extensive wardrobe along with the photo albums of Peter and Fedja, their children. In Gertrude's handbag were the fake Greek passports that she had somehow gotten from an old friend with connections at the consulate.

Olly, Gertrude's older sister, arrived with Fedja and Peter shortly after 11:30. The boys had spent part of the night at her home while their parents packed and prepared to flee Vienna. It was several weeks after the Anschluss, when the Nazis had annexed Austria, their first step towards "world domination."

When Fedja saw his mother, he began to cry. He was just seven.

"Ich habe Angst, Mutti (I'm frightened). Where are we going?" Fedja's little legs trembled in his lederhosen.

"Don't worry, Fedja." Peter, his sturdy older brother, put his arm around him.

"Shh, we must be very quiet!" Gertrude put a finger to her lips.

The train steamed noisily into the terminal, clouding it with foul smelling smoke.

Richard scanned the platform. Two Nazi troopers with rifles had left their posts on the north and south ends of the tracks and were taking coffee in the restaurant across from the trains.

"Quick," he said. "We will board the train now." He grabbed two suitcases and motioned to Peter to take the others. They walked toward the train, looking for numbers on the sleeper cars. The only other passengers were a heavy-set, middle-aged man carrying a vendor's rucksack, and an elderly couple with canes and old suitcases headed to the cheaper section of the train.

Richard was aware they were the only family boarding. With every few steps, he and Gertrude turned to see who might be observing. Only a porter and a vendor of beverages were in sight.

"We are in Sleeper Number Five," Gertrude said to the conductor.

"Where are you going?" he asked.

"To Prague, of course." Gertrude assumed the mantle of European charm she wore so casually.

"Take the baggage." She motioned to the porter with a wave of her hand.

The man, so used to taking orders, gave her a nasty look.

"Stinkende Juden," he said under his breath as he carried the suitcases onto the train.

◆   ◆   ◆

Earlier that night, Olly stood besides Fedja's bed.

"Fedja, you must get up and get dressed. Your brother is already up and I have your suitcase ready." The clock read just past 11:00.

"Where are we going, Tante Olly?"

"To the train station. Your parents are meeting you there."

Olly carefully opened the front door of her small house on the outskirts of Vienna and looked both ways before motioning the boys to come out with their suitcases.

"Komm schnell," Olly said to Peter who was lagging behind. The street was deserted except for an occasional passing vehicle. A taxi was waiting to pick them up a block away.

Fedja had trouble carrying his suitcase his mother had packed for him and stumbled. He was close to tears. The taxi drove through downtown Vienna, past the Prater where he had often gone with his parents to ride the famous Ferris wheel. When they passed through downtown, he could see the opera house, and remembered the plush crimson curtains, the paintings and gold statues that Gertrude had shown him there. They passed the Hotel Sacher where he had celebrated his sixth birthday a year before, indulging in too much Sacher Torte. Across from the famous hotel, two Nazi tanks stood next to a statue of Johann Strauss. Two soldiers with rifles and helmets stood alongside. Further on, Fedja recoiled as he saw two Nazi troopers marching behind a couple who had their arms raised. The woman was crying.

◆   ◆   ◆

The Steins followed the scowling porter to sleeper room Number Five. Gertrude ordered the porter to take down the two beds. She lifted Fedja up to one of the beds. Richard tipped the porter and hurriedly closed the sliding door.

"Don't close the curtain," Fedja cried from the sleeper compartment.

"You'll be fine," his mother said.

Just after they felt the jolt of the train starting up, there was a knock on the door of the compartment. Richard opened it cautiously.

"Billeten and Passe." It was the conductor.

Gerty took out the tickets and their Greek passports.

The conductor took the tickets, tore them in half and stamped the passports, holding them against the wall. "You are Greek?"

"Ja, we were born there," Gertrude lied.

"You speak German so well."

He gave her a questioning look, then after a moment returned the passports.

"In two hours," he said, "the border control will be boarding the train. Do not go to bed before that." He exited.

The parents settled uneasily and awaited the inevitable inspection at the border. If caught, they could be arrested and punished, possibly sentenced to death by a Nazi tribunal. They had heard rumors about the fate of some Jews in Germany—staged trials, permanent disappearances of those accused, prisons, and torture.

Now it was real for them. Two things put them at risk of exposure. They spoke no Greek, and they purposely carried no other papers that would identify them as Austrians.

The train moved on past the vast meadowlands of northern Austria. It would have to stop at the small city of Gmund on the border, now controlled by the Nazis. Once past, Richard thought, there should be no problem at the Czech border.

Gertrude took an aspirin fro her handbag. "My head is pounding."

"Try to rest a little if you can," Richard said, taking her hand.

She put her head on his shoulder and closed her eyes.

A sudden knock on the door startled them. Fedja stifled a cry from the bunk above. In that moment, the only sounds were the swish of passing telephone lines and the loud explosions of the powerful locomotive.

"Ja, who's there?" Richard tried to sound casual, but his heart beat wildly.

"Open up, please." The voice had authority.

Richard partly cracked open the door. A vendor with a cart containing coffee and sandwiches stood outside. Richard opened the door and took out some schillings. They had not eaten since late afternoon.

"Mother, I'm afraid," Fedja said after gulping down a few bites of sandwich.

"Fedja, you must sleep." Gertrude ordered him up to the bed. Her tone was harsh. The boy continued sobbing into his pillow.

Richard looked at his watch. It was midnight. He calculated the border was now fifteen minutes away.

"It's too dark in here," Fedja cried from behind the curtain.

"Sleep, sleep, Fedja." Gertrude repeated. She pulled the curtains tightly shut.

Perhaps, Richard thought, *if Gerty and I are caught, the boys might not be discovered. Maybe they could safely get through to Prague.*

He reached into his pocket and removed his billfold, casting a look at his wife. He carefully placed it on the seat so that the money was plainly visible.

The train began to slow for the border as the "GMUND" Station sign came into view. When the train had screeched to a final stop, they waited in silence. At last, there was a knock on the door.

Richard opened it. Two Austrian police officers and a plain-clothed man stood outside.

"*Passe, bitte,*" one of the officers said, reaching for the passports. The Nazi, a small stocky man with a swastika on the arm of his raincoat, was smoking a cigarette. He wore his hat low on his forehead. His eyes fixed upon the couple.

As the officer leafed through the passports, Richard stood rigidly, praying they would not discover the boys,

"Why are you going to Prague?" the Nazi officer asked.

"We're on vacation. We want to see the museums," Gertrude said.

"In order," one of the Austrian officers said.

The Nazi snatched one of the passports from the officer's hand and opened it. "This is a Greek passport," he said. His eyes narrowed on the parents' faces.

"Yes, we are Greek citizens."

"But you speak just like a Viennese."

"My husband and I were born in Athens, but moved to Vienna," she said calmly.

"DON'T YOU KNOW THAT JEWS ARE FORBIDDEN TO LEAVE AUSTRIA?" the Nazi rasped.

Richard and Gertrude looked at each other, not knowing how to respond. Richard said nothing. The silence in the small compartment was overpowering. Then they heard the marching feet of a cadre of German soldiers outside.

"Halt!" a voice called out. The marching stopped.

The Nazi moved to the window and looked out onto the platform. After what seemed an eternity, he turned back. His eyes met Richard's. Ever so slowly, Richard turned his head toward the open billfold. The Nazi's eyes followed his gaze. He regarded the wallet briefly, and then turned to the officers.

"Out! I must speak further with these people."

The officers left, murmuring to themselves, sliding the compartment door shut.

The Nazi scowled at the Steins. He took a final puff on his cigarette and blew the smoke in Gertrude's face. Then he walked to the seat and picked up the billfold. Carefully he took out all but one of the bills, and put the wallet back on the seat.

"*Gutte Reise*. Have a good trip." With a smirk he threw open the door and was gone.

Final Bequest

Martin S. Goldberg

The temperature in *The Jolly Bar* rose when the long legged blonde entered with her spiked heels, tight skirt, and impatient frown. After taking a seat at the bar and ordering a vodka Martini, she fidgeted while looking toward the front entrance.

Twenty minutes and one Martini later, the object of her wait strolled in. Six feet tall, sporting a two-day-beard growth, needing a haircut, and looking harried, Vick took a stool next to the bar thermometer's reason for a rise. "Sorry I'm late, Jamie."

"What's the excuse, this time?"

"I had to pick up Uncle Eugene's prescription."

"Why are you always the one doing things? Let your brother do something."

"Because he made it clear, I'm his favorite. There's no one else. With all his dough, I'm going to inherit some real money."

Like a schoolteacher scolding a child, she spoke loud enough for the bartender to overhear. "You spend half your life waiting for him to fade out while he still keeps on going. We get married this June, or I'm calling it quits."

"Hon, don't be angry. Just be patient. When my inheritance arrives, you and I will go on one helluva honeymoon."

"Where? Muncie, Indiana? After your jobless benefits expire, you won't even be able to finance bus fare to Muncie. I'm tired of broken promises. The more you carry his behind around, the more you look like a ghoul."

Vick frowned. "You'll sing a different tune when we head for Tahiti. He's getting worse. He told me his doctor said the only thing keeping him alive is the medicine he gets. We just have to wait."

Jamie drained her glass, then bent closer to Vick. "Maybe you can speed up his departure."

"You mean, kill him? I couldn't do it."

"I don't mean anything like shooting or stabbing."

"Well, what do you mean?"

"You could take care of his last curtain call without leaving a trace."

Intrigued, Vick whispered, "How?"

"Let me start coming over as a Nurses Aide to help you care for Uncle Eugene. I'll make sure he doesn't get his medicine. No one else pays attention to him. With his life fading, all we'll do is turn out the lights a little sooner."

"I couldn't do it."

"You won't need to. Just let me be the substitute caregiver."

Vick smiled. "All right, I'll take you with me tonight so he can get used to the idea of seeing you there. But, we'll have to be careful. He's feeble, but his mind is still sharp."

"Leave it to me, Vick."

Vick finished his drink while Jamie paid the tab. The two left the bar, arm in arm—Jamie, poster girl for a magazine cover, with her beau, poster boy for a bum.

Knute, main bartender at *The Jolly Bar,* got to know Vick as a regular who spent many evenings at the bar talking about the day coming when he and Jamie would be heading for their honeymoon in the South Pacific.

One afternoon, Vick walked in wearing a long face. Seated at the bar, he looked miserable. "Lemme have a boilermaker. Just use your bar whiskey and a draft beer."

Knute drew a draft beer and placed it alongside a shot of *Wild Turkey,* "What's up? You look like you're going to be sick."

Vick slugged the shot down, drank some beer to chase it, coughed. "It's a long story. I had been waiting for an inheritance from my uncle. Jamie and I planned to get married when he died. I was the only one helping him so I was his favorite. I noticed he was getting weaker and needed more attention. Jamie offered to help care for him. I thought it was a great idea. This gave me more free time. She started coming with me and gradually took over his care."

Knute poured another shot of *Wild Turkey.* Vick downed the drink fast, then took a gulp of beer to wash it down. His face screwed up so his features were twisted out of shape.

Knute held up the whiskey bottle as if to check for foreign bodies. "The whiskey can't be that bad."

"It's not the whiskey. It's what happened."

Knute leaned over the bar. "Go on."

"Well, she started to spend more and more time over there. I relaxed, knowing it wouldn't be long before she and I would take my inheritance and be off to our honeymoon.

"The last time I went to see Uncle Eugene, I expected to find him close to the end. Instead of finding him comatose, I found him up and walking around. I was baffled.

"Uncle Eugene greeted me with a big smile. He walked over to Jamie and put his arm around her. He told me, 'She saved my life.' I asked him how?

"'She stopped giving me medicine. It was the medicine that caused my problems,' he said.

"Jamie stood next to him and whispered in his ear. I didn't like the way she was acting so I asked Uncle Eugene if he and I could talk in private. He refused. He said, 'She can hear whatever you have to say.'"

"What did you do?" Knute asked.

"I asked Uncle Eugene to fire her."

"Did he?"

Vick looked down, on the brink of tears. He shook his head. "He fired me. Told me not to come around anymore."

Knute poured another drink. "This one's on the house. You'll still be able to inherit. All you need to do is get back in your uncle's good graces."

"Impossible."

"Why not."

"Jamie became my aunt. Uncle Eugene fell for her, despite a thirty-five-year age spread. They got married and took off, like two love birds, for Bora Bora."

Flights Of The Butterfly

◆

A Novel

Gitta M Gorman

Chapter Three

After the Christmas and New Year's holidays, Eve again sat at her desk studying. Her mother walked in. "Eve, here's a letter for you."

When Eve saw Karl's beloved handwriting, she opened the letter eagerly.

"*Mamma*! It's an invitation to his graduation. It's a ball held for the graduating Infantry Cadets. It's going to be held at the City Hall!" Eve read on to her mother, with hands trembling from excitement:

> "*On Saturday, February 20, 1954.*
> *At 1700 hours*
> *Dress—Formal.*"

"*Mamma*, what am I going to wear? I have no formal gown."

Her mother smiled at her. "I'll have to call my dressmaker. I'll ask her to sew you a pretty gown." Soon they were both absorbed in fashion magazines.

On the afternoon of the big evening, Eve felt her mother gently shaking her. "Wake up. You have to get dressed for the ball! Karl will soon be here to pick you up. I'll get your gown."

Eve could tell from her mother's voice that she, too, was excited. To savor every minute of the evening, Eve started dressing very slowly. There, on a hanger, hung the loveliest gown she had ever seen, and created just for her. She had chosen a romantic look—the same as the heroine wore in the movie *Camille* played by Greta Garbo.

But didn't Camille become deathly ill? Eve wondered. She quickly pushed the thought out of her mind.

Her strapless dress, as the fashion of the early 50's called for, featured five tiers of fluffy ruffles with white tulle, and a matching shawl to be draped over her shoulders. Long white gloves made of the softest kid leather completed her ensemble.

"How exquisite you look," Eve's mother said. "As a finishing touch I'll let you wear this necklace and matching bracelet. I also think you'd better wear my fur coat. It's very cold outside."

Eve blinked away tears of happiness when she looked in the mirror and saw the necklace and bracelet she always admired so much. The wide necklace glittered from the purple and turquoise colored rhinestones.

"It offsets the white in my gown beautifully. Thank you, *Mamma*."

Eve's father came into the living room, and stood admiring her. After a long time, he said, "These are for you, my princess. I brought these fresh white gardenias home from the flower shop. They will look good in your hair."

Eve loved their sweet smelling fragrance. She would let *gardenia* be her perfume for this special evening—maybe forever?

The door bell rang. Eve's heart skipped a few beats.

"*Mamma*! *Pappa*! It must be Karl!" She ran to the door.

When she opened it, she stood in awe. Her heart beat faster and faster as her eyes caressed the tall, young man in front of her. Karl, in the full dress uniform of the Infantry, looked more handsome than ever.

"Please come in for a few minutes and say hello to my parents," she whispered.

"You look stunning!" he said. "You look like a princess. Do you want to be mine?" His blue eyes twinkled with pride and happiness.

"Oh, yes I do."

"We have to leave shortly. The taxi is waiting."

A short while later, Eve could see the silhouette of the famous City Hall situated by the shores of Lake Mälaren. On top of the tall tower, the Three Golden Crowns, the international symbol for Sweden, gleamed against the gray winter sky.

Eve was excited and nervous. Here she was, a daughter of a florist, and she was going to one of the world's most beautiful buildings known for its Nobel Prize banquets. When Eve entered the Blue Hall of the City Administration Building, she noticed it was not blue, at all. The walls were in several nuances of red brick, instead. It intrigued her.

"Karl, how come the Blue Hall is not blue?" Eve whispered in his ear.

"Oh, I have been told that when the architect Ragnar Ostberg saw the red bricks, he liked the look so much he did not want to cover them with blue plaster. He never changed the name either." He smiled at her. "But now, I must introduce you to the senior officers. Come with me."

When she curtsied in front of them, she was happy they could not see her trembling knees under the full length skirt. Grateful that the greeting ceremony would soon be over, they continued to the stairway leading up to the famous Golden Hall. Escorted by her beloved cadet and dressed like any royalty, Eve walked regally up the grand marble stairway.

At the sight of the Golden Hall sparkling in its full splendor, Eve stood in breathless wonder. She'd read there were 18,000,000 mosaic pieces, telling the history of Stockholm, but never imagined how beautiful it would be. Dominating the wall on the north side was the large image of the Queen of Lake Mälaren, the symbol of Stockholm. Like a mother, she overlooked the banquet arranged for the three hundred graduating Infantry cadets and their guests.

After the elegant three course dinner accompanied by exquisite wines, Thore Ehrling's Big Band Orchestra started to play the very popular dance tunes of Glenn Miller.

"May I have this dance?" Karl asked, his voice filled with love. "*In the Mood?*"

"Oh, yes!"

Lifting her arms towards him, she was again mesmerized by Karl's expressive blue eyes. He took her hand and glided her onto the dance floor. Oh, how she could have danced all night in his arms.

As they left the glittering cadet ball, Eve could hear *Moonlight Serenade* playing faintly in the background. The severe cold of this February night had Lake Mälaren frozen to a large blanket of solid white ice. The contrasting black winter sky was studded with millions of twinkling stars.

Pulling her mother's soft fur coat closer to her body, Eve happily hugged Karl, her prince. "How beautiful the sky is! I wonder what's written in the stars for us?"

"Only the best, of course. We would never be star-crossed lovers, would we?"

Eve shivered, but not from the cold. She loved Karl so much. Nothing could harm them. Then why was she suddenly so afraid?

Frank Ferrari Writes His Story

Dory Rose

I was proud of my shiny forest green paint job. Jeremy, my owner, showed me off at all the fancy restaurants. Today he drove me to his usual Monday morning meeting. I was parked in the front when a dirty old Taurus bumped my fender.

"Ouch, that hurt ... right in my rear end."

A cheap looking blonde jumped out. "Sorry, didn't mean to. Anyhow, I don't have insurance and I have to dash."

Jeremy was furious. He slammed my door and ran up the stairs to his meeting.

I felt violated. I was so much more important than that cheap car.

The following week, we went to the same building. Jeremy steered me into a narrow spot. A few spaces ahead, there was the Taurus. I waited for one hour in the hot sun, which was bad for my paint job. I hate the sun. Jeremy always used a valet, and I would be in a cool spot, but this was a poor part of town.

An hour later, Jeremy walked down the steps talking to the blonde bimbo who drove the Taurus. They stopped in front of my gorgeous hood, and she leaned on me. I heard her name, Laurel Feingold. He even smiled at her.

The next few weeks, the same routine. She even parked in front of me. I hated a cheap old wreck touching me. This time Jeremy was holding Laurel's hand as they walked toward me. She sat on me. I heard them laugh. Jeremy invited her to drive with him to Starbuck's. Her cheap Target jeans touched my gorgeous leather skin. I was used to Polo or Levi's.

"I'll show him," I thought.

He turned the key. Nothing. Again he tried. No engine sound. Again he turned the key.

"Damn car!" He hit me. It had never happened before.

"This car is a lemon. I'm taking it back," he said.

I started immediately.

At Starbuck's, they left me on the street. Usually, he had a car sitter at a dangerous street like this one. As soon as Laurel and Jeremy walked into the store a bunch of tough kids engulfed me.

"Hey, nice car," one said.

They looked in my window. I was scared. One kicked my tire.

"Ouch," I yelped.

Jeremy looked out and came to save me. "Kids, lay off the car."

Laurel interrupted. "Come on, let the kids drive it. Give them a treat. It's just a car."

They jumped in me. Their greasy boots dirtied my floor. Their dirty jeans soiled my Gucci rugs. I never was "Just a car" to Jeremy. I was his life. Jeremy never had allowed scum like this to enter me, to violate me.

Jeremy used to treat me like a lover. Now that blonde bimbo was his love. He forgot about me. They held hands and made love all over me.

"I want you, Laurel, day and night. Move in with me."

"I will, Jeremy, I will, but will you let me put my car in your garage?"

"Oh, sure dear, you can park indoors and my car can be on the street. It won't hurt the Ferrari. It's just a car."

No, no, if that is what he thinks of me, my love is over. Tears poured down my windows. My windshield wipers worked overtime, but the tears poured out.

Me, just a car?

Funny Man

Carol Mann

Denny Jackson practiced the opening lines of his comedy routine. The joke about the lazy pimp had to go. He could feel it fizzle like a cheap firecracker. Tonight wasn't the night to flop. He needed something funnier.

A grimy notebook on the truck seat beside him held his material. *Denny's Babies, Jokes for the World's Greatest Comic.* He flipped through the pages for something better, a real grabber. Then he saw it, an old routine about a golfer and a gopher, *Caddy Shack* style. Why hadn't he thought of it before? It was perfect.

Satisfied, he relaxed, his thoughts on the evening ahead—Open Mike Night for Comics at the best casino in town. His dream of being a stand-up comic like Jerry Seinfeld or Bob Hope was close. All he needed was a break. He'd give it everything he had or die trying. He was ready.

The tap of metal on glass startled him. He rolled down the window of his delivery rig. Behind him trucks waited in line, their engines droning.

"Hey, Funny Man." A voice like crushed gravel whooshed in with the day's heat. "Pull your load of lumber down by those cement slabs so we can get it unloaded." Joe Fallon, the construction super, grasped a soiled clipboard and checked off Denny's truck.

The big rig idled at the construction entrance of Morgan Ranch, an exclusive housing development in the middle of sand and tumbleweed forty miles east of Palm Springs. He'd never live way out here, even if he had money. He needed the casino night life.

"Okay, Mr. Boss Man." Denny grinned at Fallon's red face, a roadmap of capillaries. Sweat pooled in the pock marks of the man's cheeks.

"Yeah, yeah. I'm 'The Best in the West.'" Fallon scratched his bulbous nose. His eyes darted over the load of lumber. "Hey, you know your load is leaning? Pull in before I got a pile of timber on my feet. We gotta get that thing unloaded."

Denny nodded and rolled up the window, fast. Late afternoon heat seared the sand and dirt, and anything in between. At least the truck for the world's lousiest job came with air conditioning.

He pulled through the gates to wait. The load of lumber wouldn't be going anywhere for the next five or ten minutes. Denny glanced at his watch. He was going to be strapped for time. What a day to get stuck doing a late delivery.

When he was done, he had to get the truck back to Palm Springs, pick up his car, and race home. He wanted to run his act in front of the mirror, a last chance to fine tune the timing and deadpan look. He'd hype himself up, then peak just right—for the Black Hawk Casino—the biggest night of his life.

His clothes were ready—the New York Yankee's cap, the lucky Hawaiian shirt with palm trees and surf boards all over it, the jeans with the baggy ass, the black high-top Keds.

The casino emcee's voice played in his mind. "Introducing the Big D.J.—Denny Jackson, the King of Dyn-O-Mite Jokes." Denny mouthed the words. The name sounded good. Better than Dennis. Better than Denver, like his buddy suggested.

He'd be on a real stage where it counted, not in a meat market joint full of sloppy drunks. Important people would be in the audience. Maybe tonight would land him a stand-up gig in the casino lounge. Or a chance to open a head-liner's act in the big room. He was right on the edge of something great. He could feel it.

The desert by night excited him. Hot chicks, big crowds, and bright lights. "Denny Jackson" pulsing in red neon on the casino marquee. He could see it, taste it.

By day, the desert sucked him dry. If he wasn't careful, the yellow polyester shirt with Desert Builders Supply stitched on the back would squeeze him into a dead-end life of dust and dirt.

"Mama," he said out loud, "this is the night your boy is gonna get noticed."

He revved the engine. Matt Larsen, from Sunshine Plumbing, pulled in behind him with a haul of pipe. Larsen got out of his truck and stretched. Denny hated to leave the air conditioning, but decided to get out. He hadn't seen Larsen since the guy had his accident.

Within moments Denny felt the polyester shirt cling to his back and chest. He ran his hand over his shaved head. Sun's rays beat like drummer's sticks on his scalp's taut skin. Heat rippled from the raw desert floor, the distant Crimson Mountains appearing hot to the touch.

"Summer in the desert's a real bitch." Larsen spat. He had a wiry build. His limp tilted him from side to side when he walked.

Denny nodded. "Glad to see you back on the job. How are you doing?"

"How do you think, Funny Man? I'm not running any races, am I? My boss don't know it, but I'm gonna sue his sorry ass. His goddamned fault the load of pipe rolled on me and broke my legs. That friggin' old truck. The side rigging was shot. Then he makes nice, givin' me a charity job drivin' deliveries." Larsen rubbed the back of his neck, eying Denny's new truck.

"Yeah, that was a bad deal." Denny squared his shoulders.

Larsen looked him up and down, a sneer on his face. "You still tryin' to be a comedian?"

Denny nodded.

"Must be kind of a come down, slummin' with the construction apes."

"Come on, Larsen."

Larsen shook his head. "You know, I had some dreams. I wanted to run the Los Angeles Marathon. Then go to Boston for the big one. Hell, now I got trouble chasin' after the dog." He spat again and wiped his lips with the back of his hand. "Dreams have a way of bein' crushed flat."

"Sorry, man." Denny looked away for a moment. "Hey, I'm doing an open mike at the Black Hawk tonight. Come on by. I'll give you a few laughs." He wasn't going to let Larsen pull him down. Maybe he could even cheer the guy up.

"So, drivin' truck ain't good enough for you?" Larsen scowled, the line between his eyes a deep crag.

Denny caught his breath. Why was the guy always tight-wired, hard to handle? "It's okay for now."

"Last joke you told me stunk up a manure yard."

"Hey, I've gotten a lot better, man."

"Says you, says you."

Denny didn't get it. He'd never done anything to Larsen. What was the guy's problem? He put his hands on his hips to air his armpits. "Tonight is big for me. Hope we unload quick. I gotta get out of here."

"In a hurry, huh, big man?" Larsen reached in his pants pocket and took out a knife. With a quick flip of his wrist, the blade flew open. "Well, I'm just gonna slow you down, let you know what it feels like to be out of the race. To miss the big one."

"Put that away. You crazy?"

"Like a genius, you fuckin' asshole."

Bright lights and fame, that's what Denny wanted. Not a knife in the belly or worse. He wasn't going to mess with the jealous bastard. What happened to Larsen wasn't his fault.

Denny turned and ran for the super's shack.

Larsen stood where he was. "Runnin' away, Funny Man? Was a time I coulda caught you easy." The words blended into the din of workmen's shouts and noisy truck engines.

Sweat rolled down Denny's forehead as he reached the shack. "Hey, Fallon, I need your help. Larsen is acting weird. He's got a switchblade."

"What the hell?" Fallon grabbed his safety helmet and motioned to another trucker crouched under a straggly palm. The man tossed his cigarette and walked over.

Larsen moved along the bed of Denny's truck. He seemed to be fumbling with the heavy straps holding the load in place. What was he doing? Alarmed, Denny ran toward him. Larsen was slashing the straps from the iron rings. If the load fell, he'd never make it to the casino on time.

"What the hell are you doing? Get outta there!"

Larsen's feet kicked up dust as he scuffed around the rear of the truck, out of sight. He moved faster than Denny realized.

Fallon and the trucker ran toward Larsen. "Leave those straps alone. Get away from that truck."

"Stuff it, Fallon. Stay away, losers, or I'll cut you, too."

"Grab him!"

Larsen scrambled back toward Denny. He chanted, "Funny Man, Funny Man." His knife waved in front of him.

Denny wished he had a piece of 2 x 4 or a hammer. His heart pounded.

Fallon's voice rose. "Catch that crazy bastard! Denny, get out of there!"

The other trucker lunged. Larsen side-stepped and, like an out of control car, swerved toward Denny. Denny tried to jump out of range, but Larsen cannoned into him. Denny lost his balance. He fell back into the side of the truck. His head cracked against an iron ring. Dazed, he saw a blurry Larsen dance away. His knees folded under him.

The lumber rumbled, an avalanche of toothpicks tumbling from an open box. The wood pressed him into the sandy pyre. He couldn't breathe. Flashes of light zigzagged, burst, and faded.

A faint voice slipped with him into darkness.

"Okay, everybody, put those hands together. Give a Black Hawk welcome to Denny Jackson, the desert's number one Funny Man."

Has Anybody Seen My Car?

Dawn Huntley Spitz

If I hadn't been so determined to buy that present for Daisy Simmons, none of this would have happened. And if I hadn't been in such haste, I certainly would have remembered where I'd parked my car. But there I was, coming out of the mall into the pouring rain with no idea where I had left my automobile. I tried to recall if I had come in through lingerie or home furnishings. Was it Robinson May or Macy's?

The moment I had pulled into the parking lot that afternoon, I realized that trying to shop in the mall on a rainy Saturday was pure folly. The lot was solid with cars, many of them still moving. They snaked in an endless stream of automotive musical chairs. This was accompanied by a prodigious amount of honking and yelling. Rain not only brings out the shoppers, I observed, but bad tempers as well. Steeling myself, I pulled into the fray. Such a test of patience is the price one must pay for not planning ahead.

My windshield wipers, which beat with the relentless rhythm of Ravel's Bolero, created a heavy pounding in my head. I tried to alleviate the feeling by focusing on the special needs reserved parking spaces. It occurred to me that there might be one I could take advantage of. Well, I certainly couldn't claim to be disabled, unless you call failing memory a disability. Four places (already taken) were designated for Takeout Only. But since there was no time limit, I wondered how this rule could be enforced. Would someone get a ticket if they did not return with food? If so, could they plead that they'd eaten it on the way?

A space appeared up ahead and my spirits rose. But as I approached, I saw it was occupied by a motorcycle. I was indignant. A perfectly good parking space wasted on a motorcycle! Why would a sensible person ride a motorcycle on a rainy day?

Next, I saw two spaces, which had been set aside for expectant mothers. My gracious, in my day we were never so pampered. I considered how a woman might prove her eligibility. Could she be just a little bit pregnant? Perhaps it would help to have a license plate that said something like HAVNKID or

MOM2BE. I had to laugh at my whimsy. Being over seventy, it was all useless speculation on my part.

Just as I was despairing of ever finding a place, an SUV began backing out. Quickly, I pulled into the available slot and turned off the engine of my little hybrid. At least, I said to myself, YOU'RE not a gas guzzler. Then I got out of the car and hastened blindly toward the mall.

Now here I was with Daisy's cologne under my arm and my umbrella shuddering in the wind while I searched fruitlessly for my vehicle. It didn't help that I had to keep dodging the ever-circling stream of cars. Some drivers were even rude enough to tell me to watch where I was going. If I knew where I was going, I grumbled, I wouldn't be wandering around in the pouring rain.

Standing behind a car, which had a Save-the-Environment bumper sticker, I got an idea. This was certainly somebody who could be trusted, I thought. I walked up and rapped on the window. A man with silver hair leaned out.

"What's the problem?" he asked.

"I have a proposal," I said.

"Really?" He seemed amused. Deep lines crinkled around his blue eyes.

"If you'll drive me to my car, you can have my parking place."

He grinned. "It's a deal. Get in."

I pulled open the door, grateful to sit down and get out of the rain.

"Where's your car?" He had a nice smell, like old leather.

"I'm afraid I don't know," I said.

It took him a moment to realize how crafty I'd been. Then he burst out laughing.

"I see," he said. "Can you give me a hint? Were you near the mall or did you have to walk some distance?"

"I'm not sure." I gave him a little smile. "I was so busy thinking about what kind of cologne to buy for Daisy that I just wasn't paying attention."

"What kind of car are we looking for?" he asked.

"A car just like yours." I said. "A silver hybrid."

"So you're an environmentalist, too." He eyed me curiously.

"A card-carrying-banner-waver."

"Who's Daisy?" he asked after a moment.

"She's the newest member of our club. We always give a bottle of cologne to a new member to help cheer her up."

"What club is that?"

"It's called the Winsome Widows."

He threw me a glance.

While we were searching, I told him about my ruminations concerning privileged parking spaces.

He laughed. "You have a great sense of humor."

I looked at him. "You know, you're terribly kind to be doing this. What brings you to the mall on a rainy Saturday?"

"Oh, just something to do. Can't play golf and I'm sick of TV."

"And your wife wants you out of the house," I ventured.

"I lost my wife a few months ago."

We were both silent until we passed the movie theatre.

"They have good films here. Do you go to the movies much?" he asked.

"Not as much as I'd like to, although I'm looking forward to seeing that new Woody Allen movie."

"I have an idea," he said. "Why don't I drive you home so you can get into some dry clothes. Later I'll pick you up and we can see that movie. After that, we'll look for your car. It'll be a lot easier to find after the parking lot has emptied out."

I was supposed to go to the meeting of the Widows that night, which was why I'd been in such a rush to buy Daisy's cologne. But somehow I felt that going to the movies with this man might be more important,

"What's your name, anyhow?" I asked him.

"Robert Crawford," he replied. "What's yours?"

"Betty Bugalopolis," I said.

But it wasn't for long, you see. Because that is how I met my second husband.

Highland Tale

Janet Davidson

Lightning sabers slashed across the dark sky, the jagged white veins slitting through angry black clouds.

It was on a night such as this that my tale begins. A tale that is repeated to this day before home fires in the Scottish village on the banks of the river Kinning.

Sir Bruce MacGregor of Elkhaven lived a lonely life behind the dank walls of his castle. Whiskey and his aged servant, Robert, were his only friends. Childless, his wife had fled years before.

"Hark, do you not hear that, Robert? It taunts my soul to come and fight."

"Nay, Sir Bruce, I hear not but the heavens growling. I'll stoke the fire and fetch another afghan."

"To blazes with the afghan and the fire and you. Bring me my spirits."

"You've finished your spirits, Sir Bruce. See, the bottle is empty."

"Then bring me a full one and be quick."

"But, Sir …"

"Now, Robert. Now."

When Robert returned with the bottle, Sir Bruce was waiting by the door clothed in a long black cape. He grabbed the bottle and pushed his servant aside.

"Do not go out there, Sir Bruce. This night's not fit for dogs."

The old man's pleas went unheeded. Sir Bruce flung open the heavy oaken door and lunged out into the storm.

"Is that the best you can do?" he cried, shaking his fist heavenward. "You'll not best Sir Bruce of Elkhaven. By my ancestors oaths, you'll not best a MacGregor."

A thunderous bellow clapped the air above him. The rushing waters of the river Kinning beckoned him, "This way, MacGregor, this way."

Sir Bruce staggered toward the urging voice. Gulping fire that burned his throat, he drained the bottle dry and slid to a ledge at the water's edge. The river rose, the ledge crumbled and the last of the MacGregors of Elkhaven was carried out to sea on a chariot of broken branches.

The heavens quieted. The river ceased it's wild ways and whispered unheard words in the grey dawn, "You've been bested, MacGregor of Elkhaven. Peace be yours at last. Farewell."

Hope Springs Eternity

Jeri Schmitz

Connie always thought she would get married, have kids and live in New York City. But at the age of thirty-seven she had already passed that section on her reality checklist. Now she found herself about to draw a line through items three and four—hopes and inspirations. It was time to seek help.

"It is called clinical depression and yes, there is medication you can take."

Dr. Grant Hughes held up a clipboard with a checklist of his own. "I can start you on Aczinol and watch you for a few months or I can refer you to an associate of mine, Andrew Osterman, who happens to be the best psychiatrist in town. It's your choice, but I recommend the latter. It may well be a long journey, but like I said, he's the best."

Connie stood on the corner looking at Dr. Osterman's business card. The path to her future was wide open with choices, but all she could see were dead ends. Up until a few months ago, her life had been a gentle breeze. But if she held to her recent holding pattern, she would barely stay afloat in the never-ending sea of confusion.

To go right would be a trip down Complacent Street, promising no adventure and reaping no rewards. Going left would subvert her worth.

"If only I had a mentor who could choose for me," she said aloud before the city noises swallowed up her delicate voice.

She looked down into the abyss of broken glass and gum wrappers, and saw nothing but Paul, his face, her motivation. He beckoned with that charming seductive smile. As the vapor emanating from the gutter cleared, Gabriella appeared. Where else would a man's wife be except by his side?

Connie should have known there would never have been a trip down the aisle for her. She should have, but she didn't.

"I can't leave her." Paul's exact never-to-be-forgotten words echoed through her reenactment of yesterday. Four words meant to stop her in mid-tracks, cruelly put together, closed over her like the long arm of a crossing gate. Four conclusive words, quietly spoken, meant to blend in with the merry-go-round music, but halting all action instead, with a screech.

Connie looked east and west across the full length of Hope Plaza, past the empty soapbox stages. She stared at endless throngs of gray statue pedestrians, positioned at bay, as they waited for green lights to grant them permission to go on with their lives. Pity washed over her as tears blurred her vision.

From north and south along Spring Street, an advancing herd of wild ponies converged on the subway entrance. To see them charge the tollbooth, day after day, and then hobble toward collision courses was to watch wind-up toys heading for disaster and settling for anonymity.

Connie shook her head, and then turned around to see if there were any knights on white horses or benevolent fairy godmothers coming from behind. When she saw none, her decision seemed the wise one and she stepped down in front of the Midtown Express.

Just Another Day

Eleanor Tyus Johnson

There wasn't a sound in the room as Janet opened her eyes. She stared at a streak of bright sunlight crossing her wall that ended on the picture of her daughter, Sydney. The light bounced around the canvas, and flicked from the child's eyes. Her beautiful eyes always seemed to be smiling. As Janet began to return the smile, her eyes dropped to the clock sitting below the picture. The alarm hadn't gone off. It was 7:10. She was going to be late.

Janet hated getting up in the morning, but she hated being late for her first period class at the university far worse. She felt that being on time was a must for a teacher and she had never been late. In one movement she threw back the covers, rose out of bed, snatched up her glasses, and headed down the hall.

She pushed open the door to Sydney's room, and stuck her head in. "Wake up, honey. The alarm didn't go off, and we're going to be late. You shower first, and I'll start breakfast."

Janet felt the chill in the air as she rushed back to her room and grabbed her robe. She loved this old robe. It was so soft from the many washings it had been through, and was the warmest thing she owned. The red and green plaid collar nestled around her neck in all the right places. Her mom thought it had seen its best days. She'd sent her a stunning yellow quilted one, but she continued to wear her old favorite. The pocket needed a couple of stitches, she admitted, and as soon as she had a free moment, she was going to take care of it.

As she passed into the kitchen Janet felt a cold, spongy tap against her ankle. Leaning down, she patted a soft, furry pair of ears.

"Be with you in a minute," she said to the other inhabitant of the apartment.

Sydney had insisted that the only thing she wanted for her eleventh birthday was a puppy. She'd also said this on her ninth and tenth birthday. So, this year Janet had relented, hoping that an eleven-year-old would help take care of a three-month-old puppy. "Muffin" had been there seven months, and it looked like she was staying.

Janet filled a pan with water and put it on the stove to boil. Then she grabbed some eggs, butter and orange juice from the refrigerator and put them on the counter next to a loaf of bread. She reached for a can of Kibbles Deluxe, scooped it into the puppy bowl, filled the second puppy bowl with cool water, placed them on the floor and turned back to their breakfast. As she was reaching for the bread, her daughter walked in completely dressed.

"The poached eggs are cooking, the bread is ready for the toaster and the juice is out on the counter," Janet said as she headed to the shower.

"Okay, Mom. I'll finish up," Sydney said.

Seventeen minutes later, Janet was back. She made a sandwich out of her breakfast, and gulped down the juice. Sydney had stacked the dishes in the dishwasher and put on her coat, hat, gloves, and scarf. Janet did the same.

It had been snowing off and on for four days. The streets were so covered with snow and ice that most motorists stayed home. The few who dared to go out stayed as close to the main thoroughfares as possible for fear of getting stuck. Janet backed their car slowly onto the snowy driveway, careful as she reached the street to roll into the two deep ridges crossing in front of her house. The Simons had already passed by. Bet they weren't late, she thought.

The car moved steadily down the street. Janet glanced at her daughter who was staring out of the window at the falling snow. It must be hard growing up without a father, Janet thought once again. It was certainly hard being a widow and single mother at thirty-five. She'd had no warning. One day Daniel was playing tennis with his buddies and the next he was gone. No one ever dreamed he'd have an embolism. He'd never been in the hospital a day in his life.

Janet sighed and concentrated again on her driving. A few more blocks and she was at Sydney's school. She needed to make up some time. Thank God the snow plows had been out.

"Goodbye," she called as Sydney jumped out of the car. "Hope you're not late."

As Janet eased back into the traffic, the snow continued to fall. Her new windshield wipers were certainly getting a rough workout today.

Janet made her last turn and wished this trip were over. Two more stop lights to go, and she'd be home free. The first light was green. She speeded up a little as she hit the second intersection. She looked and saw no other cars. The light was yellow, but it was too late to stop so she rolled on through just as the light turned red.

Suddenly there was a loud scraping noise. She braked and looked to her right. A car was pressing against her right door. Where had it come from? Had she hit it or had it hit her? The driver motioned for her to park so, gingerly, she turned her car away from the curb and pulled in front of him.

Reaching for her purse, she got out of the car. Her fender was scratched, and the door had a big dent in it.

The man was out of his car and standing to her side.

"You must have pulled out from the curb without looking," she began angrily.

"I did look," he broke in, "and I saw no one. As a matter of fact, the light was red so I didn't expect a car to come flying down the street. Anyone in his right mind knows that these streets are covered with ice and everyone has to drive slower!"

Janet felt her discomfort mounting. Perhaps she was a little bit at fault, but so was he. She had the right-of-way. How dare he suggest that she wasn't in her right mind.

"Anyone with a single brain cell working wouldn't pull out from a curb on a main thoroughfare in a snow storm without looking very carefully," she retorted.

He looked at her a moment. "All right, let's talk about this. It's pretty cold out here. Why don't we go inside the coffee shop over there."

Janet looked at her watch. She was already late. "I don't have the time, but I guess I'll have to make it," she said and carefully walked with him to the coffee shop.

He held the door for her, then followed her in.

"I've got to call my school," she said.

He nodded. "I'll get the table."

In the foyer, Janet flipped open her cell phone and punched in the university numbers, knowing that Marian would answer. Talking to Marian could be a little difficult if you were watching your time.

"This is Janet Walters, Marian, and I've been delayed. A little car accident ... No, I'm not hurt. The car will be fine ... No I don't need to see a doctor ... No, I'm not going home. I will be coming to school shortly. Please ask my class to meet me in the library. Thanks so much for your help."

She hung up, stood there a few seconds, and then walked into the dining area. The place was large, but it wasn't difficult to locate her adversary. At least she thought he was the one. The coat looked the right color. He had taken a seat at a table near the window. She headed in his direction. As she approached, she noticed that he'd ordered two coffees. How presumptive of him, she thought. Probably another control freak.

She slid in a seat across from him.

"Would you like sugar or cream?" he asked.

"Both," she replied. I might as well drink it since it's here, she thought. "Thanks," she said aloud.

As she raised her cup, she became aware that he was speaking to her. He must have drunk his coffee, and thawed out because he sounded different. He was apologizing for the accident and accepting full responsibility for it. He placed a card on the table and promised that his insurance would take care of it all.

Janet put down her cup and, with a little smile, began to thank him. Raising her eyes she looked at him closely for the first time. She caught her breath. *HE WAS GORGEOUS.*

Killer Instinct

Cheryl McFadden

J.P. fumbled in her Birkin Bag for her iPod and quickly connected it to the recessed jack on the instrument panel of her new Mercedes sports sedan. A few spins of the Click Wheel and Manhattan Transfer blasted their rendition of *Tuxedo Junction* through all nine speakers. It was late afternoon and the bouncy melody helped elevate her lagging energy. She was beginning to find that the vitality of her youth was definitely waning—pills and booze did the trick these days. "The good old fashioned way," she liked to brag, "No coke-snorting for me, that's for the kids." J.P. was a purist: amphetamines and Scotch.

Before pulling out of her reserved parking place, she flipped down the visor and checked her face in the lighted mirror. "Money well spent," she whispered as she assessed the newly taut skin and raised brows from her most recent procedure. J.P plumped her hair and silently thanked her stylist Joe-zay who could always be depended upon to keep her tawny tresses looking spectacular. Removing her Versace glasses, she squeezed a couple of drops of Visine into each bloodshot eye, instantly revealing the blue iciness hiding beneath the red.

Not too bad for an old broad, she thought. But the upkeep and maintenance of her fifty-year-plus body was becoming more expensive and time consuming every year. She didn't know how much longer she'd be able to outrun the pack of ambitious young brokers that were nipping at her heals.

But she had something they lacked—plenty of smarts and a killer instinct. It had taken both to rise through the ranks and become the first female multi-million-dollar producer in the Chicago office of Simpson, Carlton, Updike & Mifflin (jokingly referred to as SCUM behind closed doors), the largest stock brokerage firm in the Midwest. She was nearing the top of her game and setting her sights on removing the "female" qualifier from her title. After today she would be THE number one producer.

Her long, determined climb out of obscurity began with her escape from her abusive marriage to Richard Morgan some 25 years ago. She came away with the knowledge of what it took to survive and with a most serendipitous new last name. With a little applied creativity, Geraldine with a "G" became Jeraldine with a "J", and subsequently shortened to initials. Timid little Geraldine Philomena Kowalski, who sat in the back of the classroom far from the terrifying reach of the nuns at Our Lady of Perpetual Compassion in Cedarville, N.J., was erased. Shy little Geraldine, who shrank from her father's verbal assaults, ceased to exist. Frightened little Geraldine, who endured numerous beatings at the hands of the man she had once loved, disappeared. She'd toughened up. In so doing, she acquired the necessary killer instinct. J.P. Morgan was ready to take on the world.

She checked the time on her Rolex watch and realized that unless she hurried she'd be late for her appointment. That could not happen. She was about to make the most important sales pitch of her entire career—one that would catapult her to the top spot at SCUM. Today was going to be life altering—she could feel it in her bones.

J.P. turned the key in the ignition and felt the throb of the engine pulsate through her body. She was omnipotent, the mighty huntress, ready to take down the prey. Even her well known license plate, for which she'd paid through the nose, boldly proclaimed her prowess.

She pulled out into the busy traffic on La Salle Street heading for Harpo Studios on the West End of Chicago and her appointment with the most powerful woman in the world. "I must not be late. I must not be late," she repeated to herself as she pushed the pedal closer to the floor. "Faster. Faster." Adrenaline pumping, she weaved in and out of lanes, breezing by other cars, easily making up for lost time.

Ahead she could see the signal light turning yellow, then red. In a split-second-decision, J.P. punched the gas pedal and sped through the intersection. Sounds of screeching tires and colliding metal entered her safe cocoon, momentarily drowning out the Big Band rhythms vibrating through the speakers. Glancing briefly in the rear view mirror, she witnessed the carnage left in her wake—mangled cars and strewn bodies filled the street. With single-mindedness of purpose she refocused and proceeded towards her goal. *Nothing can stop me now.*

◆   ◆   ◆

What J.P did not know was that less than 24 hours earlier a camera had been installed in that intersection. In the photograph, held by the investigating officer, her car was a blur, but her prized vanity plate was not. Six perfectly legible letters spelled out: **KILLER.**

Labor Of Love

Virginia Cummings

The screen door slammed like a prison gate. As a pup, Fella learned not to mess with that flying door. The flies and moths knew to steer clear also.

Fella lay near his master's rocker as Tad watched the dark clouds gather across his west Texas Ranch. Facing east, the sky was a dark blue with no twinkling stars. Near the horizon the menacing clouds marched with sparklers celebrating their way.

Maybelle, Mama, everyone called her, stepped onto the porch and took her seat in the rocker near her husband. She watched the classic profile, knowing his intent to watch the storm's progress. He counted the seconds between lightning and thunder. As predicted, this one was coming east. There was a fascination seeing this sometimes desolate part of the country come alive because of weather.

"You know you should be in bed. You can watch the sky from your room."

"It's not the same."

"You have watched this for years. Huge black clouds filled with lightning traveling across the fields."

"I don't get tired of the sight. Beside, I have to watch in case lightning hits the barn."

"We can all help. You're not going anywhere and you know it."

Tad shrugged her off. She had made her point and he was having a difficult time dealing with it.

Mama reached into her apron pocket and gave Fella a treat. It didn't matter how pretty the dress her daughter made for her, Mama wore the apron with pockets big enough to carry treats and a hanky in case someone skinned a knee or had hurt feelings. "Please, the family will be here soon. They have dealt with weather like this all their lives. The boys said they would leave right away. I have the coffee on." she said. "Let's go in. I'll help you up the stairs."

Mama could see Tad didn't like the idea of needing help. He'd always been the one with the big heart to give help to family and friends. Mama wished she'd worded things differently, but the storm front was headed right for their farmhouse. So many years they had worked, and nights like this stripped all future plans. Rebuilding fences and barns was the usual aftermath. In the morning, Mama would hunt for the dog dish and prop up her little trees alongside the front path.

The weary door slammed its usual assault.

Mama and Tad stood at the foot of the stairs. His face was grim, and his bathrobe hung limp from his shoulders. He never liked anyone to see him in anything but his overalls. He wore them to town, and sometimes to the Grange meetings.

"You have walked beside me all these years," he said.

"It is where I've wanted to be." She placed her foot on the stair.

Tad patted her rump. "You always excite me, you know. You always will."

"It never used to take you so long to get up these stairs," she said, trying to be cute and tease him a little.

"Don't worry, lady. I'll get you in bed again."

The bed had been turned back, and Tad laid down so he could look out the window. Mama turned the light low and was laying a soft coverlet over his legs when they heard the car doors close. He knew he could rest now. He closed his eyes and waited for the on slaught of little children climbing all over his bed.

The three children tiptoed almost silently across the room. They hesitated briefly for the sign that they could spread their joy all over this big man they loved and called "Poppy."

Tad snuggled each little face and tickled the tender spots as giggles filled the room. His gaze shifted for a brief moment. He remembered stormy nights like this when he spent the night in the barn with a new calf or with the cat struggling to birth too many kittens.

A snap of lightning crackled. Thunder followed and shook the house. Sprinkles dotted the windows sill. The reality of life was very clear.

Tad knew why they had gathered this very night. He may not be with them much longer, but no one was going to talk about that right now.

Tad thought about Mama's friend, the lady painter. She'd done several pictures of the ranch. She kept talking about how beautiful it was here, and how grateful she was to have been invited to stay. She said people wanted her kind of paintings, colorful and peaceful, that showed caring for the place you call your own. People loved her pictures and she truly loved her work. One of her paintings was over the fireplace in the family room.

Upstairs in his bedroom, surrounded by children, grandchildren and the woman he'd loved all his life, Tad felt grateful.

Tad rested now, greeting his sons, holding hands like guys seldom do, and maybe even seeing their eyes in a different light. It was not the look of a scared teenager on a bronco for the first time. This was the look of love. He knew they appreciated how he had encouraged them to be the best they could be.

Tad never thought much about why you do certain things, you just do them. You got up every day, said "Good Morning", had breakfast, and took care of business. Raising a family, taking care of the ranch, and watching out for your neighbors were his main concern.

The best part of his life, though, was sharing all those years with Mama, his true love.

Letting Go

Dawn Huntley Spitz

Carter Williams couldn't stand—and it took him by surprise. He'd known for some time that this day was coming. But he wasn't expecting it so soon. He shifted his weight forward in his armchair, and made another attempt to get to his feet. His legs buckled and he fell heavily back into the chair.

He sat for a few moments, thinking what to do. He took a cursory glance around the room. There was nothing within reach he could use to support himself.

"Well, this is just great!" he said aloud. "What timing!"

The next day was his seventy-fifth birthday, and he knew Kate had invited all their friends and relatives for a celebration. She was out now, picking up last minute items for the party. Of course, everyone had heard about his illness and wouldn't expect him to be the life of the party. Still he had wanted, no, expected to still be on his feet. He didn't want to appear disabled. Not yet. No, this was definitely not what he'd expected. The doctor had given him three years. It never occurred to him he would go down so fast.

He squirmed in his chair. He had to go to the bathroom.

"What the hell am I going to do?" he mumbled.

He needed help. The damn phone was across the room. Why the devil hadn't he thought to keep his cell phone with him? Well, who knew this was going to happen?

He knew Kate would be alarmed when she discovered how helpless he'd suddenly become. Especially with so much still to do for the party. She didn't like unexpected changes. Besides, although she was fifteen years younger, his wife had health problems of her own. He was not a heavy man, but she wouldn't be able to lift him. They hadn't planned for this yet. Down the line. Not now.

"Shit!" he said.

If only Kate would come back. She could bring him something to pee in until they figured out what to do. Maybe, he thought, I can just crawl across the hall to the bathroom. But he sat where he was, afraid to move. It was frightening not to be in control of his body.

But, hey, he'd been on the tennis court less than six months ago, for God's sake. And the day he fell, he'd been playing pretty darned good tennis. He and his partner had already taken the first two sets. Then, without warning, he went down. He'd cracked his head on the court. When he sat up, he noticed immediately that his vision was blurred in one eye. In fact, he'd been so concerned about his sight that he hadn't even questioned why he'd fallen. The guys said it looked like he tripped when he went back for an overhead.

There'd been eye examinations, and the ophthalmologist had recommended surgery for a detached retina. He was ready to schedule it when the real problem surfaced. He found he kept stumbling for no reason, and would have sudden weak spells. It took a lot of tests for that one. But they finally came up with a diagnosis. A.L.S..

At first, he couldn't believe it. Why him? Kate had put up a good front, but he knew she was devastated. He'd heard her crying in the bathroom.

He was getting very uncomfortable. His bladder was full. He needed to pee. Where was Kate? She should have been back by now. But then, she always gave a lot of attention to detail. She'd have to make sure that the cake she'd ordered was just right, that the napkins and plates all matched, that the candles were the perfect color. She got a kick out of giving a party.

It suddenly occurred to him that this might be his last birthday. The thought knocked the wind out of him. He stopped mid-breath and stared into space. Gradually he became aware that he was looking at his son's picture on the desk. Craig was smiling at him, triumphant in his law school cap and gown. Craig had been born to him late in life. Still, Carter had hoped to become a grandfather. He would have enjoyed that.

His gaze shifted to two small oil paintings above the desk, the products of the art classes he and Kate had started when they first moved to Cape Cod. Kate's picture of a cranberry bog in autumn showed promise. His, of Nauset Lighthouse, needed work. Well, he'd always maintained he was better at painting walls than canvases. Damn, how was he going to finish painting the new sunroom now? He'd hoped to have it all done by his birthday, but he hadn't had the energy.

Carter had always been a doer and a fixer. Even on vacation, he was never without a project to work on. Craig had not inherited his father's manual skills. But maybe a grandson ... He didn't finish the thought. How long have I got? he wondered, not for the first time. It wasn't the dying that was tough to face. It was the dependence.

His bladder hurt. He really needed to go.

A sudden rattling at the window caught his attention. Christ, it was sleeting! He knew Kate always got nervous about driving in bad weather. He wished she'd come back. What would she say when she found him like this? He felt his eyes smarting.

"Hey, don't go feeling sorry for yourself, you jerk!" He wiped his eyes with the cuff of his shirt. The sleet pelted the windows. His vision began to blur.

"Oh, what the hell!"

He let the wetness come.

Mary Todd Lincoln Goes To The Theatre

Dory Rose

Mary Todd Lincoln was getting dressed to go the Ford Theater with her husband.

"Abraham, I will not wear this same dowdy, ugly, old dress to the theater. Now, that the war is ending, I want to dress the way they do in Paris in the newest fashion with the deep cut neckline. I will place this delicate diamond and pearl necklace at my throat."

She looked in the mirror with approval as she tried on the necklace.

"Mary, my dear wife, you know those Parisian clothes aren't appropriate for the President's wife. You will show too much of yourself to the public. It is wrong."

Mary jumped up. "I hate the role of being the first lady. I am 46, and I want freedom. I'm locked into an unrealistic budget by those darn Democrats. I don't have enough money to entertain properly. The European ambassadors' wives dress with such style, Abraham. I am stuffed into this high neck dark wool dress with a dull cameo brooch. I look like a toad."

The President turned red. "Mary, must I remind you that you have 300 pairs of gloves and many dresses and jewels. Last year you spent over $27,000 on clothes. And the senate budget committee caught it. Please, we must get ready for the theatre. Look relaxed and well composed. Please, dear wife."

Mary started to cry. "It's the servants. They steal. I know they laugh behind my back, and I am so generous at Christmas, delivering all their gifts."

The president engulfed her with his long arms as he tried to soothe her. He remembered how she easily fell into a depression. He thought about the loss of their two boys and the toll it took on her. He was so involved in the war and in slavery issues that he couldn't help her. He had so many important issues to worry about.

Mary

"Mother, I will see to it that you get a bigger clothing budget. You always look beautiful to me," he said.

The President was exhausted from listening to Mary's constant nagging and complaining. Now, he must pick his arguments carefully as he feared another bout of gloom. He must give in to her on this issue. "Come, dear, wife, get dressed so we can attend the Ford Theatre. We'll be in the President's box. Everyone will see how beautiful you look. Hurry, the carriage is waiting. This will be a night not to forget."

Mary stood on her toes and kissed her husband. "Mr. President, you will be proud of me tonight."

They walked down the steps holding hands.

Mr. Popularity

Kay Virgiel

I'm not the type of guy who's popular with other people. I don't know why. I try awfully hard to make myself adaptable in all situations. For instance, a group of guys at work stand by the water cooler, exchanging jokes. As soon as I stop pushing the mail cart and join them, they split. I'm okay looking, gargle with Listerine, and use an antiperspirant. But still, I heard some guy muttering, "What a loser. Why the hell did they hire him?"

"Hey, guys. Don't let me scare you away," I say in jest. But that's just what I have done, scared them away. People aren't comfortable being around me.

When I was a boy, my mother said I should work on my personality and try to make friends at school. I think she was tired of my hanging around the house all the time. She encouraged me to stand in front of a mirror, pretend I was having a conversation, and smile at my imaginary listener. How out of it can you be? She wouldn't understand that I didn't like anybody, including her.

Waiting in the bushes to scare some poor old lady walking by our yard gave me a kick. I lived to catch stray dogs and cats unlucky enough to come near me. I've pinched and pulled tails all my life. I love to be in charge.

So many owners complained of injuries to their pets, the van from the Animal Shelter canvassed our neighborhood on a regular basis. I avoided them if I could. If they found me, they gave me a warning.

"Watch it, kid. We've got our eyes on you." As if I cared.

My mother got fed up with my attitude. One day, she caught me in the yard holding a kitchen knife in one hand and a cat in the other. The whole neighborhood could hear her rail at me that day.

"Do you want all our neighbors to know how mean you are? You're digging a big hole for yourself, mister. Life's not a piece of cake, you know."

Shortly after that incident, she phoned my dad to tell him he had to take me. Her parting words, "You're incorrigible, and I can't deal with it anymore. God help anybody who gets in your way." Is that true mother love, or what?

Life with my father was completely different. He'd remarried and had two little girls. They were so sweet and so loving, let me play in all their games and said they loved having a brother. I felt like a normal person for a while. As I grew bigger, our play got rougher. Alice, Dad's wife, watched me with disapproving eyes.

She decided I'd grown too strong to play with them. She suggested that I go out for little league baseball. Was she on the sauce or what? I'd never tossed or caught a ball in my life. No kid would want me on his team.

"Use that energy on boys your size," she insisted.

My baseball career only lasted a short time. It ended after I struck another kid on the head with the bat when he called me crazy for sliding onto his foot at third base. He spent two days in the hospital with a concussion. My dad stopped any thought of a lawsuit, saying I was sensitive and felt bullied by being in a new environment with no friends. Can you believe they bought it?

"Christ, Alec," he said. "What kind of a problem are you? No wonder your mother gave up. I'm not sure I can do the job."

I explained that I was just trying to do my best as I always did. He didn't look convinced.

Life went on okay for a while. My school marks were decent. Nobody had to attend a teacher's conference on my account. I made an effort to fit in with everyone. But it just wasn't me, you know?

Then, everything fell apart. I had my eye on a hot girl in my 8th grade English class. I thought she liked me as much as I liked her. I pulled her into the janitor's closet, closed the door, and unzipped my pants. I just wanted to show her what a cool guy I was. She yelled loud enough that two teachers yanked the door open and pulled her out, sobbing. Me, I was taken to the principal's office before being expelled and sent home with my worried dad.

Alice nearly had a fit.

"He can't stay in this house with our two daughters. It would not be safe. Find another place for him to live," she ordered. Guess who ruled that roost.

That is how I ended up at a school for delinquents at the age of fourteen. The lesson I learned there was how to survive in an environment with kids like me. Get the first punch in, never turn your back, and be strong enough to fight off any attackers.

I got out of there when I turned sixteen and was sent to another home. The atmosphere was the same, only these people were bigger and stronger. However, so was I. I knew how to take care of myself in dicey situations.

I graduated from continuation school and attended a semester at a community college. There, I learned some skills that qualified me to get a job. Since all my problems developed when I was a minor, my records were sealed.

At age 20, I am employed at a huge brokerage firm, performing all the menial crap no one else will touch. Besides delivering mail, I make countless trips to the basement for ancient computer files. Any old fart that needs someone to run a personal errand asks for me. 'Gofer' is my middle name. I punch in for work with a time card, am never late, and at the end of the day, I go to my boarding house for dinner. A bunch of losers live there, many on public assistance. Most of them are former group house vets, just like me. I get along better with them than I do with others. They admire me because I have a paying job. You could call it the blind leading the blind. Isn't life a laugh?

Coming down the corridor this morning with my mail cart, I saw an amazing looking girl go into a big-shot's office. As she passed me, she smiled and said, "Hello." That was a come-on if I ever saw one.

"Who is that?" I asked, after she left.

"That's the boss's daughter, sonny. Stay clear of that or you'll be looking for a new job."

I always love a challenge. I could follow her when she goes to the parking garage and learn which car is hers. Then I could hide in the back seat and surprise her. I just want to be liked.

Much In Common

Alan Rosenbluth

"You come here often?"

"Are you crazy? That's the oldest pick-up line in the solar system. George Washington said those very words to Martha on her first visit to Mt. Vernon. What were you thinking?"

"I just wanted to meet you and wondered about your sense of humor."

"Well, it isn't all that funny to me, and I certainly do not want to meet *you*."

"But we already have a lot in common."

"Such as?"

"First of all, we're both movie nuts. Why else would we be waiting in line thirty-five minutes outside the Camelot Theatre to see Peter O'Toole and Vanessa Redgrave in *Venus*? The Film Festival is obviously a high point in our year."

"Mister whatever your name is, please keep your voice down. People in line are listening to us."

"Okay, but you strike me as a gal who likes an audience. I'll bet you've done some acting."

"Well, I did star in the senior play my last year in high school. Anything else?"

"You're very attractive, and I like attractive women."

"And *you* have pathetically few social skills. Furthermore, your creativity is seriously underdeveloped, especially in the area of word choice."

"My dear film aficionado, I had hoped you'd be interested in meeting me."

"I'm not your dear anything. Okay, it's fair to say that you're a nice looking guy. But you're also a clueless jerk. I can't believe we're even having this conversation. What made you think I'd go for all this nonsense?"

"Maybe it's a mistake, but standing behind you in line for half-an-hour made me feel like I knew you."

"You were ogling me all that time?"

"We also have Tai Chi in common."

"How did you know I do Tai Chi?"

"It was the way your hips swayed when you stood shifting your weight from one leg to the other."

"Very perceptive. Are you a sex pervert or something?"

"Also your (what do you call it) 'micro' mini skirt made me think you wouldn't mind being stared at."

"So you thought I was desperate to meet men? What a compliment!"

"No, no—certainly not desperate. I guess I wanted to believe you'd be friendly as well as great looking."

"All this just from watching my ass non-stop?"

"I did get a look at your eyes and noticed how they perfectly matched your gorgeous aqua sweater. Cashmere, isn't it?"

"So you also like the way I look from the front?"

"Yes I do. Wearing that sweater, you're way out in front of most women I know."

"Back to what you said about my skirt. You really think it's too short?"

"Not at all—it's not nearly as short as the skirt the girl in the movie *Babel* was almost wearing."

"That *was* a terrific film. But I must tell you that *I*, at least, have on underwear."

"Good for you. I'm beginning to appreciate *your* sense of humor. I also like your candor and spunk, which you use nicely to mask a fundamental shyness."

"It's now time, *Mr. Smooth Talker*, to ask *you* an important question. When this film is over, would you mind if I sat on your lap?"

"I'll give that possibility full consideration. Now you've reminded me, *Miss Movie Buff*, of the film where Meg Ryan meets a cop, Andy Garcia, in a bar, and within about one minute, jumps onto his lap."

"Yes, I loved that one too, especially that very scene. Just can't remember the title. And it turned out that they … oh, never mind. We *do* have a great deal in common. By the way, *Mr. Good Lookin'*, where do you live?"

"About two blocks from Smoke Tree at 1750 Avery Drive."

"Are you alone?"

"No, I live with a woman there. But she's not home, now. What about you?"

"I've been married for three and a half years. He's not home, either."

"In response to your previous question—after today's movie, I wouldn't mind if you sat on my lap."

"Oh goodie, that sounds nice! Your place or mine?"

"I didn't think an intelligent lady like you would also use such an obvious cliché. I guess you're now testing *my* capacity for humor. Where do *you* live?"

"Another coincidence—I also live at 1750 Avery Drive. The babysitter needs to leave at 5:30. I'll put little darling to bed and fix our dinner. Then we'll have plenty of time to discuss today's movie. Don't forget the Film Festival goes on for two more days. We have tickets for *Pan's Labyrinth* tomorrow. This time *you* stand in line in front of me, and *I'll* speak first. It *is* absolutely amazing how much you and I have in common."

My Best Friend

Anita Knight

Since my dear husband died nine years ago, I've kept busy, but have often been lonely. So when the chance to sleep with someone came along, I decided not to turn it down. I'm not talking about sex, mind you. What I missed was someone to snuggle with, especially as summer began to fade. It's easy to pull the blankets up when cool fall evenings arrive, but a warm body next to you feels wonderful.

You won't be able to travel … He'll want you to stay home with him … You'll be a slave again, just wait and see … These well-meaning admonitions from close friends and adult children failed to deter me. I knew I should think twice about this new adventure. But blinded by the warmth in his eyes and his personality, I'd fallen for Buck, and was eager to have him in my bed.

I went all out the first night he came to my house. Lit the fire, turned on romantic music, even made an antipasto to serve with the wine I'd chilled. Buck didn't drink any wine, but he seemed to enjoy the salami and cheese. It didn't bother me that he didn't like wine. My late husband drank too much, and usually fell asleep right after dinner. It would be fun to be with someone who might enjoy a moonlight stroll, or at least stay awake for dessert.

I didn't expect we'd end up sleeping together so fast, but we did. I went to the bathroom, and when I came out, Buck was sprawled across my bed, a huge smile on his face. As I drew close, he moved over to make room for me. What could I do? I turned down the covers and crawled in. I didn't know what to expect, or how to act, so just whispered, "This is nice."

He winked, turned over, and fell asleep.

Thanks a lot. Maybe you are going to be like John.

I remained wide-awake for ages, wondering what I'd gotten myself into.

At 4:00 AM, I roused slightly when he got up and left the room for what I figured was a bathroom run. When he came back to bed, he squeezed his body close behind mine. He'd been restless all night, and I hadn't slept well, so I kept my eyes closed and stayed perfectly still. Maybe he'd go back to sleep. But no such luck. His head touched mine. I felt his warm breath on my neck, my ear. I had to say something.

"No, Buck, no! No licking ears or sleeping so close to my face. ᴛᴇʟʟs me you're happy, but I must insist that you move closer to the bottom of the bed. And it's much too early to wake up, so go back to sleep, or I'll buy you a doggie bed of your own, and not let you in mine at all."

The stern lecture did no good. His tail thumped against my leg, and the wet kisses moved from my ear to my neck and face. My new pup only wanted to let me know how much love he had to give.

And, of course, he still sleeps with me.

Redemption

Dawn Huntley Spitz

How the hell did I know I wasn't supposed to take $8.50 from the collection plate? Now you might wonder what a Jewish guy from New York was doing in the Catholic Church, anyway. It actually has to do with my being a Coke addict—Coca Cola that is, not cocaine. I mean there is nothing quite as pleasurable as taking a swig from an ice-cold can of the bubbly stuff that chills and fires your gullet all at once. Four or five cans a day, my usual quota, can put you on a flying high.

But there's just one problem. Five cans a day adds up to about thirty-five cans a week, which is about a hundred forty cans a month, which at five cents a can for the deposit adds up to about seven bucks more or less. That's money coming right out of your pocket unless you can redeem those cans.

Now in New York we had these dandy little machines in the supermarket where you could take a month's supply of accumulated cans. You'd stick them, one by one, into the slot and then collect your seven bucks or so. Never mind that your hands got all sticky from the sugar. Or that you might have to wait while the guy ahead of you redeemed a full six-month supply of empties. You knew you were getting your money's worth—even if you were only breaking even. But in California, I'd never seen these machines in the supermarket.

Then somebody told me they were redeeming cans at a trailer up at Food For Less. So I tried that. But they just weighed the cans, which netted me only $3.25, a rip off if I ever saw one. Then one day, I saw a sign outside of a church on this sort of black billboard. It read "Redemption, 10:30 a.m. next Sunday." So I took all my cans to the church. When they passed the plate, I took what was due me. That's when I was arrested for petty theft.

What kind of redemption is that? They never even bothered to count the cans.

Returning

Phyllis Costello

Not a breath of air stirred the leaves shading the gravesite. Silently, mourners suffered the heat in their ill-fitting suits and threadbare dresses. Sweat dripped down the minister's face, staining his Bible. I saw many old friends and lots of relatives but couldn't find Abbie, my oldest friend. Marge Franklin wobbled her way through 'Amazing Grace'. Mom looked pained as Marge hit sour notes. The twins began giggling. Uncle John reached down and pinched them into submission.

My God, it was stifling in this hellhole. I tossed and turned. It was no use. I couldn't sleep in this heat. I got out of bed for a drink. A trickle of sweat ran down my leg.

Stepping out on the front porch, I found no relief. Why did people stay here? Certainly, the place offered no charm, opportunities, or esthetics. It must be inertia. I'd only returned to help because Pops was dying.

Nothing had changed … same poverty, outmoded stores, peeling houses, work-worn weary faces. The old men still sniggered and elbowed each other as the pretty young girls walked by. Housewives gathered in the church basement to gossip and count the months before the first baby appeared. The quality of pies baked, and the whiteness of the neighbor's laundry were also favorite subjects.

My God, where had these people been for the last fifty years? Had they heard of the sexual revolution? Did they ever watch TV?

Another trickle of sweat ran down my back. I wondered again if there wasn't more we could do for Pop. His pain was relentless. It was also killing Mom.

"Can't we take him into Red Oak to another doctor?" I asked.

She shook her head as she cried into her faded hanky. "He won't hear of anyone seeing him, but Doc Morgan. Says he doesn't trust all those new fangled doctors with their fancy machines and poison pills. I can't stand it when his pain is so bad. But he forbids me to do anything else."

Worry kept me awake. As I sat on the porch, I thought I saw a movement across the street in the lilac hedge. Squinting didn't bring anything into focus. I decided it must be my imagination. A few minutes later, I saw a slight movement again, almost like the rustle of leaves in a breeze. Almost, but not quite.

I looked away. Don't be silly, Annabelle, I thought. It's just your wild imagination, going crazy. Maybe it's the silence out here. You're used to traffic and city noises.

Pop was moaning again. I could hear the murmur of Mom and my sister with him.

"Do you need me?" I called.

"Not now. We can take care of this. You get some sleep."

I wondered how they slept without air conditioning or at least exhaust fans. The heat became more oppressive. I unbuttoned my pajama top to fan myself.

A sudden crack of thunder and flash of lightning startled me. Now I could clearly see someone hiding in the lilac bushes. My scalp tightened. Goosebumps raised on my arms. Why would anyone want to watch me? My entire body felt paralyzed. My breath became short gasps. I tried to get up to go in the house, but I was afraid to take my eyes off the bushes. My body wouldn't move.

Slowly he came toward me. Lightning flashed again. I began to laugh and ran to greet him. It was Phil, my old boyfriend.

"Oh Annabelle, Annabelle … why did you leave? I've missed you so." As he gazed into my eyes, I could see his pain.

"I knew it would hurt you, but I just couldn't stay any longer. It wasn't personal. I was smothering here. Needed to find a place where life was moving. Understand, Phil it had nothing to do with you," I said.

His face darkened. "Oh, but it did. I know when you left, you got rid of our baby. You didn't care that it was mine. I can't forgive you. You murdered our child. Now you will pay."

I saw the flash of the knife as he lifted it over my head.

Nothing changes in Union City. Why did I ever come back? I took a long look at the cloudless sky through closed eyes before the dirt hit them. My coffin began to sink into the grave. Not a breath of air stirred.

Rounding Third for Home

Janet Davidson

The robbery had gone down successfully. No hitches. Timing perfect. A clean get away in the crowd.

Steve Mason strode quickly down the empty hallway to room number 23, key in hand. Moving the 'Do Not Disturb' sign aside, he inserted the key, unlocked and opened the door, stepped inside and locked the door behind him.

Crossing over to the unmade bed he emptied the contents of his jacket pocket onto the rumpled bottom sheet. "Hit 'em before they knew what was happening," he mused, smirking. "Pure genius, givin' that kid the toy gun. His grubby paws were all over it. No fingerprints. Ah, just look at 'em! Eighteen sparkling beauties just waitin' to be fenced. Easy. Cool it. Gotta sit tight for a month or maybe two. Then look out Florida! Here comes old Steve."

Steve slid open the closet door. He grasped the wire protruding from the neck of the donkey-shaped piñata on the floor. From the shelf above, he took down a small box of plastic bags and a large brown bag of individually wrapped hard candies.

Seated on the bed with the piñata in front of him, Steve made a four-inch slit in the donkey's back with his pocket knife. He stuffed all but a few pieces of the candy through the slit. Picking up the diamonds, he let them run between his fingers onto the sheet again and again, relishing their cold hard touch. Finally, he carefully inserted three jewels each into five separate plastic bags, folded the bags several times, tightly creased them into small squares and secured them with double looped rubber bands. Gingerly he pushed them one by one into the slit, then covered them with the remaining candies. Finished, Steve rose from the bed, picked up the piñata, and without a backward glance, left the motel room.

As he boarded the bus, his gaudy colored piñata drew smiles and stares from the seated passengers. He found a seat next to a window and sat with the piñata on his lap. He held a front leg with one hand and placed the other hand over the slit concealed by the overlapping strips of paper.

A woman plopped herself next to him, arms resting on her grocer-bag-sized purse.

"Looks like somebody is going to have a birthday party," she said.

Steve stared out the window. "Damn, just your luck," he muttered to himself. "A gabby dame. Ignore her. Yeah, that's the ticket. Ignore her."

"Boy or girl?" the woman inquired.

"What?" Steve jerked his head in her direction. His startled brown eyes met her smiling blue ones that were set in a round, flushed face.

"The party. Is it for a boy or girl?"

"Boy," he answered sharply and turned again to face the window.

"That's nice. Well, I get off here. It was real nice talking with you," she grunted as she pushed herself out of the seat. "Bye, bye, Mr ..."

Steve offered no reply. Instead he squirmed and hunched his shoulders trying to loosen his shirt, wet with perspiration.

"Steady, old buddy," he mouthed to his reflection in the bus window. "Think Florida. Hot sands with girls runnin' around in them little bikinis. No more freezing your butt off in that lousy fourth floor cold-water walk-up you share with the damn cockroaches. You should be charging them rent. Ha! That's a good one. Think sunshine and six-packs. A cool one anytime you want." Steve licked his lips, tasting his fantasy.

A small boy slid into the vacant seat.

Shifting his body closer to the window, Steve continued his interrupted daydream. He dredged up his old lines that used to work on the young giggling girls in his neighborhood. Maybe they'd get him some of those Florida beauties.

The piñata shifted hard as a small fist slammed into its side.

Steve reacted swiftly. "Lay off, punk."

The boy folded his arms over his thin chest and glared up at Steve's irate face.

Turning away from the boy, Steve wondered if he used to stink like the skinny kid sitting next to him. Did his pals stink? Is that why the girls at PS 28 screamed and ran away from them?

From the corner of his eye, Steve caught sight of the dirty unlaced tennis shoe as it hurled in the air and struck the donkey's head.

Shoving his face within two inches of the small smirking face, Steve snarled, "Try that again, and I'll tie your legs in knots. Get it, punk? Don't even breathe if you want to live."

The boy's eyelids lowered. He shrank down in his seat.

Satisfied the boy would give him no more trouble, Steve thought again of Florida, palm trees, the ocean and a blonde on each arm one night, redheads the next.

The blinking pawnshop lights brought him back to reality. One more block to his stop. Almost home.

Steve alighted from the bus, tucking the piñata under his arm. It was a relief to see the familiar sights, even the group of swearing boys who seemed to be forever playing stickball in the street. They reminded him of his childhood, escaping from his abusive father. A policeman, walking his beat on the opposite side of the street stopped to watch the players for a minute, then moved on.

"Damn, a cop," Steve said through clenched teeth. Quickening his steps, he hurried home, his eyes reaching ahead of him to his graffiti-painted front stoop.

"Hey, man, what you got there? Does he bite?" One of the boys approached him, tapping the street with his stick.

"Out of my way, Spike. You don't know nothin'. That there is a piñata. I seen one on TV. You got candy inside, man?" asked an older boy carrying his stick on his shoulder.

"Hey, you got candy? Give us some candy, man," Spike demanded. "You tell him Stretch. Tell him he gotta give that candy to us."

"Get over here, guys," Stretch shouted. "This here bull is full of candy and he ain't gonna give us none. We gotta hit it with our sticks to make the candy spill out. It's a game, ain't it, man? A real fun game."

Steve held the piñata shoulder high as the boys circled him. No use trying to run. Beads of perspiration moved the hairs on his head. Panic squeezed his chest. He lifted the piñata high above his head. Spike snickered as he raised his stick and swung at the piñata, barely missing it. His stick hit Steve's temple a glancing blow he didn't feel, nor was he conscious of the warm blood trickling down his face.

Stretch gripped his stick with both hands. He jumped as he swung hard, connecting sharply once, twice, three times.

The donkey's paper-layered side split open with a cracking sound. Steve Mason cried out as the contents rained down on him, oblivious of the policeman running to his aid.

Scent

Anita Knight

The small cut-crystal perfume flacon sparkled with diamond-like brilliance. For the twenty years it stood on Angela's dressing table, its prisms shattered the bright morning sun into pieces of rainbow.

Angela didn't care for perfume. Allergic to most, she preferred the scrubbed clean smell of soap and water. But this was different. This was from her time with Brett.

At first, she used it daily, a drop behind each ear, a dab on the pulse inside her wrists, but after Brett was no longer hers, she stopped, afraid of the emotions the scent might invoke. Once she picked up the vial to throw it away, but something made her pull out the tiny stopper and hold it to her nose. A myriad of memories flashed through her brain. Tears filled her eyes as she pushed the stopper back in and carried the bottle to the dresser, where it had remained ever since.

The children had been young, Mary, nine, Joey, twelve, when Brett came into Angela's life. Her husband, Hal, busy trying to become a CEO, was seldom home, and had little time for his family. Angela didn't bother him with mundane household chores, and tried hard to take care of everything. She even took the kids camping. She taught Joey to do the woodsman things most fathers took care of, and showed Mary how to roast marshmallows without getting burned. It was fun, but she missed the old days when she would sit by the campfire with Hal as he pointed out stars and talked about their future.

Lonely, Angela decided to join a writing class. It inspired her to be with adults, and to think about something more interesting than daily household events. When Brett arrived, it was easy to respond. He was exciting and romantic, exactly the type of man she wished Hal were. The fact that he was handsome made him even more tempting. A fairy tale prince, who stood six-two, he was muscular and tan, had thick black hair, a great sense of humor, and a hearty laugh. What more could a woman want?

Brett. She'd always loved that name.

Angela cherished her time with him. She wanted nothing more, but still felt responsible for the needs of her family, which included the occasional wifely duty she believed she owed her husband. She would close her eyes and fantasize for the brief moments that Hal took, and then dream of what it would be like with Brett.

One night her writing class teacher handed back the final draft of the novel Angela had worked on for over a year.

"Submit it."

"Do you think it's good enough?"

"It's great, but even if it gets rejected you must submit it. It's not going to do any good buried in a drawer."

A month later, an ecstatic Angela addressed a cardboard box to a publisher who'd responded by asking for the complete manuscript. Her hand shook as she wrapped the sticky tape around the fat package. She was ambivalent about her desire to publish, worried people would find her work shallow.

Hal came up behind her and massaged her neck with his warm hand. "What're you doing?"

"Sending out my manuscript." Her head fell forward. "Mmm, that feels good."

"You've been working too hard, Angie. Maybe we can take a trip now you're done." He continued to rub her neck. "I bet it sells right away."

"It's a long shot. So many people write now."

"You've never let me read it, but I know how well you write. Am I going to have to buy my own copy?" he teased, "I am interested, you know."

"You're so busy, I didn't think you'd have time for it."

Hal bent and wrapped his arms around her. "Honey, in case you haven't noticed, I've cut way back at work. I do have time."

Angela pulled away from him and clutched the package to her breast.

"It's not a story you'd enjoy, Hal. It's a romance."

"What makes you think I wouldn't enjoy that? When we dated you said I was the most romantic guy you'd ever known."

Hal lifted her from the chair and turned her to him. "I plan to spend a lot more time with you. It took that seminar last month to make me realize my family is more important than my job." He pulled her close and kissed her.

Angela's heart raced for a moment, then she pulled away. How could she find time for Brett if Hal was around?

◆   ◆   ◆

The letter came from Heartfelt Books less than two months later. They were going to send her a contract and a sizable advance. It had been too easy!

Within a year, the book was on the market.

Brett became public property. Angela got hundreds of letters from readers who had also fallen in love with her hero, and she realized that he was no longer only hers.

She cried for a while, but as time passed, found contentment in the arms of her husband again.

Occasionally her mind would drift back to the wonderful memory of her time with Brett, but was comforted in the knowledge that she could make those moments real again. Whenever she wanted, all it took was a tiny sniff from the small cut-crystal perfume flacon, which had stood in the same spot on her dressing table for the last twenty years.

Stopping For Red Lights

Dolores Carruthers

The stocky figure seated before the small altar breathed in the fragrance of sandalwood incense. Against her closed eyelids, she could feel the bright California morning sunlight pushing away the night darkness. It was time. Without opening her eyes, she reached for the small, brass temple bell to ring an end to her morning meditation.

It was also time to move from her inner world, where all was tranquil, to the outer world where anxiety hovered. When she'd decided to leave her old self behind, California had beckoned with its freedom of choices and opportunities. She could wear skinny dresses, short skirts, skimpy tops and snappy sandals without fear of raised eyebrows. Moving had its advantages. It also had its complications.

Remembering her parent's opposition to her move dimmed the afterglow of her meditation. "We thought you would give up this crazy idea." Her father's angry words had bruised her heart, already sad about leaving without their approval.

"Dad, you know I've tried to do it your way. I can't live here anymore. Everybody looks at me as if I'm weird when I dress the way I want to. I'm not like everyone else. I'm tired of hiding who I am." Trying to lighten the tension between them, Carly added, "When you come to California to visit, you can wear anything you want. Out there nobody cares if you dress differently."

At these words, her mom had stormed out of the room, leaving her father to thunder in his loudest voice, "You know our feelings on this whole lifestyle thing. If you go through with this, you'll no longer be welcome here."

Carly swiped at her eyes, shook her head to clear away the memory, then stood up and put away her meditation cushion. Glancing at her watch, she flinched. *Damn, I'm going to be late.*

She closed her eyes, took several deep breaths and focused on releasing anxious thoughts about being late, about wasting time reminiscing, about worrying … *Stop.* "I am peaceful, I am centered," she recited. Today was a fresh start, no past

93

history to get in her way. Her new career as a meditation teacher at the Southern Cal Life Enhancement Center was an important step in her transformation.

She grabbed her water bottle, purse, car keys, and walked out the door. Her new red Mustang convertible, top already down, gleamed in the sunlight. After settling into the driver seat, she glanced in the rearview mirror to check her long blond hair and makeup one last time. That was another reason she was running late. Her makeup routine was taking longer to cover her uneven skin tones and achieve that "California tanned" look.

Satisfied with her appearance, she inserted the key and chanted the Gatha she'd read in one of her Buddhist self-help books. *"Before starting the car, I know where I am going. The car and I are one. If the car goes fast, I go fast."*

Satisfied that everything was under control, she turned on the ignition. After backing out of the driveway, she eased into the fast moving traffic. Everyone was in a hurry in California. When she first arrived in Los Angeles, she'd kept up with the moving traffic, not paying much attention, until one day she'd glanced at the speedometer. She'd been driving 85 in a 75 mph zone and up ahead a traffic light had turned red. Just remembering gave her goose bumps. *No more of that. Even if I'm late I'm keeping an eye on the speedometer.*

Once on South Boulevard, she relaxed enough to think about the other big change she'd made. It had started when her high school buddy, Alan, asked for help with a Buddhist meditation class.

"Are you kidding? You know how I feel about any kind of religion."

Impatiently, Alan said, "Look, I just need someone to help set up the room and take registration. I'm not asking you to become a Buddhist, although I think you'd be interested in its teachings about compassion and Oneness."

It was the word *compassion.* Without thinking, "Yes, I'll help," came out of her mouth. Fascinated by the idea that a great spiritual leader believed compassion was the way to reduce a person's suffering, she began studying Buddhism and meditation. Here she was five years into …

Glancing down at the speedometer, she saw the car was going too fast. *Oh shit. Oops! Cancel that thought. Cripes, the traffic signal is yellow.* She stepped on the brake, but was already half way though the intersection as it changed to red. In her rearview mirror she saw a motorcycle cop pull out of a side street, and heard the siren.

"Not now, not now, please," she pleaded under her breath.

The cop motioned her to pull over. She did and turned off the car, which also turned off the CD player and the soothing music of Enya. The peace was shattered by abrupt silence.

A tall, slender figure slowly dismounted the motorcycle and walked to the car. Carly took a deep breath. *I am surrounded by Love.* Lowering the window, Carly flashed her brightest and most serene smile at the officer, who stood looking down at her through dark sunglasses. It dawned on her that it was a police woman. Instantly she relaxed. *Women were more sympathetic and understanding than men.*

"What's wrong, officer?"

The officer raised her sunglasses and looked hard at Carly as if she couldn't believe the stupid question. "Do you know what the speed limit is?"

Carly hesitated. *Damn! If I say yes …*

Impatient, the officer answered her own question. "It's forty-five and you were doing fifty-seven. Mustangs are snappy cars so you should be watching your speed."

Without taking time to breathe, Carly reacted. "Are you saying you targeted my car because it's a Mustang?"

The officer glared at her. "I'm saying you were speeding *and* ran a red light."

Carly's heart raced, her attempts to be peaceful deserting her. "It wasn't red when I started through, but turned red after. You're harassing me because I drive a red sports car. Are you jealous?"

Officer Stearns stiffened. "Show me your license. Now!"

Oh no. She was in for it unless the officer didn't look at the license too closely. She reached in her purse, pulled out her wallet, and started to hand it to the officer.

"Take the license out of the wallet," said Officer Stearns, her name tag now directly in Carly's vision. *Boy is she named right. Even her face looks stern.*

Carly yanked the license out of its slot, and thrust it out the window. The officer walked back to the motorcycle with the license, rested her hip against the seat, and spoke into her two-way radio.

Glancing in her rearview mirror, Carly could see the officer shaking her head as if she didn't agree with what she was hearing. Perhaps if she concentrated on their Oneness, she could overcome her angry reaction to this annoying woman.

Oh, oh, here she comes.

"How long have you lived in Los Angles? This license is registered in New Jersey, you wear glasses, have brown not blue eyes, and are male not female. What's going on?"

Carly glanced away from the cold eyes glaring at her. She'd hoped for more time to become comfortable in her new lifestyle.

Hesitantly Carl said, "I'm transsexual. I just moved here a couple of months ago and haven't had time to change my license."

He could see Officer Stearns surprise although she quickly assumed a neutral mask. After all this was California, home to all kinds of sexual orientation which was why Carl had moved here. *Maybe she's never stopped a cross dresser before.* He smiled hopefully—after all they were One.

After a long silence, the officer said, "In the future watch the speed signs and the warning signals before starting through a light. And get your California license! Welcome to Los Angeles." Striding back to her bike, the officer quickly mounted and raced away as if the hounds of political correctness were chasing her.

Stunned by his escape of a ticket, Carl breathed in and out, and started the car. "*The car and I are one. When the car goes fast, I go fast.*" After a contemplative moment he added a new stanza. "*The car and I stop for red lights.*" Peaceful inside and out, he eased back into traffic. Life was good. Compassion and Oneness existed in sunny California.

Tell Me 'Bout Love, Granny

Janet Davidson

"Tell me 'bout love, Granny."

"Love? Why you're just a child."

"I'm almost ten, Granny."

"'Most ten? Already? Seems like you was born only yesterday. Well, I know 'bout lovin' one man. That be your great-granddaddy. Child, that be a long, long time ago."

"You forgot him?"

"No, I ain't forgot him. Not 'til I die."

"Tell me. Tell me 'bout you and great-granddaddy. I'm waitin', Granny."

"Child, it was a day like today. I could smell the earth bustin' to start spring, and the air so clear after rainin' you could hear it if you listened real close. I was standin' on this here porch. It was pretty then. Had paint. This here rocker was pretty then, too. I was lookin' up yonder hill at that big ol' tree and I seen him. He was standin' under it starin' down at the house. Child, my breathin' stuck in my throat, and when he started walkin' t'wards me I wanted to run, but my legs just wouldn't move. He asked me where my pa was and I couldn't answer him right off 'cuz I was looking at him so hard."

"Go on, Granny. Go on."

"Oh, he was a handsome sight to see. I remember how his big shoulders shut out the sun, and his brown eyes smiled at me like he was laughin' inside. I was warm all over lookin' at him."

"Why was you warm?"

"Don't know. Just was. Him standin' that close and all. Well, Pa needed a hand so he put your great-grandaddy on that very day. He worked for meals and a blanket, he did."

"Then what?"

"Your Granny was happy all the while knowin' that man was here. Know what I'd do? I'd leave Mama with the chores and sneak off to the fields to watch him workin'."

"Why would you want to watch him workin'?"

"Felt good watchin' him, Child. Know what else I'd do? When I was helpin' Mama put down supper, I always set a meat plate right in front of him. Know what he'd do? He'd pat my head or pull my hair a little."

"You let him pull your hair? I'd never let him do that. Keep goin', Granny."

"One day after supper I was washin' up the dishes and quiet as a mouse he untied my apron strings behind me. Then ... he kissed me."

"On the lips?"

"No, right here on my head. That night I put my doll in a box and shoved her way under my bed. I never took her out again 'til I gave her to your Grandma."

"I'd never do that to my doll."

"You will, Child, one day. Wait and see. One day you will."

"What happened then?"

"Let your Granny think a minute."

"You done thinkin' Granny?"

"I'm done. Pa liked him 'cuz he was the best worker he had. That man could work like a mule, he could. Mama liked him, too. She know'd I was sweet on him."

"You was sweet on him?"

"Yep, and he was sweet on me. One day he asked Pa if he could marry me. Pa told him he sure as thunder could if I was agreein' to it. When I told your great-granddaddy I'd be pleased to be his wife, he let out such a holler folks could hear him clean to Creek Tree County. Know what he did? He picked me up and carried me to the trees yonder and laid me down on the cool grass and kissed me on the lips 'til I wasn't thinkin'."

"Is that love, Granny? All that kissin'?"

"More to love than kissin'. There's lookin' at each other and there's touchin' ... I reckon love is waitin' for your man to come home and missin' him so much when he's gone that you just plain ache."

"You got a headache missin' him?"

"No, Child. Can't rightly tell you just where."

"I wish you had a picture of great-granddaddy. I wish I could see what he looked like."

"Wishin' don't cost a penny."

"Don't you wish you had one, Granny?"

"No need for me wishin' that. I got his picture right here in my heart."

"Tell me more. Tell me more than kissin' and missin'."

"Well now, there's makin' babies. That's a sweet time for sure. That man was gentle with me like he was with baby kittens. He was a good man, your great-granddaddy was. He know'd how to make me happy. But ... his feet couldn't stay in one place. They just couldn't stay."

"You cryin', Granny?"

"Still got tears left in me thinkin' 'bout that day. The snow was all but melted. Little patches here and there. The kitchen was nice and warm from Mama cookin' breakfast. I recollect the apple cakes and syrup tasted special good that mornin'. Pa was itchin' to start turnin' the ground and he was eatin' fast as he could.

"But your great-granddaddy was pokin'. He was lookin' all around him like he'd never been in the kitchen before. He was eatin' real slow like he was puttin' off goin' to the fields. Pa told him to hurry, but he paid him no mind. When he was done eatin' he walked out the door and up the hill. He stood under that big ol' tree a minute lookin' down at me and then he was ... he was gone. Child, your grandma started kickin' inside me somethin' fierce, just like that little baby know'd her daddy was leavin' and she would never see his face. I was standin' here when he came and standin' here when he left."

"Where'd he go, Granny?"

"Don't know. 'Spect I never will."

"I don't like love, Granny."

"You will, Child. One day you will."

The Bingo Game

Dory Rose

Molly held her purse close to her body. This was the first time that she won $50.00 at the Senior Center Bingo Game. She'd had to wait until the end of all the games to collect her money, and now had to walk home in the dark.

Molly kept looking back to see if anyone was following her. Suddenly she felt a bright light surrounding her 110-pound body. She was lifted straight up to the sky where she landed in a small, stark white room. A loud voice invited her to sit in a chair.

"Molly, do not be afraid. We will not hurt you. We are aliens from another planet. We had to pick a human being from earth to study. Your head looked so large that we knew we would have a lot of material to work with."

Molly laughed. "My head isn't big. I was at George's Beauty Parlor today. I always get my hair done in a bouffant when we go to play bingo because a cute widower sits next to me. If you want my bingo money, take it and send me back to my apartment. I'm tired."

"We don't want your money, Molly. We will not touch you. Put on this blue robe for the X-ray machine."

Molly jumped up. "I never wear blue. I went to a color expert at J.C. Penny's and I was told to wear green. Blue makes my skin yellow."

The robe turned green.

"That's better," Molly said.

"Molly, I'm going to put a few wires in your hair."

Molly shook her head. "Oh, no, I spent $25.00 on my hair. You're not touching it, and besides, Buck Rogers, I'm starved. I'd like eggs, a lightly toasted bagel, apple jelly and crisp bacon."

The plate of food was in front of her. She pushed it away and pulled back.

"These eggs have a hard center and the bacon isn't crisp. Take it away. I want to go home right now. My boys will wonder where I am. They call me every night from Chicago to check on me. They're good boys."

"Molly, we must get more information. What do you like to read? Don't earth people read Shakespeare?"

"No, I hate thees and thous and sires. I read *People* magazine when I am at the super market. Once I read a Sidney Sheldon book. Besides I'm having cataract surgery, if you ever let me go, and then I will read another book, maybe."

The alien voice grew low and shaky. "Molly, one more test. We know humans look at TV, and have computers and cell phones. Will you help us to learn about those machines?"

Molly stood up. "My boys, they are such good boys. They gave me a computer, but I can't use it. I do look at TV but only two stations. My favorite is about the gay guys. They decorate houses really pretty."

The voice came back. "This must be a happy program if they are gay all the time."

Molly laughed and laughed.

The alien disappeared. The room disappeared. It didn't take but a twinkle of another bright light before Molly was back in her apartment clutching her bingo winnings.

Immediately she dialed Chicago. "Saul, you'll never believe what just happened to me. I had the most amazing experience tonight. I won $50.00 at Bingo."

The End of A Fish Tale

Dawn Huntley Spitz

Joe Santini leaned on the railing of his boat and stared into the water. The wind felt cool on his face as the trawler chugged slowly down the Sacramento River.

"Come to me, my friends," he whispered. He was approaching the delta, the place where the Sacramento and San Joaquin converge on their way to San Francisco Bay. Fish had always been plentiful here, fine striped bass and salmon and delta smelt.

Forty years ago, when Joe had started fishing with his father, a man could take his quota in a couple of hours. Now, a whole day could pass without catching a single bass. Now, he might collect a smattering of smelt or threadfin shad. If he was lucky.

Were the fish angry? Is that why they had gone away? Had he not shown enough gratitude for the rich bounty that had sustained him for so many years? Joe was superstitious, like all men who worked on the water. Fish, they knew, could easily be spooked. Who knew why?

Something in the water caught Joe's attention and he tensed with hope. But it was not a fish. It was something that waved in the current. Water hyacinth! Joe spat in disgust. These damned weeds choked the channel. What good were the herbicides?

A sharp scream sounded overhead and he looked up. Seagulls were circling in greedy anticipation of a share of Joe's catch.

"Patience, feathered ones," Joe called, waving them away. The seagulls retreated to pilings at the edge of the river where rows of new condominiums stood, close as corn stalks.

Joe's teenage son, who had been standing in the stern, moved forward. He was strong and had the sea in his blood like all the Santinis.

"Those gulls are fat and lazy," he said.

Joe looked at him. "They know fishermen will feed their hunger."

The trawler swept through the waters for hours.

"Let's bring 'em in," Joe said.

Together they watched as the winch pulled up the net. The seagulls returned, shrieking with excitement.

The net hung slack. The gulls circled, suddenly silent. There were no fish. No fish at all. Only weeds. While the boat idled, a mass of debris—garbage, plastic and dead fish—floated by.

The boy looked at his father. "How could this happen?"

Joe shrugged, his hands outstretched in silent apology.

"You must feed yourselves, hungry ones," he called to the circling gulls.

He moved to the wheel and the boat headed upriver. In its wake, the gulls descended on the swill with glittering eyes.

The Fury, Deleted

Carol Mann

The lifeless form lay face down among the peonies. Taking a deep breath, I raised the iron sledgehammer above my head. It fell back between my shoulder blades and, as my elbows straightened, made its return arc.

Take that!

The words ricocheted through me. The hammer, powered by my newfound maniacal strength, slammed into the remains. With a surge of hurt, anger and adrenaline, I quickly swung again. Sweat welled on my temples and neck. It slid down my cleavage and the small of my back.

I should have done it long ago. I hated Toshie, the superior acting bastard, with his constant abuse—never acknowledging my intelligence. He thought the keys to the world's knowledge were his and his alone.

I stopped to brush away a tangle of hair. The long cotton tunic and black tights I wore clung to me. Heavy dangling earrings pulled on my earlobes. Their swinging annoyed me. I dropped them in a pocket. I thought I'd feel exhausted. Instead, a rush of pleasure slid over me, a garment of smug satisfaction.

I used to enjoy the well-groomed peony bed. Pink, magenta, and white flowers bent stems of bushes imported from China many years before. The garden, on the downside of a gentle slope, highlighted Lakeside Park, a town landmark. I'd brought carnage to the pride of the community. I didn't care.

The blooms, eerie in fickle moonlight, surrounded a white lattice gazebo. Worn white wicker chairs sat under its protection. Toshie and I idled there on summer afternoons, becoming acquainted, before things turned sour. I thrilled to his gentle touch, the excitement of a new relationship, the exchange of ideas. We wrote short stories together—a themed collection about love.

Feelings of inferiority edged over me gradually, dull at first, then honed like a razor on a strop. Toshie's incessant badgering beat into my confidence and pounded it to smallness. I could still hear him.

You're not good enough. How many times do I have to tell you? When are you going to understand?

I swung the sledge.

Gauze-like clouds rippled in front of a pale moon, brushing the night out of focus. It was a few minutes past midnight. I stood alone with my revenge. No one would know my secret after I buried the remains, smoothed the dirt, and gentled the surrounding peonies to their former glory.

I heard my name.

"Leah, what in the hell are you doing at this hour?" It was snoopy Lester Baumgartner, the town gossip monger, peeping around the neighborhood on his late night walk. On an occasional afternoon he had joined Toshie and me in the gazebo.

I kicked dirt on my handiwork. Passion, kindled by Toshie's thoughtless degrading treatment, and disregard for my talent, now mixed with fear. I hadn't planned on my neighbor's inopportune nosiness. He usually took his walks earlier.

Lester appraised the hammer dangling from my hand. I knew he liked to roll rumor around town about me. Now he'd have more oil for his gossip wheel. I could hear him—*Leah's wandering around in the peonies at midnight.*

People already thought me eccentric. I'd heard the talk. I wore my hair and skirts too long. Off shoulder, peasant blouses showed too much skin. My tunics and tights appeared clownish. Too many jangling bracelets and piercings adorned my body. My liberal ideas jarred the town mindset.

After I'm a famous writer, they'll grovel. They'll flock around me, instant friends. I'll spurn them.

Toshie, the traitor, had been on their side. Even he hadn't believed in me.

Lester drew closer to peer at the battered carcass, partially buried, lying at my feet. "Geez, Leah, what in the hell are you doing?"

I tried to shield what lay in the peonies. He brushed me aside.

"Well, now I can say I've seen everything. Wait'll the guys down at Hava-Java hear this. Leah's in the park—at midnight—smashing her new laptop!" A great guffaw emanated from his belly.

My artistic soul withered. Gripping my sledge, I stepped toward him. A final deletion.

The Hair On Her Chin

Dory Rose

Small villages dot the green rolling hills of southern Ireland. Folklore and legend thrive in these quiet, innocent towns. O'Toole's Pub on the edge of town was the center of storytelling over a mug of beer.

Every year in the late fall, the sun hit the hill where a mystery had taken place many years ago. The hill was shaped like a woman's face. The flat top was the forehead. The bottom of the hill was the chin. The point was the nose. The folks called it Fat Molly's Hill.

At every pub heated arguments took place. Who were these lovers who hid in the hills? Occasionally fistfights took place (after three beers). Each fighter had his or her own version of the scandal on Fat Molly's. Mary Kate, who worked at the pub, believed the lovers were 16, too young to be on the hill alone. Pat, the town mayor, insisted that the boy was a stable boy and she was from a landowner's family. Erin, who only drank Irish coffee and ate boiled potatoes, argued the boy was a Protestant and the girl was Catholic.

The legend evolved over many years. In the long history of storytellers in Ireland, the story changed. Everyone agreed that the lovers met on the hill (that was shaped like a chin of a woman) secretly as the sun went down. The town folk were sure that they embraced under a bough, warming each other in the chilly mountain air.

One night, when the October moon was brilliantly bright, a young shepherd hunted on the hill, trying to catch a hare for his Mother's rabbit stew. He chased it up the hill that was shaped like a woman's chin. In the bushes, he saw a movement and discovered the young couple embraced at the chin of the hill.

He raced down to the town to the closest pub. The story spread to the church, to the schools and even to all the cottages that dotted the town.

The next night, the town fathers marched up Fat Molly's Hill with flaming torches. They cut the thick bushes away. Under the light of the moon, the two young people were wrapped in each other's arms. Pat, the mayor, tapped his foot across them. Their bodies were still. Their skin was blue. There was no move-ment.

Were they murdered? Did they commit suicide? Did they die of broken hearts?

Even today, the folks in O'Toole's pub debate about the legend that took place where a hare was found on the hill shaped like a woman's chin.

The Magic Glasses

Shirley Gibson

Marvin made a profound discovery one day as he was browsing around his dad's antique shop. He found a pair of old round glasses. Being nine years old, he was inquisitive.

Where did they come from? How long have they have been there? I don't remember seeing them yesterday, he thought.

He put on the glasses, but immediately pulled them off. That was weird, he thought. Once again he put on the glasses. He saw a man in an old fashioned suit standing in the room. The man was wearing the glasses. When Marvin removed the glasses, the man disappeared.

"Where did he go?" he asked his father.

"Who are you talking about Marvin?"

"There was a man standing over by the window."

"Maybe it was someone outside," his dad said.

"No, I saw him inside."

"There's no one here."

"But I know I saw him. He was wearing a pinstriped suit and a hat with the rim turned down. He had a mustache and he was wearing these glasses."

"Hmm, that sounds like this picture of Mr. Robert Anderson." His father held up a faded black and white photo.

Marvin's eyes lit up with excitement. "Yes, that's the man I saw."

"Son, he's been dead for twenty-five years."

"What happened to him?"

"The story goes that he lived on the edge of town and was owner of the mill. He had a daughter Emily who got sick and died. She was about eleven. Having lost his wife only a year earlier, Emily was all he had left."

"Do you think these are his glasses?"

"They could be. There're exactly the same as in his picture. I received this box of pictures and glasses from the estate of Mr. Anderson."

"Can I have the glasses?" Marvin asked.

"Sure, they're not a salable item so go ahead."

Marvin placed the glasses in his pocket and headed out to the mill. The mill was one mile from town. The old mill needed repairs. Some boards where missing as well as the paddles on the water wheel.

Marvin pulled open the door. The hinges gave out a squeaking sound that caused the pigeons on the rafters to scatter. The floor, as well as the remaining equipment, was covered with dust, the remains of a once thriving business. He saw the ramp where the trucks brought in the corn to be ground into corn meal. He looked at the structure to see how the water wheel outside connected to the machine that turned the turbine that ground the corn.

Marvin reached in his pocket and put on the glasses.

Everything came to life like a motion picture from the past. There was Mr. Anderson sacking up the ground corn, Emily by his side, reading a story as he worked. His wife was seated on a stool with a cash register that showed the numbers as she punched them in, one at a time. Her long blue dress matched her eyes. Her hair was tied neatly in a bun. The top of the dress had a white ruffle around the neck where a heart shaped locket hung.

Marvin could hear the sound of the water outside, turning the wheel. The sunlight streamed into the mill, catching the dust particles as they danced aimlessly though the air. The sunlight cast shadows on the floor.

Emily stopped reading, and looked across the room. She seemed to be staring at something. Then she got up and started toward Marvin. "Can she see me?" he wondered.

"Who are you and what do you want?" Emily asked.

Unsure of what to do, he jerked off the glasses. Once again the old mill was deserted. Only the sound of the pigeons could be heard.

Putting on the glasses he now saw Emily standing in front of him.

"Who are you? I don't remember seeing you before."

He decided to play along to see if he could get more information about what happened to Emily and her family. Emily was the only one who could see him.

"Oh, I'm just here visiting my uncle for the summer. Would you like to go for a walk?"

"Yes, let me get my sweater."

Marvin and Emily found a log near the water stream. They spent some time talking and agreed to meet there the next day.

Each time they met, Marvin found out more about what life was like for Emily. She told him that she liked to write poetry, and wrote a poem for him. Her voice was sweet and cheerful as she repeated the memorized words. Her blue eyes accented her smooth flawless skin. The sun's rays reflected on her brown hair, giving it a reddish tint. When she smiled, Marvin could see her perfect teeth.

But she seemed to tire easily and developed a wheezing sound in her chest followed by a cough. One day Emily did not show up in their favorite spot. He went to the mill. When he arrived, he found it closed.

What is going on? he wondered. He went to the house where Emily lived. There he saw the doctor telling her father he had done all he could for her.

"I know this is hard to take Mr. Anderson with just losing you wife last year," the doctor said.

Mr. Anderson sat staring into space. Marvin entered the house and went to Emily's room. She lay on the bed, dressed all in white and looking like an angel. Carefully, he touched her hand. It still felt warm. How could he make these glasses go back in time so he could say goodbye to her? He thought of all the things they talked about, the laughter they had shared.

How could he ever explain the grief he felt as she died before he was born? He felt lost, helpless, and decided to bury the glasses in a box under the tree where they shared so much.

When he returned to his father's shop he searched through the box from the Anderson estate. He found many of Emily's poems. There in the midst of all her poetry was the poem she'd written to him along with her mother's locket. Inside was a picture of Emily. He grasped it hard in his hand and brought it close to his heart.

No one would ever know of his secret of the magic glasses.

The Male Effect

Kay Virgiel

Theresa Thompson and Amy Massoudi, members of the senior center's Widows and Widowers Club, were good friends until handsome Carl Parker joined their Monday group meetings. Friendship walked out the door once he walked in. When each woman decided he was the man for her, all hell broke loose.

They were seated side by side, as was their custom on Monday mornings. Theresa, a petite blonde, and Amy, an olive-skinned brunette, looked forward to the shared gatherings held throughout the year. They enjoyed the sociability of others who were in the same position of having lost a spouse. It was a safe place to meet new people and talk. Popular excursions were held monthly and attended by most members.

The room grew quiet when a tall, handsome man poked his head through the door. The program hadn't started yet, but his arrival piqued interest. Suddenly, every woman in the room sat up straighter and put a hand to her head, in case a stray hair had invaded its perfection.

Secretary Namzie Graham smiled at him from her chair. With a tiny gesture of her fingers, she beckoned him to sign in at her desk. Then he walked to the nearest empty chair and sat down. It happened to be in front of Theresa. He sat up straight and was so tall, Theresa had trouble looking over his shoulder. He abruptly turned around to face her.

"My name is Carl Parker," he said. "I hope I'm not obstructing your view of the stage. If so, I'll move."

Theresa shook her head and smiled. "No, you're fine. I'm Theresa Thompson." She noticed his blue eyes, which matched his shirt. He had a deep cleft in his chin. She was a sucker for any man with a chiseled chin. It reminded her of her late husband, Hal.

She turned to Amy and whispered in her ear, "I know I swore I'd never marry again, but my mind could be changed."

Amy stifled a laugh. "No way. You're too sensible to be that silly at your age. Now, me, I'm younger and warm-blooded, so it's natural for me to have erotic thoughts."

Theresa sat back and folded her arms over her chest. "I'm not that much older," she muttered.

Out of the corner of her eye, Theresa saw her friend studying Carl. Was it possible Amy was interested in the newcomer? It had been months since such a handsome male specimen came to their meetings.

The guest speaker, a representative from the local hospital, started his speech on preventative health. Theresa had heard it before and didn't pay attention. Instead, she stared intently at the back of Carl's head and at the muscles on his arms. How did this older guy still have muscles at his age? He must go to the gym everyday. She was daydreaming when the program ended.

The treasurer said, "Remember, lunch is at the Blue Iguana today at noon. Those of you with reservations, you gotta show up. Newcomers can pay me now. The manager's tired of no-shows."

Theresa got up her courage and touched Carl on his shoulder. "Would you like to join us for lunch? The Blue Iguana offers good food. If you have a hearty lunch, you won't have to worry about dinner."

"I'm up for it. Am I dressed okay? No jacket," Carl said.

"I can tell you're new to the desert. This is as formal as we get." Amy stood and pointed to her denim pants and flowered blouse. She took Carl's arm possessively, and said, over her shoulder, "How about it, Theresa? Are you coming? Get those old bones moving."

Amy started walking away with Carl.

Theresa was too shocked to respond. She'd approached Carl first. Where did Amy get off with this pushy behavior? Well, it wasn't going to work. She picked up her pace and grabbed Carl's other arm.

Amy said, "We'll take my car. It's newer and has more room. You can sit in the back, Theresa, while I point out the sights to our passenger. How long have you lived here, Carl?"

"I moved a month ago from Minneapolis. This weather is a real change from the mid-west. I'm looking forward to hiking the Indian Trails. Do you ladies hike?"

Before Theresa could say, "Are you kidding us?" Amy spoke up.

"Being an Oregon native, I love to hike. I haven't had much opportunity since my husband passed on. Theresa likes a more leisurely form of exercise. Don't you, Theresa?" She looked back and smiled at what would soon be her former best friend.

Meanwhile, Theresa was contemplating some form of homicide, preferably on Amy, who was showing a side she'd never seen. Was she always this mean when it came to men?

It would be another three weeks of jealous bickering before the two former best friends learned the truth. Carl Parker's late spouse was named Charles.

The Patient

Jeri Schmitz

A layer of fog moved in at dusk billowing over the coastal city like a magician's black cloak. Not happy to be out on a night like this, Marjorie squirmed as she entered the empty parking lot. The open space did not feel threatening at first, but with the ominous-looking sky looming closer, she began to sense a foreboding.

As if on watch for deer in the roadway, she maneuvered her new 1965 blue Ford station wagon slowly over the asphalt. The crunch of the tires moving across the blacktop cast a safety net over the silence. She held on to the sound as one would a companion. Her attention soon focused on the shadows surrounding the Laguna Beach Children's Medical Center until a bump into a wooden-beam barrier broke the spell. Suddenly the parking lot was huge, bigger than it was both times she had been here before. But, then it had never been on a Sunday and never at night. Although Marjorie was overwhelmed by thoughts of fear and doubt, there was no turning back.

Maybe I've got the date and time wrong. No, I'm certain that's what Dr. Sanford said. "Can you come alone on Sunday?" Alone, meaning without Sam, of course. "I'll be finished with patients at 7:00 PM." Those were the doctor's words. She was clear on that. Sam hasn't been my husband since last year, but his embarrassing behavior at our appointment last week still strongly reflects on me.

Lately, Marjorie had questioned the clarity of her mind. So many problems at once, her own doctor had prescribed Valium. To have a son with neurological problems was overwhelming. On top of that, she had to look for a job when she had absolutely no skills. It was easy to see how indecision could cloud her good sense.

I need one of my pills, now. I can't swallow. My heart is beating so fast I can't hear anything and my throat is closing. Why is this happening?

The fingerprint covered glass doors to the Children's Center were unlocked. The right one swung open with reassuring ease, confirming the time and date. At first, the familiar reception area renewed the importance of the evening's objective, but her logic soon vacillated.

The waiting room for well children was on the right, the one for the contagious ones on the left. Disarray at the end of the day meant a busy clinic. A busy clinic meant a great doctor, but that was no excuse for clutter to Marjorie. She wanted to pick the books up off the floor, put the toys in the toy box and throw the tiny paper cups in the trash.

Stop. I'm not here for that purpose. What am I here for? Sam and I already had the consultation for Josh, but this time the doctor wants only to see me? Call me ambivalent, but after all, he is the doctor and Sam did make an ass out of himself last week. I almost ran out after he screamed at the top of his lungs, "There's nothing wrong with my son."

Marjorie could see Dr. Aaron Sanford at the end of the long hallway. A smirk wrinkled his boyish face. He was shorter than she was, decidedly handsome, if you weren't standing next to him.

His body motioned left as he spoke, "Mrs. Rosten, come in. It's a pleasure to see you again."

The hall lights were as low as aisle dimmers. Marjorie's eyes would have adjusted quickly had she had been in a theater, but this building offered no let up to the endless black. Like a Catholic church on a weekday afternoon, these halls were laid out in somber stillness. Finally, rounding a corner, a flashlight-sized beam came into view. The light emanated from a door that was slightly ajar. Marjorie moved forward, hoping and praying that another person might be behind it.

Can this be the same lively place I visited three weeks ago for Josh's testing? And last week for the consultation? It seems so different.

"Please, please sit down." After following Marjorie into the room, Dr. Sanford peered straight into her eyes.

She never could hold her own in a staring contest. Head down, a thank you was all she could mutter. In an instant, she stumbled to the closest chair. Now it was as if she really was in a church … on the inside of a confessional.

Just give me my penance and get it over with. I know I have been a horrible mother just like I know it's my fault my son has behavior problems. God gave Joshua to the wrong mother. I'm not cut out for this.

"Why is it you wanted to see me again, Doctor? I'm grateful for the opportunity to apologize for my ex-husband's actions, but he's adamant about not giving medicine to kids. I admit he also refuses to take our son's problems seriously, but I do want you to know I was going to continue the treatment for Joshua on my own." Marjorie shredded a tissue through her fingers. "The pre-school director, the woman who gave me your card, said you were the best doctor for children like Josh. To be honest, the school wasn't going to accept him without medication and the divorce court judge ordered me to find a job."

I'm talking too fast. This will give me away. I've got to keep a handle on my emotions or they'll give custody to Sam. I know they will.

"Mrs. Rosten, may I call you Marjorie?"

Marjorie's chin remained in a downward tilt. Slowly, she lifted her face toward the doctor.

He didn't wait for a reply. "Marjorie, here is a book I have written on hyperkinetic children, plus a medication schedule for Joshua. Additional tests may be necessary later on, but that is not what I wanted to talk to you about." Dr. Sanford set the book on the desk in front of Marjorie.

"Wha … what do you mean?" She didn't usually stammer, but her words wouldn't come out right.

"I wanted to talk about you."

This isn't just strange anymore, it's creepy. The pounding in my ears is worse. I can't breathe. Please God, get me out of this place, I'm not safe.

To rummage through her purse for a pill would give away Marjorie's secrets so she bit her bottom lip. "Dr. Sanford, I don't understand. What do you mean—me?"

"I know you're going through a rough time. I can also see that you don't have emotional support from anyone. I'd like to help you, if you'd let me."

"It is true, I have panic attacks, but I recently started on medication … so really I'm doing fine. This evening has been difficult, and I am having trouble breathing. My heart feels as if it's going to explode."

There it is. Out in the open. Now he knows I have mental problems. He'll recommend that Josh go live with Sam.

The doctor came around the desk. He removed his stethoscope from his neck and positioned the earpieces. Putting the diaphragm next to her chest, he bent over, listening with one hand up by his ear. "I can't hear," he said, while starting to unbutton her dress from the back.

I can't believe this is happening. What is going on? How can I be screaming … yet silent? Where are my words of protest?

Dr. Sanford slipped the dress off her shoulder, and then did the same with her slip and bra. When all her clothing had been sufficiently loosened, he came around to her front and began prodding her chest with the stethoscope.

He's a doctor. He's a doctor … but he's a children's doctor. Oh my God, does he think I have designs on him? Have I sent him the wrong signal? This building is empty, but for the two of us. Dear God, help me get out of this and I'll be the best mother in the world. Please.

"Dr. Sanford, I'm okay. Really, I am okay."

"Well, your heart is. I just don't know about you. Now tell me, how can I help?"

"I'll be fine, really I will." She thought about telling him she'd be okay once she found a job, but she took the thought back, afraid he might offer her one. Marjorie adjusted her straps, pulled her sleeve up in time for him to come around and button the dress back up. In one final move, she picked up her purse to walk out.

"Wait," he cried out. Grabbing her by the shoulders, he kissed her on the mouth for what seemed like five minutes. "That's for luck," he said to Marjorie. "And don't forget the book. I signed it for you."

On the way to the car, the ex-Mrs. Marjorie Rosten made a lonely dot in the wide parking lot. The clouds had evaporated so that her tear-streaked cheeks glistened in the dim glow of the risen moon. She turned around to look at the building for what she knew would be the last time.

Luck? Luck? What's luck got to do with anything? Why do these things always happen to me? Now, where in the heck do I find another pediatrician?

The Virtuous Diana Bolton

Judy Cohn

Diana looked around the ballroom of the Breakers Hotel. It was a winter wonderland, with snowflakes hanging from the ceiling and puffs of simulated snow covering the trees and potted plants. Women dressed in bright gowns, and men in their tuxedos, added color to break the monochromatic décor. The theme was fitting tonight, as it was unusually cold and windy for Palm Beach in January.

As she studied the crowd, a chill ran through her. *I've been here before, haven't I? So many awards, so many testimonials. Well why not? I've been a dedicated volunteer giving my time and money. David and I helped build wings on hospitals and museums when we lived in New York, and now Bennet and I are doing the same here in Palm Beach. Of course I deserve to be honored. But, oh, if they only knew.*

Diana Crane had moved to Florida three years ago when she married Bennet Bolton. Her first husband, David, had been a founding partner in one of New York's most prestigious law firms. After graduating with a Masters in Fine Art from Columbia University, Diana went to work at the Metropolitan Museum of Art. She met David when he was part of a guided tour that she was leading. Statuesque, blonde, wafer thin, with blue eyes and flawless skin, it was not surprising that David was attracted to her. It wasn't just her physical beauty. Diana was a compassionate person with a keen mind and witty sense of humor. She and David married, had three children, and eventually settled in a large English Tudor home in Rye, New York. The Cranes were famous for their elegant dinner parties, globe-hopping travels, accomplishments in tennis and golf, and their charitable endeavors. Diana's friends often commented on her impeccable taste in clothes and jewelry. The Boltons lived diagonally opposite the Cranes and were part of Diana and David's inner circle. When Alyssa Bolton died a year after David, Diana and Bennet drifted together. Within a short time they became reliant on each other for companionship. Marriage and the move to Florida followed.

Before retiring, Bennet had been an investment banker with many international clients. Still somewhat involved in business, he enjoyed playing the stock market. In this age of e-mail, fax machines, and cell phones, it was easy to keep in constant touch with associates. Bennet shared Diana's interest in art, music, and politics. They were avid golfers, spending a lot of time at their country club where they'd made numerous friends.

These people are all here for me. So much preparation has gone into making this evening a success. Soon I'll be introduced. The chairperson will talk about me in glowing terms. I'll walk to the podium. I should feel very confident. Bennet said I look stunning in my yellow and carnation red dress. I'll tell them how thrilled I am to accept the Humanitarian of the Year Award. I promised to keep my speech short so I'll glance at my watch and know when it's time to stop. Yes, yes, the watch. Cartier I think it was. One of my favorite venues for picking things up. I was in a hurry that day. I saw it, liked it and took it. So simple. No one was even aware. Well, they'd never suspect me anyway.

I'll smile as they all applaud. Bennet will tell me how proud he is, just as David always did. No, they will never know my secret. I'm a master of my art. A woman of virtue. A woman of deception.

Toadshade

Bill Hinthorn

"Karen, I really think you should drive up here," Jeff said into the cell phone. "The local sheriff hasn't made any headway with this woman. We may have a serial killer on our hands, and it certainly seems to me that there are mental problems involved. Is there a particular disorder in which mothers kill their children?"

"Jeff, that could be anything—long-term psychosis or psychotic episode, schizophrenia, postpartum psychosis, anything. We wouldn't know without an in-depth examination."

"This may also be complicated by an odd take on religion. We really need you here."

"You don't know what the schedule in Atlanta is like. Work has us completely buried, and the state simply won't assign funds for more people. I'm swamped. I'm working a fifty-hour week and I don't see how I can get away."

"Then is there somebody else there at Mental Health that could come? Unless we can get to the bottom of this, these baby-killings are going to continue just as long as this woman can have children."

"I'll try, Jeff." Karen's voice was weary. "I'll try."

"Good girl. You've got my cell phone number. Call when you get here."

On an ominously gray and hot summer morning two days later, Karen eased her Camry into late-morning Atlanta traffic. A sudden thunderstorm made driving slow as she headed north on I-75. The drive to Dalton was almost two hours, but she knew there were more miles of difficult back roads before arriving at the woman's home. By the time she reached Dalton, the rain had stopped, but the heavy overcast remained and the oppressive humidity was high.

Jeff was waiting at the motel. "Do you want lunch before we go? There's not much of any place to eat once we leave here."

Over lunch, Jeff told her what he knew of the case. "We got involved when the local sheriff called our office. It seems that a local midwife had driven the woman—a Mrs. Griffey—to a hospital in Chattanooga, when Mrs. Griffey developed complications giving birth. I don't know why an ambulance or medical helicopter wasn't called. Anyway, the Chattanooga hospital got her and the child through the complications and she successfully gave birth to a baby boy. Mrs. Griffey was in the hospital for one day after giving birth, and then took her baby and left without signing out. Nobody knows how she got home from the hospital. The doctor was concerned for Mrs. Griffey's health as well as the health of the baby. The midwife who'd driven her to the hospital gave a local address, so the doctor called the local sheriff. The sheriff drove out to see Mrs. Griffey. He said that she had apparently just gotten out of bed, but there wasn't any baby. She claimed she didn't have a baby."

"You said the midwife told you that Mrs. Griffey had already had about a dozen children?"

"Yes, when I got to the sheriff's office, we went to see the midwife. Apparently Mrs. Griffey is a regular breeding machine. The midwife said that Mrs. Griffey has been having a child almost every year and a half for the past twenty years or so."

"But you say that there is no Mr. Griffey?"

"The midwife said that she thought that Mrs. Griffey was married at sixteen and her husband died a year later."

The ride further north was over increasingly difficult roads. With Jeff driving the SUV, Karen looked out the window and tried to relax. But the hill country scenery seemed offended by their presence. The tall trees bore a resemblance, in Karen's mind, to giant green beasts. Karen had always enjoyed the Blue Ridge Mountains, but this time the entire scenario seemed decidedly threatening.

On their arrival at the sheriff's office, Karen expected to find some yokel who resented their intrusion into his territory. Instead, she found a tall, well-built, and well-dressed man in his thirties, who was articulate and seemed genuinely concerned that a series of crimes might have been committed.

"What can we do to help?" was his first question after Jeff introduced them.

"Karen's area of expertise is mental health. Of course, she'll have to talk to Mrs. Griffey," Jeff said. "But first I'd like her to hear what the midwife has to say."

"Certainly. Let's go see if we can find Mrs. Barger."

They left, this time in the sheriff's car, with the sheriff at the wheel. More back roads that eventually became little more than trails led to a ramshackle house trailer propped up on cement blocks. A half dozen hound dogs lay under the trailer amid a considerable amount of trash, and with the arrival of the sheriff's car, the dogs bayed as they emerged. As the sheriff got out, the trailer door opened. A paunchy and overweight man, probably in his 50's, stepped down the cement blocks that served as doorsteps.

"Hi, Bo," the sheriff addressed the man. "Is Rachel at home?"

"Yeah," Bo said. He didn't sound happy. "She's inside. What y'all want?"

"We just need to talk to her."

"Well, jist a minute. I'll git 'er."

Bo returned to the trailer door and yelled for Rachel. A thin and graying woman came to the door wiping her hands on a faded and threadbare apron. When she saw the sheriff, she came down the steps.

"I think you know Jeff," the sheriff said. "He was with me the other day. And this is Karen. She's from the State Mental Health Department."

"Mental health?" Rachel asked. "My land! What does the State Mental Health want with us?"

"We just want to ask you some questions about Mrs. Griffey, the same things we asked about a couple days ago," the sheriff said.

"Well, I don't know what else I can tell you."

"She done told you everything the other day," Bo put in.

"Karen wants to hear what you told us, and then she may have some questions," the sheriff said.

Rachel repeated what she'd told the sheriff and Jeff, essentially that Mrs. Griffey had been giving birth to a child about every year and a half for the past twenty years. Rachel had been midwife to almost all of them. No, she didn't have any idea as to what had happened to the children, but she thought they were dead, that they all died shortly after birth. No, Mrs. Griffey hadn't said much about it. They had just disappeared, and when she asked, Mrs. Griffey said that each of the children had died.

"How did you know when she was going to give birth?"

"She come and seen me four or five days before, and then I went up and checked on her every day 'til it was her time."

"Did Mrs. Griffey seem depressed in any way?" Karen continued. "Was there anything she said or did that made you think she didn't want the baby?"

"No, she didn't say nothin', not with any of the babies."

"Well, thank you," Karen said. "Maybe we can find out what happened to them and assist Mrs. Griffey with her problems."

"I don't see how I been much help," Mrs. Barger replied.

"You have been. And thanks again."

The three of them got back into the sheriff's car. Thunderheads were forming again, and it seemed to Karen that the humidity had increased.

The impending storm heightened her apprehension. "I don't feel good about this at all."

"Karen, nobody feels good about murder," Jeff said, "particularly the murder of infants."

"It's not just that. This whole thing seems evil. This place gives me the creeps."

"Ma'am, this place really isn't all that bad." The sheriff's tone was defensive. "We have some bad people here, but there's a lot more good people."

"I know, and you probably have less bad people per capita than we have in Atlanta. Still, there's something about this that really makes me feel uneasy." Low hanging tree branches clutched menacingly at the car. Karen shifted uncomfortably in the back seat and continued to watch the dark shadowy landscape pass by. "How far is it to Mrs. Griffey's place?"

"Not far." The sheriff was concentrating on driving on a road that was little more than a trail. As if being true to his word, the sheriff drove around a curve and stopped the car in front of another trailer house. This time, however, there weren't any dogs. No sound disturbed the absolute quiet. There was no wind in the trees, no bird calls, no sound of running water from a creek, nothing at all. An eerie silence pervaded.

"What is that terrible smell?" Karen asked as she got out of the car. "Smells like something has died."

"No," Jeff said. "It's actually a low-growing plant—a trillium, sometimes called "stinking trillium" because of the smell of the flowers. The common name is 'toadshade'. It's called that because people believed that toads sat in its shade. The name does have some legitimacy in that toads do sit under the plant, not for shade, but to catch the flies attracted to the bad smell of the flowers."

"But the smell is really strong. Can a few plants really smell this bad? Jeff, I think there's more to this than just plants. There's something dead and decaying here."

"This seems to be a particularly large and thick stand. You can see them all over." Jeff pointed them out. "They're all around here."

Karen covered her nose. "This must be what purgatory smells like."

The sheriff knocked on the door of the trailer. Getting no response, he knocked again. He waited, knocked the third time and then yelled, "Mrs. Griffey?"

The door opened a crack. A voice asked, "What you want?"

"We need to talk to you."

"You ain't got no right to be here. This is my place."

"Mrs. Griffey, I'm the sheriff."

"I talked to you before and I know who you are, and that don't give you no right to be on my place."

"We'll leave just as soon as we can talk to you. But we can't leave until we do."

A few large drops of rain splattered on the leaves overhead.

"Mrs. Griffey, can we come in?" The sheriff was persistent. "We could talk outside, but it's starting to rain. Or we can talk in my car."

There was no response other than the sound of Mrs. Griffey moving away from the partially open door. The sheriff motioned to Jeff and Karen to follow him up the three rickety wood steps.

"I don't like this at all, Jeff." Karen voice was apprehensive. "If I believed in such, I would say that this place is the gate to hell."

"You're being silly. I've never seen you like this."

"That's because I've never encountered a place as malevolent as this one."

The sheriff pushed the door open. Jeff and Karen followed him into the dark trailer. The foul odor of spoiled food permeated and mixed with the odor of the toadshade coming from the outside. Karen felt her stomach churning. There was obviously no running water, no electricity, no telephone. Aluminum foil covered all the windows, a lone exception being one small window in what appeared to be a kitchen area. The dirty window provided little light. The only other illumination came from a foot-high plastic statue of Jesus, apparently with a battery-powered bulb inside. The brightness of the lighted statue was enough to see outlines, but few details of the trailer's interior were visible. There was a single bed, but no bed coverings other than two pillows without cases.

Mrs. Griffey slowly rocked in a rocking chair, the only chair in the room. She was a thin woman and Karen thought she looked older than she probably was. Her hair didn't appear to have been washed or combed for some time. The room was too dark for Karen to determine much about her clothing, hair or eye color.

The sheriff sat on one end of the bed. Jeff motioned to Karen to sit, but she shook her head and remained standing.

"Mrs. Griffey, we know you had a baby in the hospital in Chattanooga," the sheriff started. "Where is the baby?"

Mrs. Griffey made no response, but sat rocking with her thin hands folded in her lap.

"We have to find the baby," the sheriff insisted. "If you don't help us, Mrs. Griffey, we'll have to bring other people in here to search."

"Jesus took the baby home to him," she said.

Apparently, Karen thought, she didn't want people digging around.

"You mean the baby died? How?"

"Jist died. Jesus took it."

With a chill, Karen noticed Mrs. Griffey's referring to the baby as "it".

"Mrs. Griffey, who was the father?" she asked.

"Jesus."

"Jesus," Karen repeated. "Jesus was the father? Mrs. Griffey, that's not possible."

"Yes, it is. Jesus can do anything he wants to."

The rain had increased and the loud hammering on the metal roof hammered on Karen's taut nerves as well, but she persisted. "You were married at one time, weren't you? Where is your husband now?"

Even in the dim light, Karen could see an expression of hate cross Mrs. Griffey's face.

"He's burnin' in hell, that's where he is."

"He's dead, then?"

"He wouldn't be in hell if he was livin'."

"How and when did he die?" the sheriff asked.

"Jist died. Died 'bout a year after we got married."

"Where is he buried?"

"In hell!" Mrs. Griffey venomously spat out the words.

"Mrs. Griffey, where is his body?"

"I jist told you. In hell."

"Mrs. Griffey," Karen put in, "would you ride down to Atlanta with us to talk to some people at the mental health department? We'll drive you down and back, and put you up at a hotel while you're there, at no expense to you."

"You can go to hell, too. I ain't got nothin' more to say to the lot of you. Now git off my property."

"Mrs. Griffey," the sheriff said, "we're going to have to find your husband's body, and we're going to have to find your babies. Now, you can help us, or we can get a court order to search. It would be in your best interest to help us."

Mrs. Griffey stopped rocking and stared straight ahead. She said nothing. Total silence held sway while the sheriff waited for a response. A feeling of dread crept over Karen, covering her like a dark and suffocating blanket.

After a couple of minutes, the sheriff rose. "All right, if that's the way you want it. I'll be back with a court order."

The rain had stopped but the drive out required all the sheriff's attention. Little was said, and the silence only increased Karen's uneasiness. Once at his office, the sheriff said he'd be getting a court order and would take a team in to excavate around Mrs. Griffey's trailer. Jeff told the sheriff they'd be in touch tomorrow, and Karen and Jeff drove back to the motel in Dalton.

"Jeff, I really have to get back to Atlanta tonight. I've got a meeting tomorrow I can't miss. I can come up again day after tomorrow. But I really have to go back tonight." That wasn't exactly true. She did have a meeting the next day, but it wasn't absolutely necessary that she be there. She just felt that she couldn't bear to stay overnight there. "We really do need to have a professional talk to Mrs. Griffey."

That night back in Atlanta, Karen had a hard time falling asleep. She finally got up and found an old bottle of over-the-counter sleeping pills. She drank a cup of warm milk and finally drifted off. But she had nightmares of a devil in the form of Mrs. Griffey, of babies being slaughtered and covered with blood, of murder and visions of a hideous underworld every time she slept. She woke up once sitting upright in bed, screaming. At 4:00AM, she gave up, got out of bed, took a shower and tried to concentrate on her day's schedule.

The following morning Jeff called to say that the sheriff expected to have his men start digging the next day. If the sheriff's men found anything, he'd immediately be arresting Mrs. Griffey, and Karen would probably want to have a psychiatrist talk to both Mrs. Griffey and the prosecutor. If the sheriff's department didn't find anything, then they were back where they started. Jeff suggested that she come up the following day.

Although Karen hadn't slept much since returning to Atlanta, and when she did sleep she had monstrous nightmares, she called Jeff the next day to say that she was on her way.

Jeff was waiting for her at the motel. "The sheriff took some men up late yesterday afternoon. Out behind Mrs. Griffey's trailer, in the woods, they found something that registered on a metal detector. Of course, that could mean anything—an old tin can, anything, but the sheriff thinks it's a good place to start. Mrs. Griffey apparently wasn't home. She does occasionally buy groceries in Dalton, but nobody knows how she gets from her trailer to town."

"On a broomstick."

Jeff laughed. "I'm glad to see you're not as uptight as you were about this."

"Jeff, I'm even more frightened than I was. I'm almost serious about the broomstick. I really think she's some sort of fiend, and when the sheriff digs into the ground around the trailer, the flames of Hades are going to burst through."

"You're kidding, of course."

"No, I'm not. Jeff, this place is wicked."

The sheriff and his men had already left for Mrs. Griffey's trailer, so Jeff drove the SUV the rest of the way. The sheriff's car was parked in front, and the sheriff and one of his men were at the trailer's door.

Karen and Jeff climbed out of the SUV and were immediately threatened with huge swarms of black flies. Flies settled on the two of them, on the car, everywhere.

"Jeff, what is it with all these flies?" Karen's sense of dread grew.

"They're drawn to the stinking odor of the toadshade flowers. As you may have noticed, the odor of decaying flesh is even stronger today. The rain increased the humidity and the plants seem to be in full bloom."

"Jeff, this place really is horrible. Call it intuition or whatever you want, but this is evil incarnate. I don't think I can stay here."

Jeff put his arm around her. "You'll be okay. We'll be out of here shortly. In fact, as soon as we've talked to the sheriff, we'll head back to his office and wait for him there. Later he can bring Mrs. Griffey down to his office."

Karen didn't respond, but she was trembling. The sheriff came down the steps to where Jeff and Karen were standing.

"What's happened?" Jeff asked.

"We were able to dig a little last night after I talked to you. We found a skeleton, a male in his twenties, we think. The back of the head had been crushed—or more accurately, a hole had been chopped in it. It appears that he was killed with an ax. He was wearing a belt with a large buckle, which had "Hubert Griffey" etched on it. The belt buckle was what showed up on the metal detectors. We're going to check to see if we can find a marriage license that links the victim with Mrs. Griffey. We've also found a skeleton of a baby, but we can't tell how old it is. Since a baby's skeleton is mostly cartilage, we may not find the earlier ones. But we'll keep digging. Mrs. Griffey wasn't here last night and the door was unlocked, but when we came back this morning, it was locked. We're trying to force the door now."

The flies continue to settle on everything. The hood and windshield of the SUV became almost black. Between the snatches of conversation, the only sound in the ghostly silence was the buzzing of the flies. Thunderheads blotted out the sun and the large tree branches created a feeling of a black grotto.

"One thing we still don't understand," Jeff said, "is who the father of Mrs. Griffey's children could be."

"Well, if you believe Mrs. Griffey," the sheriff answered, "it's Jesus. Maybe there's somebody dressed up like Jesus living in these woods somewhere. We don't know."

The sheriff's man at the door motioned that he had the door open, and the sheriff went to check the trailer. Karen and Jeff started to return to the SUV, when Karen's foot struck a bone that was half buried in the dirt.

"Jeff, what's that?"

"A bone of some kind, probably an animal bone." He pulled the bone out of the dirt.

"That's not an animal bone." Karen felt her fear and hysteria rising. "Jeff, that's a small human bone—a tiny arm or leg bone. I just tripped on a baby's skeleton!" She was almost screaming.

"No, you didn't." Jeff tried to reassure her. "Come on back to the SUV."

They escaped some of the flies, but some managed to get inside the car with them. Jeff was trying to calm Karen when the sheriff returned. Jeff opened his window.

"Well," the sheriff said to Karen, "your services won't be needed now."

Karen felt another wave of terror vibrate through her.

"Why?" Jeff asked.

"Mrs. Griffey apparently committed suicide. We suspect that she took some sort of poison, probably from some plant around here. Jimsonweed grows down below in a clearing, and there's some wild foxglove as well as other poisonous plants. We'll have an autopsy done. Right now, I think you should take a look at what we found."

Jeff turned to Karen. "You don't need to see this."

"No, I don't." She was holding onto Jeff for support. "Yes, I do. I'm a grown woman and even though I'll admit I'm terrified, I think my report should probably include this."

They climbed the rickety steps to the open door. The sheriff's men had set up a battery-powered lantern that probably gave more light inside the trailer than there had been for years. The sinister buzzing of the flies that had invaded the trailer along with the odor of the toadshade and the heat and humidity made the place almost unbearable.

Mrs. Griffey, dressed in a faded print dress and wearing dirty white socks, lay on the small bed on her back, her eyes half open and one hand clutched at her hair. Flies were already settling on her body, congregating around her eyes, nose and mouth. Her head was on one pillow. On the pillow next to her lay the plastic statue of Jesus. The battery had been removed and the statue was dark.

Trilogy

◆

Fargo—Savannah—Hollywood

Mary Burton Olson M.D.

Fargo

Hi! I'm a firecracker named Yankee Doodle. Have I got a story to tell you! Once upon a time, July 4th 1943, in Fargo, North Dakota, the finest city in the world, I, a talented, wise, and loving soul, rescued myself from explosion and certain death.

I, a mere pile of gunpowder wrapped in red tissue paper, sang my heart out. *I'm a Yankee Doodle Dandy! Yankee Doodle do or die!*

I learned about Fargo at fireworks school where I studied with friends, two-inch studs like me, little one-inchers, and teeny ladyfingers, sparklers, Roman candles, and cherry bombs. I graduated top in my class. The principal awarded me first prize so I got to go wherever I chose for the 4th of July. My fuse sputtered with excitement.

I picked Fargo for the holiday food, comforting specialties and up home dishes. They outranked the down home delicacies of Dixie. No wonder the North won the Civil War.

Seriously, home, up or down, north or south, means comfort. In Fargo it smells of hamburgers grilling, sounds like teeth typing along an ear of corn and glows with color, red and green of garden tomatoes and cucumbers. Textures—the crunchiness of coleslaw, potato salad and cucumber or the soothing feel of mashed potatoes, creamed soups and soft macaroni coated with thick golden cheese—bring back memories of youthful joyous times.

Hey, remember, I named the feather in my hat, Macaroni. When I was a kid I used to thread those noodles on my fuse.

Back then, homemade vanilla ice cream topped with hot fudge sauce reigned as the number one dessert on Fargo's 4th of July menus. Contrasts of dark brown on white and hot on cold added to the beauty of the sundae's soft texture.

In case you're not familiar with it, I'm gonna tell you the story of how sundaes were invented. It began in the late nineteenth century when at the behest of the clergy, a law was enacted forbidding ice cream sodas on Sunday. The righteous poured syrup over scoops of ice cream. In honor of the Sabbath, they named the dish, sundae. Back in school, this kind of knowledge impressed my teachers. My fuse stood straight up doubling its height.

We fireworks were legal in Fargo in 1943. The town was the home of the most elaborate family displays in the nation. People saved any kind of empty cans for weeks to place over a firecracker with a lighted fuse. They listened for the sounds of explosion and predicted how high the cans would fly. What fun! Firecrackers ruled! They were kings for a day!

Fargo kids in 1943, like those throughout the country, had experienced nothing but war their entire lives. Fathers and older brothers in Europe or the South Pacific fought to preserve freedom. Their mothers worked in factories making war supplies or, at home, knitted sweaters and rolled bandages. Kids went along to the train station when fathers, brothers, or friends departed for war. They watched newsreels at The Fargo Theater. They didn't know grocery shopping or filling the gas tank without ration books.

I arrived in Fargo in June, 1943, and was purchased by Rick Olson, the father of two boys. The older son was in the Navy in the South Pacific and the younger, Bobby, was a student at Roosevelt Grade School.

Mr. Olson unpacked his fireworks and stacked them on the dining room buffet. Impressed with his massive array, I, Yankee Doodle, felt at home, like I was in fireworks school among my fused classmates.

"Wow, Dad! This is the best 4th ever," Bobby said, picking me up. "Can't we light one now?"

"No, we can't."

"The 4th's a long way off." Bobby ran his hand over me gently. I worried I might not survive to see the 4th of July.

"It'll be here before you know it. Look, but don't touch."

Bobby put me in his pocket. He climbed the stairs to his room where he placed me in his bottom dresser drawer. Well, a firecracker like me couldn't stay imprisoned in a drawer. I escaped more than once and visited my mates on the buffet deck. I never got caught.

The week passed quickly and on the morning of the 4th, Bobby returned me to the buffet, placing me way in back. In Bobby's room, I'd feared detonation, before the celebration day. Now I figured I'd go last. I'd get to see the celebration from beginning to end.

She's a grand old flag, a high flying flag,
and forever and ever she waves,
the emblem of, the land I love,
the home of the free and the brave.

At 7AM Bobby's parents joined him in the dining room. I watched Dad take three firecrackers from the front of the buffet and Bobby take three cans from the box next to the refrigerator. They ran outside. Boom! Boom! Boom! The tinkling sounds of cans bouncing on cement and an exuberant exclamation from Bobby filled the air.

"Let's have breakfast," Mr. Olson said.

"Can't we fire a few more? We've got millions."

"We'll pace ourselves and save the best for last, Bobby."

All day long, I listened to the sounds of fireworks exploding throughout the neighborhood.

I only heard the fireworks, but I saw Mrs. Olson. She tirelessly worked in the kitchen. I paid particular attention to her making of the hamburger patties, which when cooked, would be placed between buns and adorned with a bewildering array of condiments. No wonder they're the icon of American food, like me, the icon of Independence Day.

I watched Mrs. Olson shuck corn, slice tomatoes and cucumbers and make potato salad and coleslaw. She hardboiled eggs, simmered potatoes, chopped scallions, celery, red and white cabbage, and carrots. She put some things in one bowl and others in a second. She finished with seasonings and dressings, made lemonade and set the porch table. I saw happiness in her face, joy in her heart, and pride in her accomplishments. I sang, *She's my Yankee Doodle sweetheart.*

Mr. Olson kissed his wife on the cheek. "Are you ready for me to light the camp stove?"

"Sure, anytime."

"Now's the time! I'm hungry."

It wasn't long until I smelled kerosene. I worried about detonation, but the aroma of grilled beef replaced that of kerosene. Soon I was able to watch the Olsons enjoy a perfect up home meal. It seemed an ideal holiday of shared love—except for the empty chair across from Bobby's.

"Great meal," Mr. Olson said, leaning toward his wife.

"Thank you, my dear."

"It's almost dark, time for the big finale. Everybody, grab the fireworks and come outside," Mr. Olson said.

Bobby jumped up first, Dad not far behind. Mother had to hurry to keep up.

Bobby cradled me in his hand, slipped me into his pocket and piled heaps of explosives into his arms. When everything was outside, the neighbors came over. I, Yankee, hummed my familiar tune. Scared to death about detonation, my voice wavered. It was barely audible through the fabric of Bobby's pocket.

Everyone loved loud noises. To me the boom-boom detonation of firecrackers, the screeches of Roman candles and the squeaky sizzles of sparklers were scary. Everyone shouted with joy as they watched flying cans, colored lights of bursting rockets and flickering orange glowing sparklers.

When the fireworks show ended, I remained in Bobby's pocket. I have lived on in Robert's memory box, of a time when big brothers were in the South Pacific and firecrackers were legal in North Dakota.

Savannah

I, a juicy melon, orange in color, fell in love on a blistering Georgia day. My love blossomed in a Winn Dixie brown paper sack. She and I bounced along Magnolia Avenue, warming to each other. My rough, netted skin collided with her smooth yellow-green wrapping.

"I hope I'm not hurting you. What's your name? Where are you from?" I asked.

"My name's Honey Dew. I'd share a bag with you any day! I love the feel of your undulations, your thick skin and coarse netting."

She made me so happy I was speechless. "I'm an Old World winter melon," Honey Dew said. "If it weren't for Christopher Columbus bringing my ancestral seeds to Haiti in 1494, I'd not be here today."

I felt my seeds swell with each of her sensuous touches. I was in love. I guess that's why I remained mute.

The more we snuggled, the warmer we became. The air was tight, hot and humid, preventing evaporation and its cooling effect. I watched a cloud form around her. It grew denser by the second. She slipped like an angel over my rough netted skin. I breathed Honey Dew's heavenly aroma. I felt her ripening flesh lose water and become softer, more fragrant.

Honey Dew asked again, "What's your name?"

"Cantaloupe," I said.

Her sides caved in, like an accordion, over and over. I thought she'd lose her figure, laughing so hard. "Can't elope?" she said.

"You're making fun of me!"

"No, I'm not. I love you! We've eloped. We're running away from Winn Dixie, off to get married, you and me, plus two little fellows, the yellow lemon and the green lime, and a plastic bag of mint leaves." Honey Dew showered me with her juice.

"How romantic!" I bumped her, my idea of a hug.

"We'll have oodles of good times. What would you like to be, a drink, an appetizer, a salad, a dessert?" she asked.

"A melon margarita with salt around my glass's rim. I'll swim in tequila, triple sec and lime juice, and splash the salt. On second thought, whatever I am, I want you, Honey Dew, snuggled up, warm and close."

"Prosciutto wraps are out, then. We don't want drippy Italian ham slices separating us. We'll sit next to each other, orange and green chunks, with a sprinkle of lime juice and a sprig of mint or a dab of whipped cream cheese. I'm dying to see your flesh, bright orange, oozing its sweet aroma," Honey Dew said.

Just then a bolt of light blew into our bag. "You may see it sooner than you thought."

We were lifted onto a counter next to the lime, the lemon, and the bag of mint leaves. "It's much cooler. The temperature's dropping. I'm feeling better already," I said.

I watched in horror as Honey Dew was halved by a giant knife and big chunks of her beautiful flesh were scooped into a bowl. I was surprised that she didn't scream.

"It's wonderful to be freed," Honey Dew said. Lime juice dribbled down her sides, mint leaves stuck to her flesh. She looked lovely, totally refreshed. "Oooh! This feels good." She shivered.

I tried to jump out of my skin and into her bowl.

Someone must have read my mind. The giant blade quartered me and a spoon ladled my pieces into another bowl, one exactly like Honey Dew's. "No, no, I want to be in her dish, mingled with her pale lime-green parts."

I heard a voice answer. "Hold on buddy, you'll get to mingle soon enough." What did that mean? Who spoke those words?

As I pondered answers, I felt a shower of lemon juice slide down my flesh. I peeked over the edge of my bowl and got a better look at Honey Dew.

I swallowed hard. Fright gripped my acid-drenched flesh. I saw chunks of Honey Dew bombard the sides of the plastic whirring contraption. She disintegrated, as did the mint leaves. Finally the top of the chamber opened. I heard her screams.

"It was so much fun! Do it again! What a ride! You'll love it!" she said in a high-pitched squeaky voice. It was still Honey Dew. Her shape had changed, solid cubes irrefutably liquefied, but her green spirit lived on in a clear glass pitcher.

My thoughts ended abruptly when I was dumped into the contraption. Unfortunately, no drops of Honey Dew remained. I whirled at cyclone speed banging into the sides and losing shape with each collision.

"What a ride! A once in a lifetime experience!"

I hit the bottom of my glass pitcher and saw wave after wave of swirling orange, sloshing against the sides of my new home. Too dizzy to focus and unable to see through the orange, I couldn't find Honey Dew. Suddenly motion stopped. I felt a chill.

My vision cleared. I saw through my walls and into hers. There we were, side by side, Honey Dew and I, in separate pitchers in a refrigerator. We spent more than three hours there, talking and professing our love. As time went by, I felt myself thicken. Honey Dew said she did, too.

"What do you suppose we are? Juice or Soup?" she asked.

"I don't know. I just hope we get to share a pitcher or a bowl."

"Me too," she said.

Our wish was granted four times over. When we got out of the refrigerator, we were simultaneously, poured into four small bowls. It was amazing. Honey Dew sat in half of each bowl and I in the other half. We touched in a straight line down the center of the bowls, joined together in perfect unity. Exclamations of our beauty and the miracle of the hard straight line linking us, but not allowing us to cross over, filled the air.

Honey Dew and I thought we'd never get any closer, but we were blessed by the spoons. They quickly disrupted our lines and joined us in love and eternal happiness.

Hollywood

Death row, what a place! Not home for me, an egg, the son of a chicken. It's cold and dark in here. When the door opens, the lights go on. Warm air wafts into the box, carrying sounds and scents of sizzling burgers, bacon, and other kitchen delicacies. To think I will spend my last four hours on God's earth in a refrigerator.

My time elapsed in the icebox of the original Brown Derby Restaurant on Wilshire Blvd., not far from Hollywood. It was1937, nighttime. I sat next to a mouthy avocado. Each time the door opened, I gawked at his bulging black eye and green wrinkled skin.

"So, egghead, what're you doing *aqui*?" he asked.

"Waiting, waiting for another transformation. Thinking," I said.

"Gad Zooks, are you nuts, *mi amigo*? I didn't know eggs thought. What do you think about?"

"Sexy stuff, like fertilization and transformation. I once had soft insides; they hardened in a sauna. I got the boiling bath treatment, 15 minutes at 212 degrees, followed by an icy pool dunk, and now in my cold stay of execution, I'm hard boiled."

The door opened, the light came on. A cluster of fellow inmates, a head of lettuce, bunches of watercress and chicory, and a half head of romaine were pulled out. "Did you catch the name tag? *Bob Cobb, Owner*," I read.

"Si, senor. What's he doing with the green stuff? I grew up with leaves. I hold a soft spot in my pit for foliage, for all that's green." Avocado sighed.

I shuddered. "Chopping, I hear chopping. I hate chopping."

"Probably another transformation. Maybe the next time the door opens, I'll be swallowed up by a mastodon or a giant ground sloth," Avocado said.

"Fruit! Nut head! What've you been smoking? Do hallucinogenic mushrooms chill here?"

Avocado shook his head. "No, no, no! Humpty Dumpty, it's not far fetched. My ancestors traveled from Mexico to South America, before the Central American land bridge existed, flew over the sea in the gastrointestinal tracts of large birds. Pits survived undigested. When the birds did their thing, pits were excreted. They grew, or as you'd say, transformed into new plants."

"That's not all." Avocado preened, which wasn't easy considering his thick skin. "My history goes back millions of years, to when all the continents were one. Avocados, like me, came from Africa, migrated north over the Spanish land bridge, and traveled west across the Atlantic on North America. That's when North America separated from Europe and drifted to its present location."

"You've sprouted quite an imagination," I said.

The suction sound interrupted us again. Bright lights made it hard to see, but I recognized Bob Cobb. He extracted two breasts of cooked chicken from our cell.

"Look at that," cried Avocado. "Part of your history just exited."

"My mother was a chicken. Those could be her breasts." Condensation dripped down my shell.

"Cheer up, old egg. She's more likely a distant cousin. Did you see what Mr. Cobb had on the kitchen counter?"

"Yeah. Our cellmates, the leaves, guillotined, sitting in a big bowl. Don't let Mr. Cobb dice me. It would upset my inner geometry, my yellow center, like the sun, master of our solar system."

"You're certainly full of yourself." Cyclops's skin puffed out. "You know, I grew on a leafy tree. In Mexico, chefs simmer avocado leaves in mole sauces."

I quickly changed the subject. "How about the hot juicy tomato snuggling up to the bunch of chives next to the chopped leaves? My yolk would sure look nice beside her."

"Cuddle up to that dish and her red would reflect off your shell. You'd look like a pink Easter egg. *Huevos Rojo*! After a few days, you'd smell worse than the Roquefort cheese I saw on the counter."

"I got a whiff of that too. Horrible! It must have been electrocuted a month ago," I said.

The door burst open, lights went on and a bottle of French dressing vanished. The door closed. "Did you see anything?" Avocado asked.

"Not a thing. We should get some sleep. It's past midnight."

"Good idea, Humpty. We'll need to rest up for a big day, *manana*."

"Tomorrow's already today."

This time the door opened wide. Mr. Cobb stepped aside. Our vision cleared and we saw IT. A huge round plate sat on the counter, divided into five sections, like a pie, chicken wedge next to greens wedge, greens wedge next to tomato wedge, and two empty triangular spaces. Chives had been sprinkled over the tomato, bacon over the greens, and Roquefort over the chicken.

"We're next," Avocado said.

I addressed Mr. Cobb, "Slip me in that space next to the tomato." I didn't think he heard me. I watched him skin my green wrinkled friend and remove his giant pit.

"Don't throw away my seed! *Es usted loco*? Bury it in a bowl of guacamole. It'll keep the dip bright green. Or, suspend it with toothpicks over a tumbler of water, just wetting the lower third. My pit will crack and sprout. Before you know it, a new me." Plop! The pit hit the bottom of the garbage pail.

I breathed a sigh of relief when my friend slid in next to the chicken, leaving a space for me beside my sweetheart. I wished I could be sprinkled all over her like the lucky chives. As the thought crossed my mind, I heard my shell crack from head to foot. Denuded and quickly chopped, my beautiful yellow yolk and white albumen crumbled into pieces, but I didn't care. I rested between my good friend, Avocado, and the love of my life, Tomato.

"Hey, Sid, come and see this salad," Bob Cobb shouted.

Sid Grauman of Grauman's Chinese Theatre examined IT as Mr. Cobb show-ered us with French dressing and tossed. "Looks wonderful!" Sid said.

Bob Cobb served two plates and they feasted. His salad almost finished, Sid said, "This is so good, you should put it on the menu."

Bob did. Hollywood celebrities loved the mouth-watering salad. Movie mogul Jack Warner regularly sent his chauffeur over to pick it up in a take-out carton. Although the original Brown Derby has been demolished, reproductions of the famous restaurant in the Disney resorts at Orlando, Anaheim, Tokyo, and Paris still serve Cobb Salad today.

Troubadour

Kay Virgiel

In the year 1976, a young male entertainer clad in white, stood alone on a London stage. He raised his hands in triumph as he sang the final notes of his encore. His glorious voice captivated the audience, and he bowed time and again to tumultuous applause. After blowing a kiss to his fans, he left the stage, trembling from excitement and pride at his achievement. At the age of 23, Teddy Well's first starring appearance in Albert Hall had come true. From the wings he could hear voices shouting, "Teddy, Teddy, Teddy!" The sound was sweeter than he ever imagined.

◆   ◆   ◆

In his armchair, 54-year-old Ted Wells shook himself awake. He must have dozed off while watching the telly. Ever since Rita's death eight months before, he found it harder to concentrate, no matter how interesting the program.

He sighed and looked at the empty chair beside his. He could cry with loneliness, but it wouldn't bring his wife back. Misjudging a narrow curve on a rainy night in the French Riviera, Rita lost control of her Porsche. She died immediately. When told of the accident, Ted wouldn't believe it. "It can't be true. She's not gone," he kept saying, as if the words would bring her back. He closed his eyes, remembering his beautiful golden wife. He hadn't appeared publicly since her death.

The pulsing music coming from the television roused him from his reverie. He'd almost dozed off again, his mind drifting into the past. *FUTURE STAR* flashed across the screen, and photos of young entertainers were displayed. Ted sat up. This could be an interesting program. No one knew the life of a star better than Teddy Wells, whose own story had been told in every tabloid. He could tell the winner about fame. It followed you everywhere, judged your actions and then tossed you aside on a whim.

Teddy had begun his career singing in small clubs during his late teens. Even then, he had the ability to thrill women with his romantic voice and charismatic personality. Demand for his appearances grew greater each year. Every woman watching thought he sang just to her. When he walked on stage, an aura of excitement filled the room.

He'd demonstrate his sly sense of humor halfway through the performance by teasing his audience and saying, "I'm a little warm. Do you mind if I take something off?"

The crowd would go wild while he removed his white scarf and threw it into their midst. The lucky recipient screamed upon catching it. When his hit song, *I Want to be Your Teddy Bear* hit the charts, women carried stuffed bears to his performances and threw them on stage. His agent donated them to the Great Ormond Street Children's Hospital.

He heard a familiar sounding voice coming from the screen. Ted edged forward. He shook his head in disbelief. "Bloody hell, this kid sounds like me. He looks like me, too."

The young man sang passionately. Dressed in white, his vocal rendition of the enduring song *Unforgettable* proved to be just that. His voice carried the same timbre and sensuality as Ted's. The appreciative audience shouted, "Ronnie, Ronnie!"

"Damn good vocals, kid. At least you stole from the best." The camera moved in for a close-up. For the first time, Ted saw the performer's vivid blue eyes, reminiscent of blue eyes haunting his past. He was intrigued. Teddy would have his agent reserve a seat for the next show.

Teddy had traveled extensively for his career. His performances in the States drew huge crowds. During his Las Vegas tour, he met Julie, a California girl. Memories of their time together never left him.

Seated in the front row during his performance, Julie was one of those selected to come on stage. She was charming and funny in their repartee. When he put his arms around her and sang her a love song, she blushed. Her vivid blue eyes and sweet personality enchanted him. The physical chemistry they felt for one another ended in passionate love one night. From that time on, they were inseparable.

He learned that she was born in Napa Valley, the daughter of a vineyard owner. He told her he was a Manchester lad, whose parents worked long hours for their only son.

"They encouraged my dreams, even during the worst times. I'll always be grateful to them for their support," he told her.

Teddy was consumed by his love for Julie. He thought she felt the same way about him.

A few days before leaving for his East Coast engagements, he called her hotel, only to find she had checked out. Teddy was stunned. He was unable to locate her before his scheduled departure. Sweet Julie had disappeared from sight. He looked back on their time together as something precious that slipped through his fingers. He never felt the same passion for another woman.

In England, Teddy met Rita at a friend's wedding reception. Exotic and fun-loving, Rita, a Jamaican girl, was a back-up singer for an American rock band. Within a year they married, and she retired from public life. The union produced no children, but Ted and Rita were content. It didn't matter what messages other women heard in his songs. He was faithful to his wife, who did her best to make him happy.

Ted longed for someone to fill the loneliness he'd felt since Rita's death. He needed to find his way once again. With a sigh, he returned his attention to the screen. Who was this young Ronnie?

When the program ended, Ted called his agent. For the first time in months, he looked forward to something.

◆   ◆   ◆

After the usher escorted him down the theatre aisle, Ted took his seat and smiled at the delighted woman in the seat next to his.

The lights dimmed, and the emcee for *FUTURE STAR* strolled on stage.

"Ladies and gentlemen, we're honored to have Teddy Wells in our midst." He gestured to Ted, who stood and bowed. Thunderous applause erupted from his loyal fans.

"I have a question for you, Teddy," the host said. "Those following our show have noticed that one of the contestants resembles you. Quite a lot if I may say so. Is there a secret you're keeping from us?"

"I don't think so." Ted grinned. "But I'm here to make sure. You'll be the first to know." His answer was met with laughter.

"Our judges hope that one of these young persons will entertain the world in the same fine manner as Teddy has done. Let's show them our support as they come on stage." The host began to clap his hands.

Ronnie's outstanding performance captivated the audience once again.

When the show ended, Ted went backstage. When he shook Ronnie's hand, he suddenly felt shy. Standing side by side, they were mirror images of one another, except for the age difference. Ted looked into blue eyes so much like Julie's. What he was thinking couldn't be possible, could it?

"You were brilliant tonight." Ted gripped Ronnie's hand a little tighter. "You have a fine voice, and great stage presence. The audience loves you. Where are you from?"

"California, sir. My mother's family owns a winery there. I'm a student at Cambridge University. I was sent to England to broaden my world and become civilized." He grinned.

"Is Ronnie your given name?"

"My full name is Ronald Ward. My mother thought this experience in London would give my singing career a boost. If you'd like to meet her, she's in the audience."

Ted hurriedly summoned the usher.

"Please find Mrs. Ward before she leaves," he asked.

"She's gone, sir," the usher said when he returned. "People seated near her said she left as the lights dimmed."

"Too bad Mom missed the whole show. Maybe jet lag caught up with her. She's probably taken a cab back to the hotel. She told me I look a lot like you, Mr. Wells. She's always admired you and has all of your old records."

"Is your father in London with her?"

"My father died three years ago. I'd love to stay and talk, but I have a date. If I keep her waiting, she'll think me a rude American prat."

"I have a favor to ask. I want you and your mother to dine with me tomorrow night. It's possible that we share some family connections. Would you mind giving me the phone number at your hotel?"

"That would be great! I can use any advice you could give me." Ronnie hastily scribbled on a piece of paper.

With the precious number in his pocket, Ted walked away, his heart pounding. At home in Chelsea, he dialed the number Ronnie had given him. The phone rang several times with no answer. Disappointed, Ted was about to hang up when a woman's voice came on the line.

"Hello?"

When he didn't answer, she asked, "Is someone on the line?"

Ted could feel his heart beating rapidly. He recognized that voice from the past. He'd waited so long to hear it, he had difficulty speaking.

"This is Teddy Wells. I was at the theater tonight and watched Ronnie Ward perform. May I ask who this is, please?"

"This is Julie Ward, Ronnie's mother. Is this really Teddy Wells? I'm not in the mood for jokes right now."

"This is Teddy. Julie, it is you, isn't it? You must remember our meeting all those years ago in Vegas." There was silence on the line again. "I've never forgotten you. We saw one another every day and then you disappeared. Where did you go? What happened?" Ted asked.

When she still didn't reply he said, "I think I deserve an answer."

She hesitated a moment. "When we met, I was engaged to another man, my wedding date set. The last thing I expected was to fall in love with you. I didn't know what to do. Everything happened so fast."

"I fell in love with you, Julie. How do you think I felt when I couldn't find you? You never mentioned anyone else. I thought you loved me, too."

"Teddy, my wedding took place within four weeks of my return home."

"How old is Ronnie?" he asked, his voice rising. "Is it possible that he's my son? A son I never knew existed? My God, Julie, I found out about it when I saw him on the telly last week. How could you keep a secret like that from me?"

Her voice trembled. "I'm sorry, Teddy. When I learned I was pregnant, I panicked. I couldn't tell anyone. My family had no idea I'd met someone else. I couldn't hurt them that way. You were a big star from another country, and always on the road. How would I fit into your life? When I saw you enter the theater tonight, it brought all the old memories back."

"Ronnie has no idea I'm his father, has he?"

"No one knows except you and me. It would have killed my husband if he knew. He was a good person and a good father. He didn't deserve that heartache. I'm sorry, Teddy, I'm so sorry. Please forgive me." She began to sob.

"We have to get together, Julie. I suggested to Ronnie that we three have dinner tomorrow night. I hope you'll agree."

"Yes, but don't tell him about this conversation. You must promise me."

"I promise. Neither of us needs any more grief. You took a huge piece of my heart when you left, Julie. To see you again means the world to me."

"I still love you, Teddy. I've never forgotten those days."

"Until tomorrow, luv." He put the phone down, at once exhilarated and exhausted.

When Big Ben chimed eight the following night, Ted sat in a Knightsbridge restaurant, his table facing the entrance. His nervousness grew as he waited. At last, he saw the two persons whose future meant the most to him. Ronnie held the arm of a stunning brown-haired woman. Ted's heart skipped a beat.

He stood as they approached the table, his excitement keen. His eyes followed her every move. Julie was even more beautiful than he remembered. Ted stepped forward, took her hand in his and kissed it. Gazing up at her, the years separating them seemed to vanish, and he was young Teddy Wells again.

He turned to Ronnie. "Somehow, I knew you would have a beautiful mum. I hope this is the first of many evenings together, and we three become real friends."

Ted sat next to Julie, holding her hand tightly. Her fingers wrapped around his. They stared into one another's eyes as if they couldn't get enough of each other.

"If I didn't know better, I'd swear you two had met before." Ronnie said.

"You might say that," Ted said. "Sit down, son." He patted the chair beside his.

Trouble In Paradise

Phyllis Costello

I could have avoided all that trouble if I hadn't lost the envelope.

I remember the day Lola Mae Britton moved in. What a grand entrance. A long tanned leg emerged slowly from her T'bird. Her thighs were firm and her ankles, slim. With gaping mouths, we stared, like gawky young boys. She wore a yellow halter and scanty white shorts that revealed more than they covered.

Suggestive eyes gazed back at us. We were each granted a radiant smile from her full lips. We welcomed Lola Mae to the Palms Senior Park with nervous eagerness.

Computers hummed that day as we all ordered Viagra. Lola Mae reawakened the young boy in all the old men. Accustomed to seeing aging faces belonging to sagging butts and lengthening boobs, she bloomed, like a rosebud, in the onion patch. And she moved next door.

My wife wasn't pleased. Wives in the Palms protected their property from female predators. Widows guarded the few single men left. Lola Mae wasn't invited to neighborhood parties or for patio cocktails. Backs turned as she drove her racy little red car through our park.

On the other hand, men surrounded her as she visited the Clubhouse for lunch. She laughed at our jokes as she stroked our egos. When she gardened in her bikini, traffic became heavy on my street. And any male who could hobble worked out at the gym during Lola Mae's scheduled time.

Roger Richardson suffered a fatal coronary that first week, pushing his 72-year-old body too far. "A guy has to keep in shape," he gasped to Lola Mae, as he dropped to the floor.

At the Loyal Ladies Book Club, Mrs. Richardson was heard saying, "Poor Roger would still be here, if *she* hadn't moved in. That Lola Mae is no better than a whore. You better watch your husbands." Eyebrows rose at this bold statement. The seed of poison had been planted.

I'd been happily married to the same woman for 52 years, until Frances heard that damned remark.

"Bill, where are you going?" she started to ask.

"To get the mail."

Frances would always dash to the window making sure I came straight back. No detours for me.

One morning I came back with the mail, and turned back toward the open door.

"Where do you think you're going, now?" Putting her hands on her hips, she defied me to challenge her authority.

"The roses are looking tacky. I need to do some trimming."

She glanced at the wall clock. It was 8:30. Gardening was allowed between 9:00 and 10:00 each morning, the exact time that Lola Mae went to the gym. "Let's have another cup of coffee," she said.

She wasn't fooling me.

"Want to go to a movie today?" she then asked.

"I told you, I have a golf game scheduled with Dirk."

"Let's go out for dinner. How about Mexican?"

Sighing, I agreed. I'd hardly had a moment alone, or with any of the guys, since the Richardson witch made her remark. I've always been faithful to Frances. But shit, she doesn't even want me to window shop. Maybe I should buy some horse blinders.

Finally outside, I worked on the roses. Stepping back to admire my work, I heard Lola Mae's voice. "Billy, hi there, stranger. Could you come here a minute? I can't get my old garbage disposal to work."

I tried not to run as I crossed the lawn.

Down on my knees, I gave the disposal another twist and it began to hum. I turned and saw those gorgeous legs leaning close to me. It would be a tight squeeze to get up, but I'd try. Stifling a groan, I stood up. I could feel the heat of her body and smell her gardenia perfume. She hadn't moved an inch.

"I don't know how to thank you. I'll have to think of something special, just for you, Billy." She smiled.

I looked toward her upturned face and was rewarded with a perfect view down her low cut shirt. Lola Mae stood on tiptoe, put her arms around my neck, and pressed her body close.

Moist red lips were slightly parted and moving toward me. Things were moving a bit out of control.

"Bill, where are you? Bill?" My wife's voice came from our back door.

"Gotta go." I rubbed against her to get out.

"Now don't you forget. Come back and collect that thank you anytime, Billy." She ran her fingertips along my arm.

I rushed out the door, stumbling over the sill.

"What have you been up to, Mr. Rose Trimmer? Did you transplant some roses in her kitchen?—or maybe the bedroom? Stay away from her, Bill. You're my husband."

"Jesus, Frances. I was fixing her disposal. The woman is alone and needs help."

"That woman is never alone. She's about as helpless as a thousand-pound gorilla. You stay the hell away from her."

"Oh, get over it." I stalked away.

Frances was right. Lola Mae was never alone. I saw men coming and going. Some were my buddies. They all left smiling. I became obsessed. I wanted to dip into that honey pot. My wife tightened the reins even more. I felt pussy-whipped. How did I ever think we enjoyed life together? At night Frances snored beside me while I tossed and turned, thinking of that beautiful body and who was with her.

One night, I crept out of bed, slipped across the lawn and peeked in the window. What a glorious sight. Lola Mae was lying on the bed, nude. My God, I hadn't seen a body like that for thirty years. All the right curves. Rosy little nipples, standing upright. I let out a silent whistle. Feasting my eyes on velvety skin, I began to fantasize.

At that moment, something knocked me to the ground. I felt the poodle's teeth sink into my calf. Screaming, I managed to shake him loose. I kicked the snarling mutt. Yelping he ran away. Immediately the entire neighborhood appeared. There I stood, in my underwear, with ragged bloody flesh hanging from my leg. Frances glared, Lola Mae clucked—the rest all whispered.

"For Christ sake, Frances, get my robe, woman. We have to get to the hospital. The rest of you better start looking for the prowler, before he gets away."

It was embarrassing as hell. No one believed me.

The next morning, there Lola Mae stood, at my front door, smiling sweetly at Frances. "I've baked brownies for Billy. How is he?"

My wife stood her ground. She didn't invite the predator inside. Opening the screen slightly, she grabbed the brownies with a curt, "Thank you. He's fine."

Bang the door slammed, and the brownies were dumped into the garbage.

Locked inside with my jailor for several weeks, life became a living hell. Frances was tight lipped with a ramrod stiff back. Oh, she waited on me, as I sat on the couch, with my injury. She waited and watched. Charles Manson couldn't have been guarded any closer. She never yelled at me about the incident. She never spoke to me again.

That winter, Frances succumbed to a flu bug. Hospitalized with pneumonia, senility set in. They transferred her to extended care. She ranted and raved obscenities about her husband and some hussy. The language was color-ful—unbecoming a lady. When I visited, she became silent. Upon leaving, her mad raving would begin once more. "That son of a bitch is—" It could be heard all over.

"We're so sorry, Colonel. Sedation doesn't help." The small staff always seemed glad to see me. It was the only time Frances stopped her lewd babble.

Meanwhile, left alone at home, I remained faithful to Frances. But the memory of Lola Mae, naked, haunted me. My fantasies became urgent and lurid. After all, my wife had gone bananas and was no longer available. A man had a right to one last fling before he's planted in the ground.

I began to formulate a plan. It must be perfect. Lola Mae would find me hand-some and irresistible. She'd choose me, while scorning all others as a bunch of horny old goats.

Double order of Viagra, massage, work out, tanning salon, walks, haircut and color, shave, teeth whitened, new clothes, new underwear, hairpiece. Carefully I made the list. A military officer knows the importance of strategy.

Sticking to that plan took discipline. I watched my buddies come and go. It became agony, but I strained, sweated, tanned, colored, and cut—I worked at the plan.

L-Day arrived. I began early, with my walk and work out. A relaxing massage and shave at Marty's for Men. Waking up from my nap, I took a long hot shower, polishing it off with cold water and brisk rub down. I felt ready for any-thing. Flexing and looking in the mirror, I saw flat abs, a virile, handsome man. The hairpiece looked natural. I applied *Old Spice* liberally, paying special atten-tion to areas below the waist. I pulled on new red bikini briefs and T-shirt. Next came walking shorts with my print silk shirt. As I brushed my salt and pepper hair, I admired the newly acquired mustache. I looked quite distinguished. With my dark tan, who could resist?

I decided to reread my avowal of undying love to Lola Mae, before sealing the envelope.

My dearest sweet darling, Lola Mae,

I confess my undying love for you. You are a sweet rose among cactus.

My darling, I must have you. I won't be satisfied until you are only mine. I have traveled the world. I know secret ways to hold your hot body and love you like a real man. You're driving me out of my mind with desire. I am desperate.

Your love slave forever,

Billy, your bad boy from next door

Sealing the envelope liberally with *Old Spice* Cologne, I was ready.

Knocking smartly, I practiced my smile. "Lola Mae? Are you home, darling? It's your Billy. Lola Mae?"

The door stood slightly ajar so I went in, eager to find my love. I walked toward her bedroom, "Lola Mae? Where are you, my angel? Your true love is finally here."

She was lying on the bed. "You little minx. Were you hiding from Bad Billy?"

There was no answer.

Then it smacked me, right between the eyes. Someone had planted a kitchen knife in my darling Lola Mae's heart.

My legs wobbling out of control, I backed out of the room. In shock, I slunk out the back door and crawled across the yard. Shaking all over, I dropped into a chair. My God, who would do such a horrible thing to sweet Lola Mae?

I sank to the bed and began to undress.

Suddenly I remembered the letter. Where was it? I'd put it right in my pocket. I searched my clothing, the bedroom and bath. Not there. I looked in the kitchen. Crawling and searching the yard turned up nothing.

I knew I'd have to go back inside. I steeled myself to return to the grisly scene. My hand on the doorknob froze when I saw nosey, Mrs. Larson watching me from her window. Turning rapidly, I headed back home. In my panicky state, I had forgotten, I was half undressed.

Pacing, I looked at the clock. Better wait until at least 3:00 AM when everyone was sleeping. I glanced out the front window. My God, there was a car parked in her driveway. What could I do now? Better have another. *Johnny Walker*. My nerves were shot.

A dark figure hurried out the front door. The car shot out of the drive and around the corner before I could see more.

I'm screwed, I thought. I polished *Johnny Walker* off, straight from the bottle.

Dawn finally came. I continued my anxious vigil. Briefly, I felt a reprieve when nothing happened. Then I saw George Sloane make his way to her front door. My stomach dropped into my shoes.

Ten minutes later, two squad cars pulled up. Four officers entered the house on a dead run. Yellow tape went up. The whole neighborhood came out to speculate about what was happening. *Johnny Walker* and I went stumbling out to the street. The men looked concerned. Couldn't say the same for the women with their smug smiles and knowing nods. The damn bitches.

There was silence as they stared at me. When they began to talk, no one seemed to know anything. I swayed a bit and grabbed the mailbox.

Mrs. Larsen, the bearer of all park dirt—vindictive could be her middle name, gave me a dirty look. "How's Frances doing, Bill?" she asked. She would sing long and loud to the police.

"Hello folks. My name is Phil Gibson, Investigator for the Palm Springs police. We have a serious situation here. Your neighbor, Lola Mae Britton, I'm sorry to say, was murdered last night."

Faces reflected shock. They all began talking at the same time.

The detective held his palm up. "Quiet, please. We'll be conducting an investigation. Try to recall anything you might have seen or heard. I'll be talking to each of you. But I can't answer any questions, at this time." He turned back to the house.

Confusion and babbling filled the air. Maude Larson gave me a nasty smile and whispered to Naomi Wegstrom. As I let go of the mailbox and wobbled toward home, I felt their stares boring into my back.

Lola Mae's beautiful body was carried out. Goodbye, my love, I thought. I'll find out who did this.

A memorial service at the clubhouse was customary when a resident dies. Should Lola Mae be denied this courtesy, due to the disgraceful way she died? The board couldn't come to an agreement. They called an open meeting. A brawl would be more accurate. The women voted against the memorial, claiming it would draw negative publicity about our park. The men disagreed. Wives began screeching at their husbands. It escalated into shin kicking and hitting. The male vote eventually won. The memorial would be held.

Not a single woman attended. Many men came limping in with black eyes. A life-size picture of Lola Mae rested on an ornate easel, flanked by two urns of white lilies. Her apparel consisted of a simple sheer white scarf. I blinked back tears, as my eyes feasted on her blonde perfection.

Phil Gibson stood at the back of the room, his eyes constantly shifting, observing whatever detectives observe.

A strange woman entered. Beautifully dressed, slim and elegant, she wore a heavy black veil, concealing her identity. She walked slowly to the picture of Lola Mae and studied it intently. Suddenly, manicured hands scribbled wildly with a red magic marker, defacing that blonde perfection. Running out the side door, she vanished.

Everyone retired to the bar after that unsettling display. Soon everyone returned to the memorial. As different men spoke, I noticed they all said the same thing. How beautiful … how sexy she'd been. They described her body. It was tasteless … no respect. They were a bunch of sex crazed old fogies. Some guy stood up to sing. His voice quavered and threatened to fade away. I hoped it would. He wheezed out a medley of *I'll See You In My Dreams* and *She's A Red Hot Mama*.

This wasn't a memorial. It was a desecration. I couldn't take much more.

Worrying about the lost envelope distracted me. Who had it? The police? That unknown dark figure? George Sloane? Maude Larson? My mind ran in circles.

Detective Gibson paid me a visit later that day. "Did you see anything out of the ordinary that night?" He leaned forward, giving me a penetrating look.

I tried to look relaxed. "Well, a noise outside woke me." I felt nauseous. I couldn't breathe. I had to pause before I could continue. "I recall a dark shadowy figure rushing out and driving away."

"Hmm—how well did you know the deceased?"

I looked out the window. "Hardly at all. My wife is in extended care. I've been busy trying to get her well."

"So you had no relationship with Lola Mae Britton?"

"No sir, just speaking. No friendship."

"What were you doing at her back door, in your underwear, that night?"

"Gosh Detective, I always check to see if her door is locked at night. You know, being a woman alone, I am concerned for her safety."

He gave me a long sideways look. "I'll have to take you downtown for further questioning, Bill."

That damned Mrs. Larson had done her work. I wanted to take the knife out of poor Lola Mae and stick it in Maude Larson.

"Am I under arrest?"

"No, not yet. I need to check out some information."

They grilled me for two hours without any mention of the letter. Talk about needing *Johnny Walker.* I tied one on.

I woke up late that night and my mind was clear. The old military training was kicking in. I would find the guilty party. Start at the crime scene.

Dressed in my Colonel's uniform, I crossed the yellow tape. Boldly, I walked up to Lola Mae's front door and pushed it open, pausing to give Mrs. Larson the finger. Onward, to the bedroom.

She turned slowly and gave me that dazzling smile. "Hello, Billy." She searched my face. Her eyes gave her away. They were the appraising eyes of an opportunist.

"Lola Mae? But … but you're …" My voice trailed off as I attempted to unscramble my brain.

"Dead? No, I'm alive and well." Her mind continued to judge my reactions, and calculate her next move.

How in hell did I ever think she was warm and loving? This was a dangerous bitch. "But I saw your body."

"You saw Lillie Ray, my twin sister." She gave me a cold smile. "We were both living here, as one person. She was hiding from the law—wanted for a bit of confidence work in the Bay Area. Worked fine until she began blackmailing me. Threatened to expose my past as a Vegas call girl."

I listened to my illusions being destroyed. Lola Mae rubbed up against me. Disgusted, I pushed her away.

She continued her story. "I confronted Lillie Ray, telling her to leave. She laughed. Said she was going to tell Bennie Rocco where to find me. That did it. Benny is a mobster and my old boyfriend. I lost it. We began to wrestle. I grabbed a knife I kept in the bedroom for protection. Then I left. I only came back for my diamond watch." Her arm glittered as she held it up.

"Keep your hands up. Lola Mae Britton. I arrest you for the murder of your sister, Lillie Rae."

Detective Gibson stepped into the bedroom. "I heard the whole story from the den while waiting for the killer to return. Boy was I off base. Thought it was you, Bill. Better keep your dick in your pants and your brain in your head. Mrs. Larson gave us quite a flaming tale."

A week later, I noticed that scruffy poodle trotting around carrying a worn piece of paper. It looked like my love letter.

"Here Fifi, here." I held out a large patty of raw hamburger.

The old boy eyed me with suspicion. Gingerly, he grabbed the meat and I grabbed the letter. A fair exchange, I thought.

Fifi didn't agree. I ran to the house with that vicious beast hot on my heels. As I reached the door, he ripped the seat right out of my pants. Mrs. Larson would have another story for the park. I didn't give a shit.

Couple of things still bothered me. The guys all dipped into that honey pot. I never did.

And I've always wondered who really died? Lola Mae? Or Lillie Ray?

Under Bridges, in Crystal Balls

Bill Hinthorn

"There are bodies under the bridge." Diane's tone was positive. But then Diane was almost always positive, and the less she knew about the subject, the more positive her tone became.

"What bodies?" I asked. "What bridge?"

"I don't know. I just know there are bodies under a bridge."

"*How* do you know there are bodies under a bridge?"

"Taueret said that there are bodies under the bridge."

Ah. Taueret. Taueret, a friend of Diane's, had been born Mary Jane Smith about thirty years before. She grew to be an adult and apparently a rather good secretary; a better secretary, some thought, than an adult. She seemed stuck with what she saw as her unsatisfactory life—and name—until her grandmother died and left Mary Jane a small inheritance. The inheritance wasn't enough for Mary Jane to live the high life, but it provided a yearly income sufficient to meet her most basic needs.

On receiving the inheritance, Mary Jane rummaged around in what she considered appropriate ancestors and found an Egyptian goddess named "Taueret". With that, she chucked both the job and the name of Mary Jane Smith, reincarnated herself as Taueret, lion-headed Egyptian goddess, and opened a soothsayer's shop in a seedier section of Riverside. There she dabbled in the occult arts, spending part of her time staring at a myopic crystal ball. It wasn't that Taueret marched to a different drummer. Rather, I always thought, it was a case of her not hearing any drummer, at all.

However, if her ancestral research had been more thorough, she would have found that only infrequently did the deity Taueret appear as an avenging lion-headed goddess. Taueret was actually a goddess of childbirth and suckling who almost always appeared in the form of a female hippopotamus. Childbirth and suckling were hardly suitable issues for Mary Jane Smith. On the other hand, given her size and general configuration, her being a female hippopotamus was quite appropriate.

But I digress. My point here is that I believed very few of the visions revealed to the latest incarnation of the Hippo Goddess.

"Where, exactly, did Tauret get her information about the bodies under the bridge?" Patience is a virtue when trying to get any accurate information from Diane.

"I don't know. From some of her friends, or maybe from her crystal ball."

"You know," I said, "there seems to be a short in that crystal ball's connection to the nether world. Taueret should restrict her prophecies to whatever she can find in the evening news."

"You're not very nice." I could almost hear Diane pouting. "This is serious."

I was about to say that any information coming from Taueret couldn't possibly be serious, but there are times when silence is, indeed, golden, and I usually know when to keep my mouth shut. I told Diane I'd talk to her later, and ended the call.

I was out and about the next day, a Saturday, when Diane left a cryptic message on my recorder saying, "It's Susan. I just know it's Susan," and that I was to come to her place just as soon as I could. I drove over to find her trying to fry chicken.

"Why are you ruining that chicken?"

Diane, an attractive gray-eyed blonde in her mid-twenties, took care to keep herself in good physical condition and that usually precluded eating fried chicken. Besides, Diane was an even worse cook than I, which certainly put her close to the top of the Worst Cooks in America list.

"Well," she said, "I thought that since we would be going out checking bridges for bodies, we might make sort of a picnic trip out of it."

"Wouldn't it be simpler to just stop by a fast food place and grab something?"

It was a foolish question, far too logical and I didn't expect an answer. But I couldn't imagine a picnic while out looking for dead bodies.

"What's this about your friend Susan?"

"Susan has disappeared. I'm sure it's her body that's under one of the bridges."

"What do you mean, disappeared? I thought she had a boyfriend in Sherman Oaks. How do you know she isn't there for a long weekend?"

"Because Susan would never go out of town without telling me." The positive tone of voice again. "I just know something has happened to her."

"When was the last time you heard from her? And if she's really missing, shouldn't you file a missing person's report with the police?"

"I heard from her on Tuesday. She said that her friend from Sherman Oaks was coming here and I haven't heard from her since. I called her home phone and didn't get an answer. I just know he's killed her. We've got to go check."

"What's this "*we*" business? This has nothing to do with me. This is between you and Taueret."

The "*we*" business was simply that I drove a 1950 Willys Jeep that I'd bought for a few dollars and refurbished, and if we were to be off the road, we'd need the four-wheel drive capability of the Jeep. Diane's only vehicle was a 1982 Cadillac convertible, which had pieces continually falling off it—pieces she never bothered to retrieve. How she kept it running was a mystery. The only explanation I could think of was that Diane's part-time boy friend, a full-time mechanic, must have kept the car running for her. Anyway, the Cadillac would get hopelessly stuck in the sand.

I really didn't have anything to do that morning, so I gave in. We loaded the fried chicken, such as it was, along with other picnic items in the Jeep, took our light jackets and off we went to the bridges of Riverside County, desperately seeking Susan.

It was a late winter day. A few high thin clouds wisped across a pale blue sky, doing very little to dull the brilliant sun. We hadn't had much rain all winter and most of the streambeds were dry. In fact, most "bridges" were freeway overpasses. It was a simple matter to pull off to the side of the road and wander around.

We went from bridge to bridge. Diane poked around in small piles of trash under some of the bridges, piles so small that they couldn't have covered the body of a human being, even a dismembered one. I couldn't help but wonder what microbial and fungal perils Diane might be exposing herself to, or if she was going to come down with a case of "trashitis" and start growing skin tumors that looked like Styrofoam hamburger containers.

At one bridge, we interrupted a small mangy stray dog snuffling around in a little pile of trash. The dog avoided me but barked continually at Diane. Each time she approached, the dog trotted off in that peculiarly skewed dogtrot some dogs have, moving sideways while going forward. He stopped every few feet to turn and face Diane so that his barking could be aimed more directly at her.

"Well, he's hungry!" Diane said.

She dug around in the picnic supplies and hauled out a piece of her fried chicken. She offered it to the dog. The dog refused to take the chicken from Diane's hand and barked louder. She laid the chicken on a paper napkin on the ground and backed away. The dog stopped barking long enough to sniff the chicken. He backed away from it, growling.

"What's wrong with that stupid dog?" Diane asked. "He was up there licking hamburger wrappers but refuses to eat good fried chicken."

The dog obviously had better taste than Diane. Just keep quiet, I told myself.

"He can't be very hungry after all," Diane said.

I knew better.

After a few hours of poking around under what seemed half the bridges of Riverside County, our search revealed nothing more than some women's and men's underwear, aluminum cans and other windblown trash. By two o'clock we decided that we probably weren't going to find anything—which I had known in the first place—and quit. I felt pretty silly looking for dead people that Taueret had conjured up in her dysfunctional crystal ball.

We really hadn't needed the Jeep after all. We could have taken Diane's Cadillac—assuming, that is, that too many vital parts hadn't fallen off.

We couldn't find a suitable place for a picnic either, and finally returned to Diane's apartment to eat. The chicken was even worse that I'd thought, something the dog had realized without the help of a crystal ball. Diane was still concerned about the bodies and she didn't eat. I didn't eat much either, but it had nothing to do with dead bodies, other than that of the chicken. After a few bites I gave up on the chicken to try Diane's dessert concoction, a sort of custard-pie-gone-wrong thing. But that wasn't any better. The custard was tough and hard to chew.

"Look," I said, "if you're really sure that Susan is missing, the thing to do is to file a missing person's report."

"What good would that do? Besides, I don't think Susan has been gone long enough. You have to be gone for weeks before the police consider you a missing person."

I explained that filing a report would do far more good than our messing around in trash under bridges. After all, the police had far more resources than we had.

"Maybe we should talk to Taueret," Diane suggested.

Talking to Taueret didn't really make a lot of sense to me, but maybe we could find out some of the details so it was worth a try. But telephone calls to several places failed to locate Taueret. She was nowhere to be found. Like a hippopotamus in a river, sinking below the surface of the water, Taueret had sunk somewhere out of sight, presumably below the level of intelligent society.

I finally decided I *did* have better things to do with the rest of the day and left Diane to her murderous problems.

◆   ◆   ◆

A friend called early Sunday morning to ask if I'd like to go skeet shooting. After killing most of the morning—and a number of clay pigeons, although given my marksmanship, more clay pigeons lived than died—we wandered along to Sunday lunch. Later I checked my cell phone, which I usually have turned off or just ignore, and found some cryptic messages from Diane. I was to be at her apartment as soon as humanly possible. The second and subsequent messages all asked why I wasn't there. I called to assure her that I was on my way.

It was another beautiful day, not quite so cool as the previous one, but with a sky full of bright sunshine. The open Jeep made the trip pleasurable and I was almost reluctant to end the drive for the emotional chaos that I suspected was waiting in Diane's apartment.

When I rang the bell, she opened the door immediately. "I'm glad you're here."

She let me in, closed the door, then opened it immediately to look out, checking, it seemed to me, to make certain I wasn't followed.

"What's happened now?" I assumed there were some new developments, although making any assumptions as far as Diane was concerned was usually a mistake.

"Well, I did what you said. Last night I went down to the police station and filed a missing person's report about Susan. The detective, a Mr. Olson, took the information and said that they didn't have any reports of Susan being in an accident or in jail. Why would they think she's in jail?"

I really didn't see any point in trying to answer that nor did I see much use in arguing that Susan had probably just failed to call.

"I told Mr. Olson about the bodies under the bridge," Diane continued.

"You didn't."

"Well, yes, of course. The police would certainly want to know about people being murdered."

"Diane, there aren't any bodies under a bridge. This is all a fantasy of Taueret and a crystal ball that's as cracked as she is."

My arguments were too disgustingly logical for Diane to even consider. She continued to insist that Taueret knew what she was talking about, that there were bodies under a bridge somewhere.

Mercifully, the telephone rang before I became as confused as Diane. Thinking that it might be the police, I answered it. It was Susan, just returned from Sherman Oaks.

"I'm glad you're there," Susan said. It seemed that just about everybody except me was glad I was at Diane's apartment.

"I had the strangest call on my recorder," Susan continued. "I'm supposed to call a Detective Olson at the police station. I called, but he wasn't in. He'll be back in an hour. What do you suppose that's all about?"

"Well," I said, "I can explain most of this, but it will take a little time."

Susan listened while I told her the story from the start.

"The business about the bodies under the bridge was something that Taueret heard at a party," Susan explained. "I wish Diane would quit blindly accepting everything that Taueret says."

"What, exactly, did Taueret have to say about the bodies under the bridge?"

"She apparently overheard part of a conversation about two people who were killed and their bodies dumped under a bridge."

"Do you know if she notified the police?"

"I doubt it. This was just another party conversation, and the people discussing it may have been talking about a story or book or something else, although Taueret seemed to think that real intelligence might be involved."

"I doubt that Tauret would recognize intelligence if she fell into it. Didn't she tackle the story tellers and ask for more details?"

"Apparently not."

"Who is it?" Diane wanted to know.

I told Diane that Susan had returned from Sherman Oaks, and handed her the telephone.

She talked a few minutes and hung up. "Susan said that Taueret said that both bodies are men."

"That obviously eliminates Susan as one of the murderees."

Diane looked at me as if I were an idiot and I'll admit I felt like one for getting involved in this absurdity in the first place.

"We really should go down to the police station and talk to Detective Olson," I said. "Susan said he would be back in an hour and since Susan isn't missing, we need to clear this up before a bad situation becomes a real mess."

When we arrived, Detective Olson had just returned to his office. He was a trim and fit man with a no-nonsense attitude, and a face of chiseled granite that looked as if it would crack if he smiled. I explained the strange story from the beginning, and he listened patiently without interruption, his attention all mine.

"Well, we've already had a call from your friend, Susan," he said. "We did only preliminary searching, so there wasn't a lot of time and effort wasted. And, by the way, we found your bodies."

"Under a bridge?" Diane breathed.

"Under a freeway overpass."

"What were the sexes of the bodies?" Diane's question was hushed.

"Both male," our granite-faced detective answered.

"See!" Diane exclaimed. "Taueret was right! She understands these things. I knew it!"

"But Taueret got her information from a party conversation," I argued. I turned to the detective. "Do you have any other details?"

"Yes," Detective Olson smiled, and I was surprised to see that his face didn't crack after all. "We had an accident report this morning of a two-car collision at a freeway overpass. No one was really hurt, but at the scene of the accident, the investigating police officer noticed a foul odor, like something dead and decaying. He walked down under the overpass to investigate."

"And?" Diane asked eagerly.

Detective Olson's granite face broke into a very broad grin. "There the officer found the bodies of two wild alley cats, both male. Apparently they'd been fighting over territory, and had wounded each other so badly that they both died."

Violets Are Blue

Eleanor Tyus Johnson

The body lay face down on the floor. A tumble of red ringlets almost completely covered the perfectly chiseled face for which Violet was famous. Also out of sight were the gorgeous lavender-blue eyes that had given her the nick-name, Violet. Covering her world famous body was a sheer shroud of muslin, a far cry from what it was accustomed to wearing.

When Violet made her debut into the world of fashion, she was heralded as possessing the most anatomically perfect body in the world. Her picture, along with detailed accounts of her every measurement, flooded fashion magazines. Her career skyrocketed and designers all over the world built their finest couturier collections to fit her. *Harper's Bazaar* did a five page feature story that carried over ten different outfits modeled on her body. Each outfit was created by a different "famous" designer. That issue of *Harper's* was sold out before it hit the news stands.

Violet was selected to display the first line of bikini bathing suits for *Catalina*. On Violet's body they looked great—even better than great. The designers had fitted the suits so that everything that should be hidden was, and everything that could use a little sun got it. Violet's well-toned body guaranteed that nothing was out of place or where it shouldn't be. That issue of *Vanity Fair* was well received, and only a few readers thought the suits were too revealing. The consensus of opinion was "bring them on." The bikini was here to stay.

One of the most unforgettable events in Violet's career was a Christmas performance at Marshall Fields in Chicago. She was draped in a white full-length ermine evening coat that floated around her like a cloud that had just dropped from heaven. There was the suggestion of a lilac gown under the coat, but one's attention was drawn to a circle of stones that covered its top edge and seemed to be part of the coat. Likewise, her ears were covered with jewels that appeared to be accessories for the coat. Violet was standing on a moving saucer that took her up and down the streets of a miniature snow covered village. The coat was priced in the six figures, and it was reputed that the store had sold out its total stock in three days.

Yes, she had been the "Queen" for almost ten years. And she probably wouldn't mind giving it up to a worthy opponent—But, Miss Skinny!—The new model in the dressing room ... no arms ... no hips ... no boobs ... no belly ... no butt. Nothing that even faintly resembled a human female body. Well, maybe it was just a fad and wouldn't last.

The door was pushed open. A hand reached in and flicked a switch. Light flooded the room as an elderly man pushed a cart through the doorway. He glanced around then headed to a corner occupied by a tall waste basket. He pulled out the plastic liner, tied it and dropped it in his cart. He replaced it with another liner and moved further into the room.

It was a large room and one wall was lined with tall cabinets. Each cabinet had a glass door. Some were standing open. Large flat tables covered the middle of the room and several waste baskets were slid under them. The janitor moved between the tables emptying and replacing the baskets as he passed. When he reached the back wall he closed the cabinet doors that were standing open. That's when he looked down and saw her.

"Damn," he said aloud. "This is the second time this week a store mannequin has fallen out of its case and hit the floor. I bet those designers will want to blame me if it's broken."

He gingerly picked Violet up, deciding not to replace her in her cabinet. Instead he placed her on the table in the middle of the room. After he finished his duties in the room, he walked past the table and glanced at her. She sure was pretty, he thought, as he switched off the lights.

What's Your Pleasure,
Red or White?

Virginia Cummings

The coastal redwoods and natural stone wall gave me the impression of a fortress as I drove through the huge iron gates. Approaching the house, I couldn't help but feel slightly overwhelmed by the Santa Cruz Mountains from a height I'd never seen them from before. Why did I accept this invitation? Armida's request made me wonder who would respond if Peggy needed someone. Of course, she'd never be so far from the city, and hopefully not for the same situation.

The main house had been restored and rooms added by various owners, but the style remained consistent. Smaller cottages near the trees left the house a commanding view of the mountains. Peggy would love to come here, not just to see Armida, but also the gardens, the view and the house, itself. The entry door, though tall and elaborate, fit the stately picture and friendly atmosphere I'm sure it was meant to express.

I entered and was asked to wait wherever I felt comfortable. Armida would be with me in a few minutes.

Inside, the house retained the same casual and elegant atmosphere as the outside. It was easy to see it took time, plus a lot of money, to create the desired look. Each room unobtrusively displayed paintings and other expensive collectibles. For all the effort, the house still felt steeped in mystery. I could see one man trimming trees, while another cleaned the pool. They looked more like security guards than ground keepers.

What could Armida Heim want to talk to me about? I'm sure Conrad Heim had taken care of the family details long ago. He wanted our firm to take care of any business contracts. I generally kept business and social contacts separate. Why did I make the exception this time? If we had not met for dinner, I wouldn't be here right now.

What was keeping Armida? I hadn't planned to stay here all day. I took off my glasses and rubbed my neck with my right hand. I didn't feel much better.

"I'm sorry to keep you waiting." Armida appeared unsteady as she crossed the foyer. "There are so many details to take care of. We will have tea on the patio." She paused and invited me to follow. I could see she had been crying.

Our conversation moved smoothly, limited to discussing the remodel and changes in the gardens. Armida thanked me for listening. "I wanted to talk to someone who knew Conrad. Working all the time, we didn't have a chance to meet any of the people who lived near here."

Walking through the gardens to the front of the house, I took Armida's hand to say goodbye. "Call Peggy next week, she will be glad to hear from you. Get away for a couple of hours and come into town."

The Skyline road made my trip a little longer, but it was a clear cloudless day, a rare chance to view the city and the East Bay hills. Now in the heavier traffic downtown, I moved slowly toward my destination. My thoughts wandered, and I recalled vividly how the Wine Master had given each of us a chance to taste the wine he suggested for our chosen entrée, that night

◆   ◆   ◆

Peggy had deserved a night out. Husband, business, and young children can be a tedious drain on your energy. She and I were the first to arrive. When Conrad and Armida were seated it was easy to see the women would find much to talk about. I had not met the other couple that would join us. They were friends interested in the Arts and charities Armida found worthwhile.

Everyone decided to have wine with dinner except for Peggy, Armida and myself. I stayed with my usual vodka tonic. Peggy and Armida chose water with dinner and coffee later.

During dinner, a waiter filled Conrad's glass for the second time. Conrad lifted the glass as a toast to everyone. Smiling briefly, he took a sip and suddenly dropped the glass. Other diners, startled by the sound, stared as Conrad clutched his throat, fell into his food and then onto the floor.

The diners, shocked by the scene, started talking loudly as the maitre d' hurried to our table. Things moved so fast that it was hard to remember what happened next. I have relived the scene over and over. It seemed to come to mind when I least expected it. I did remember the last waiter was one I hadn't seen in the room before. At the time it didn't seem unusual. He couldn't be found after the 911 call.

Now, opening the door to my office, I could see the phone light flashing. I pushed the button on the machine. There was one message. "Mr. Stetson, this is

Detective Roberts. Will you please call me? I need you to come downtown and identify the waiter that served the wine. I will meet you in the lobby when you get here." My thoughts raced as I gave a sigh of relief. Good, maybe we could get this over with, and I could get back to soccer, basketball and any other activities my teenagers could conger up.

Detective Roberts was waiting near the entrance, and indicated we would be taking the elevator. The down arrow gave me a clue this was not what I expected.

"The waiter is dead," he said as the elevator door opened.

The Detective unlocked the door to the morgue. It was just like on TV, stark and clinically clean. "I've been on the job for twenty-two years and I hate this part. It is never easy. Do you think you can handle it?"

We went to the gurney and he rolled back the sheet.

"That's the man," I gasped as I turned my back to the corpse. I wasn't sure if I would be able to control the sudden cramping in my stomach.

"Let's go to my office where I can tell you what we know so far."

"The man in the morgue is a known assassin who usually works the East Coast," Detective Roberts explained once we were seated. "It was unusual for him to get so close to his target. Time must have been running out and he had to do something quickly.

The body guards did a good job of protecting Heim until you went to the restaurant. We think one of his men may have taken out the waiter. Smuggling is a tough and dangerous racket, no matter which side you are on. It is a good thing you aren't involved more than you are right now."

I could tell the detective was watching all my reactions. These guys were always checking if your eyebrows twitched at the wrong time. I thought his words indicated I was not in question other than identification.

"I don't think we need to talk again. I'm turning this over to another division. Thank you for coming in."

As I walked to the car I wondered if Armida was aware of her husband's business interests. I'd leave a note for Peggy to talk to me before taking a call from Armida.

I didn't handle confusion well. A dedicated legal accountant only thinks in numbers. They say numbers don't lie. Two and two equals four every time, no matter how many zeros you add. Clean, how can anyone be totally clean, when you deal in mega numbers all the time? Being involved disturbed me. Would the totals add up when or if some "Hot Shot Lawyer" was drawn to this case?

All the family members, drug and shipping guys, could only want to split the take and move on. Cash in and move on, that was my motto. How many lofts, condos and storage units would we put on the market? Work, and then take a vacation.

Peggy came into the office with my lunch, chicken salad on wheat, from the Deli near the Bart Station. She said Armida had not called, and she wanted to know why I left the note on her desk.

I had to think fast. How much should I tell Peggy? Who could have tipped the guy that told me Conrad moved in suspect circles?

Our company typed, filed, faxed and recorded the Real Estate transactions after the bargaining was complete. It was Peggy's job to screen dates, errors or misspelled names. She was in charge of the Heim's account. I guessed it was only time before some one would find that out and realize Peggy could lead them to Conrad.

Ignorance is bliss, I thought. I'll just tell Peggy that Armida didn't need to know any details of Conrad's business. We'd close out that part of the business, and look for another client.

I pushed the sandwich to the far side of my desk. "Peggy, let's you and I go to lunch, have a glass of wine, and make a toast to Conrad," I said. "Go get your coat."

Wilma's Escape

Shirley Gibson

This past week has been more excitement than I care to ever experience again. My name is Wilma Hall. I live in a nursing home in Louisiana. I have seen and been through a lot in my ninety years, but the past week has been the most difficult and challenging ever.

On the television set in the recreation room, we saw pictures of yellow and orange swirling images, which represented hurricane Katrina coming our way. All night long I could hear the wind and rain beating on the window above my bed. At seven in the morning I was awakened by voices coming from the hall outside my door.

"Hurry, we must move quickly," Louise shouted. She was the nurse in charge of the wheelchair patients. Built sturdy, she could lift most of us without any help, but she wasn't as friendly as the other nurses. "We need to evacuate and evacuate now."

There was much confusion and fear as we were not sure how this was going to take place. Some wanted to stay. They had to be convinced it was in their best interest to leave. The nurses scrambled to make sure anyone who needed medicine would have it with them. I had on my purple robe, a birthday present from my granddaughter. I was reaching around for my glasses when Louise shoved them into my hands. Everything seemed a blur as she wheeled me down the hallway to the waiting bus.

Just two days before, when we first heard of Katrina, we all gathered in the chapel for prayer. Now it seemed our prayers had fallen on deaf ears.

This has been my home for the last eleven years since I fell down some stairs. My family consists of two grandchildren. Walter is thirty-three, a writer living in New York. Elisa, thirty-five, is a lawyer living in Huntsville Alabama. Samuel, my only child, died of a heart attack three years ago.

We were evacuated in groups, those that could walk and those who needed assistance. The group who could walk out was picked up by relatives or friends.

166

The group on oxygen was put on a school bus. I was in a bus that had wheel chair access. There were only five of us; we were the last to leave.

It seemed that we had only gone a few miles when we encountered water. The bus engine began to stall. As we sat there helplessly, I thought, is this how I am going to die?

My thoughts returned to only a month previously when I celebrated my birthday. My two grandchildren surprised me with a chocolate cake. On top were nine yellow roses, representing my ninety years. There were green leaves cascading down the side of the cake. As we ate our cake outside, a pair of butterflies danced around the flowers along the walkway. The air seemed so clean, while the sun was warm as if a blanket around my shoulders. I enjoyed the surprise visit.

The sound of the engine starting up brought me back to the present. Thank God we were moving again. We then encountered long traffic lines, as we were about to enter the Interstate. Jake, our bus driver for many years, decided to take a short cut. Being raised and living here all his life, he knew all the back roads. He had taken us to many events and we could always find a laugh or two from his jokes. This time there were no jokes, just his word that we would arrive safely.

"Now Miss Wilma don't you worry your pretty head about anything. You and the others will be safe," he said.

I don't remember how long the trip was because I fell asleep. When I woke up I looked out the window and saw the sign saying, *Welcome to Huntsville Alabama*.

It has been a week now since that fearful night's escape. But, you know, God did answer my prayer as I am now in a better place. My granddaughter comes to visit me several times a week. I also have wonderful nurses to take care of me. I am happy here making new friends.

I guess my story turned out to have a happy ending, but the people who were on oxygen were in the bus that caught fire. They will be missed by all of us.

Poetry

A Poem and a Prayer

Jeri Schmitz

My needs are very simple, I want
No noise and no fine print
No double talk, just leave me alone
My dog and I are content.
Let us be.

No significant other in my life,
Energies elsewhere spent
Grandchildren maybe, maybe not
Long as I can pay the rent.
Let me have just enough.

Tolerable traffic, gone to the future
Chaos in the streets
Leave me to lie, hopefully safe
Under my Martha sheets.
Let me rest.

Hallmark quality television
Rubber shoes for the rain
I long for signs of yesterday
But you can't go home again.
Let me look in both directions.

I'm not saying I'm not content
But leave me inside my cocoon
To emerge some day to bicycle

In front of a rising moon.
Let me fly

A Silent Concert

Alan Rosenbluth

October
Is aflame, but fading,
November, impatient on the horizon.
It's almost over.
Mountains of leaves blanket the soil,
Mostly golden, some red, bronze, and rust.
A desperate few still green, cling fiercely to their lifelines.
Brilliant colored ones descend on fragrant breezes,
Gently rocking side to side,
Spinning lazily counter clockwise.
Singles twirling, twisting, tumbling, and drifting on cascading waves.
Dozens dangling and dropping in clusters,
In tune with the air's unpredictable, invisible currents.
A surprising minority rebel and swirl upward for a moment,
Until they comprehend and respond to the gravity of the situation.
Suddenly, without warning, the trees hold their collective breath,
And so do I.
Without a gasp,
The wind disappears.
Gone is the gentlest breeze.
Motionless and silent,
Not one leaflet flickers or falls,
For half an expectant minute,
Seeming like an hour,
Until breath is restored.

Branches again sway and shimmy seductively,
Enticing each clinging leaf to enter a frantic unrehearsed ballet,
Finishing like a tiny plane executing a delicate landing,
Celebrating with a bow,
Its life's last magical cycle of grace and color.

Butter Not Eat It

Jeri Schmitz

I haven't had a croissant since 1982
About the time the sweets I love all became taboo
I don't drink real cola as per my inner voice
Coffee black, for thirty years, has been my beverage choice
Eggbeaters and veggie burgers, berries without cream,
Healthy choices all around me, steak is but a dream
Cooking styles have also changed since I began to diet
Calorie counting, a game I play, means I can not fry it
Cheese is out, so are carbs, hummus and eggplant … in
No trans fats or butter means pie … only if you're thin
Chicken, as a protein, is used in every home
For years now, I've had no skin nor have I seen a bone
Mashed potatoes, Wonder bread, white rice—out the door
Gluten is the way to go and it's soy I'm shopping for
Processed foods, verboten now,
No salt,
No spice,
No fun
Herb-filled, no-fat, multi-grain is now my breakfast bun.
As I contemplate my overweight and pull my bathrobe tight
My bathroom scale sticks out its tongue as if to say, "I'm right."
For the truth remains exactly the same as the digital display
In spite of the effort I put forth, it's the same, day after day.
Menopause, hormones, thyroid disease, all enemies within,
To fall off the old chuck wagon is a very grievous sin

So instead I climb on the treadmill and dream of foods I want
The list is long, but it always begins
With my favorite … the croissant.

Classroom Folly

Cheryl French

Walking into class, feeling about three feet tall,
Taking my seat, hoping on me the teacher won't call.

As she scans the room quickly, I pray our eyes won't meet,
"Have I prepared my lesson?" she inquires from her seat.

I turn my head quite slowly and finally answer "yes",
Shuffling anxiously through my papers, hoping I can be the best.

I open up my quivering mouth to deliver the first line,
Glancing around the crowded room, I think I'm doing fine.

Excitement makes my heart race as the minutes tick away,
At last I am finished, and now I want to stay.

How I love that class and that darling of a teacher,
I'd give her a great big hug if only I could reach her.

For boldness now permeates every pore within my flesh,
Do I love to read my stuff in Class? Of course, the answer's yes!

Creative Juices

Cheryl French

There are so many things I want to say,
But finding the right words can really get in my way.

Where oh where shall I ever find,
Just the right words to fit the right rhyme?

Expressions of thought run rampant but unable to connect,
Searching and pursing, but they aren't right yet.

Looking out of boredom upon a magazine on the desk,
I spy a lovely creature looking very statuesque.

A vision is created by that glance upon the page,
Rearranging my thoughts like displaced actors upon a stage.

My vision is directed now and so I can create,
Thoughts, which pour forth at a most astonishing rate.

The joys of creative adventure are at last mine,
As the plot thickens and develops with the passage of each line.

At last I know the secret to make the words all blend,
Creative juices flow like wine, each time I look again,

Gazing upon that captivating image entranced me from the start,
Allowing me to paint a picture on the canvas of my heart.

Dreamlights

Janet Davidson

I dream by candlelight
    Of days past
Love's soft whisper
      While shadows cast
         The image of his adoring face.

I dream by moonlight
    Of long ago
His warm embrace
      The music low
         Caressing tenderly our space.

I dream by firelight
    When he was mine
Blending sweet kisses
      Sharing white wine
         Veiled in love's exquisite lace.

I dream by starlight
    Of gone-by years
I loved and lost
      Midst mourning tears
         Memories time cannot erase.

During the Night After

Cyndy Muscatel

What was it?
The coffee?
I can't sleep;
The brandy?

When the clouds were mean,
Emily Dickinson wrote
Poetry.
I used to.
When I was young.

It's 3:20 and
I can't sleep.
Tomorrow, 5 and 8, by 7, will
Clammer, hammer for
Cherrios.

When you are 46 and only
Someone's
     mother,
     daughter,
     wife,
What can you do when
THEY are all asleep?

I read an article.
It's fashionable to write

down

    your

        thoughts.

I always liked e.e. cummings
and goings
and puns.

At dinner, I sat next to a doctor.
He said he was lazy.
If so, what am I?
He'd operated at 7.
I couldn't even get the kitchen
Cleaned up … all day.

4 years of college, magna cum laude.
Then a Masters Degree.
All that training
to become a maid?

5 o'clock. I'd better try to sleep.
It'll be the morning after.
Soon.

Golden Gate

Anita Knight

The fog swirls and clings to raised arms of steel
that rise above the blue Pacific
as it rolls into the bay.

The bay where crowds waft like the fog
but stop to gape in awe
at majestic vistas that await them
atop the steep hills.

The steep hills where houses stand
joined like Christmas garlands.
Cherished by owners who outdo each other
with colors not found on Glidden charts.

Charts in wharf shops depicting tides.
Used by sailors centuries ago,
many lost before their feet touched the land.

The land joined by this golden span.
This symbol of our life
oft threatened by miscreants
who never find the joy of peace.

Peace. Such a simple answer
to the endless woes of our enemies who
fight and kill, yet never seem to move
beyond the fog.

He Loaded 16 Tons

Jeri Schmitz

"Come quickly, see this," my husband called, the TV was all aglow,
How could I tell him the program he watched was just an old sideshow?
For his eyes were full of wonder, in fact, they almost sung,
As he gazed at the infomercial he cried, "This salsa is tingling my tongue."

"Oh no, you're not getting sucked into this?" with mockery, I said,
In utter desperation, I moaned, as I slapped my head.
"You can't fall for this hyperbole, it's worse than a politico's bite,"
I gently tried to talk him down with all my wifely might.

But Satan lured as a little machine chopped up everything in sight,
Using words like "ultimate" meant I was losing the fight.
My husband's lust for spending on long insomniac nights
Was not only leading to the loss of his soul, but also his civil rights.

The maniac on the TV screen stuffed in celery, peppers and rice
He chopped up nuts of every kind and poured in whole allspice.
Then, lo and behold, this guy threw in a tube of Polident,
Even I sat up straight as an arrow, when he added hard cement.

I wouldn't have given a tinker's dam, but my blender was on the blink
So together we dialed 1-800, as I felt my resistance sink.
The huckster on the telephone was worse than the guy on the screen
'Cause I ended up buying attachments that I had never even seen.

One for my daughter, one for my sister and one for an unknown friend,
There was no hint in sight that this spending would ever end.

A few days later when the packages came and I sheepishly open the door
The UPS driver grinned at me like he instantly knew the score.

"Should I wait for a bit or come back after while when know what you want to
keep?"
I wanted to reach for my baseball bat, but I was buried in boxes too deep.
I ended up keeping nothing—they were chintzy products, all.
So when the $600.00 came off of my card, this moral I hung on the wall,

"Never buy products you can't put your hands on, and never, I repeat,
Try to get rid of shipping and handling, those charges you'll have to eat."

In Love

Virginia Cummings

What is it about the way you walk?
We talk
And then you move and talk
to other people.

Often we meet, and others share
our conversation.
It is always good.
They are our friends.

What is it about the way you walk?
It's late. It's dark.
You are the gentleman, and walk me
to my car.

And then one day you walk toward me.
What is it about the way you walk?
I scare myself.
I find I care.

No Lunar Tunes

Dawn Huntley Spitz

My gift of rhyme is quite sublime
I versify most all the time
That is to say that day by day
I gaily rhyme the time away.

Well, what I mean is week by week
I daily doublet so to speak
Or more precisely by the minute
I can rhyme to the infinite

But never, ever month by month
.... Not oneth.

Poetry Defined

Cyndy Muscatel

Poetry cushions the sadness.
Writing gives shape to the despair,
> Contains it
> Inside Out,
> Outside In.
Nerve endings vibrate atop my skin.

Poetry narrows the Eye
Sharpening the focus
From thou to I.
Intellect clashes against Intuition.
The cauldron boils over, spilling out fever.
Hot thoughts and cold dreams.
Replaying all my life themes.

Poetry is a shotgun.
I am the shooter.
I draw a bead on the torment
And pull the trigger.

The Carpool Lament

Cyndy Muscatel

Hurry, hurry. We're going to be late.
And don't forget to shut the gate.
Put on your seatbelt, lock the door.
Remember your lessons start at four.

We've got everyone now, the car is full.
Jake, your door's not shut, give it a pull.
Hey, you three, stop that fighting.
Zach, I told you, no more biting.

Please, it's raining and it's dark.
Quiet Rambo. Get him not to bark.
It's hard to see and it's rush hour.
I'm all sweaty. I need a shower.

Don't sit on that blouse, it's made of silk!
Watch that cup, you're spilling your milk!
What's that on your blouse, Lynn?
My Phi Beta Kappa key for a safety pin?

There's the school, just up ahead.
Did you bring your shoes as I said?
… You can't find them? Wait 'til I park.
We'll use the flashlight; it's so dark.

Shhhhhh, please, the windows are fogging.
And I almost hit that man out jogging.

Okay, we're stopped. I'll look under the seat.
Come on, kids, you can at least move your feet.

You remember now, you left your shoes at home?
They're in the bathroom, right next to my comb.
BE QUIET and don't ask why I'm counting to ten!
Just get in the car so we can drive home again.

The Wedding

Shirley Gibson

Upon her finger slid the ring.
How lovely the choir did sing.
This was her wedding day.
This was the first of May.

She met him in the park,
From the sound of his dog's bark.
When she saw his eyes of blue,
She knew he would be true.

The goodbyes were said,
Looking forward to the life ahead.
As they stepped into the car,
They knew there love would go far.

The Wrinkled Shirt

Cheryl French

Wrinkled shirt hanging carelessly from his tall lanky frame,
Sleeves rolled up halfheartedly, but just the same.

A narrow collar folded over twice,
Each small button woven in and out like a fast game of dice.

Rumpled hair hanging thin and grey,
A mischievous smile almost gives him away.

Dancing grey eyes twinkle with such sweet delight,
Yet he still hides his feeling far out of sight.

His steps are labored with the weight upon his back,
And he finds no clear direction to assault an attack,

To set himself free from the shelter of his soul.
Becoming all he longs to be, now becomes his goal.

Old wrinkled shirt longs for some care,
To be unfolded and pressed and given it's due share.

Of love and affection like a gentle soul,
So the once wrinkled shirt would finally feel whole.

Where once his stature had blended with the wall,
He now straightens upright and starts to stand tall.

Oh, the freedom that love can proudly possess,
For the once wrinkled shirt is now well dressed.

The tie and jacket wrapped neatly about,
"Love conquers all," the three of them shout!

The Yellow Haired Stranger

Cheryl French

Don't fence me in as I want to be free,
Don't fence me in, she shrieked with glee.

I got my spurs hooked to my boots,
And them deer saddlebags are loaded with loot.

I'm a gonna ride out of Texas and never look back,
'Cause over yonder a fellow waits for me, named Jack.

He'll be tall and handsome, and as smart as can be,
He'll have that yellow hair and he'll be waiting for me.

Away from him I'll never want to run,
With that hair of his, shining like the noonday sun.

I finally spied him one hot summer day,
With the leaves a scorch'n,
And them rocks real gray.

Lean'n against an old hickory tree,
Looking so tall and handsome as a man ou'ta be.

Pickin' his teeth, and a' cleaning his gun,
I just kinda knew he'd be the one.

He told me I was witty with a steel trap mind,
He kept walkin' and reaching to grab me from behind.

A' thinking he could catch me with that worn out
Rope of his, planting both feet firmly and a'
Whirling his rope overhead.

Holding on tightly with one hand to a tree,
That rope started unwinding and soon broke free.

I laughed out loud, 'til I seen his face, knowing he was
A hurtin', sure put me in my place.

So I walked over slowly and kicked up some dirt,
Just to let him know I weren't no flirt.

I gave him a hug and a quick gentle kiss,
As he held me close, we both sensed our bliss.

That a love flown between us made me want to cry,
'Cause my feelings were show'n and that I couldn't hide.

Intelligence and talent he said he admires,
But the depth of my soul ignites him with fires.

He wants to possess me for all he thinks I am,
But there ain't no true possession in possessing a friend.

So he lets me go free to find my own way,
And if I come back then he knows I'll a' stay.

With that yellow haired stranger that I spied one day,
And then surely he'll know I will never more stray.

The Brothers Grimm

Anita Knight

They let me down
those writers who weaned me.
At seventeen I went to the ball,
thought my prince had come.
but his hot breath
urgent hands
pounding heart
frightened me.
He kissed me
but didn't wake me.

Mother said
I had a lot of nerve
wearing a white dress,
but at least I was married.

I cleaned house,
emptied cinders,
hid my growing belly
until, with no choice, let it show.
Fingers moved,
months counted.
I lifted my head,
tried not to care.

Tired, overworked, worn,
with dwarfs of my own

but no mirror to declare me fairest of all,
I ran away.
But at the last minute
remembered to drop
breadcrumbs.

To Be All That You Are

Shirley Gibson

"Take a chance," the voice said.
The voice was in my head.
"Go that extra mile,
It will be worthwhile."

Become the person you long to be,
And success is what we see.
Wash away those doubts and fears,
For tomorrow's way is clear.

I know of a man,
Who I can't hold in my hand,
For he belongs to another.
How will we ever get together?

I don't plan and I don't scheme.
I take things for what they seem.
If love is to grow,
How am I to know?

The time we spend together is so good.
I think of him more than I should.
He brings out the woman in me.
The total sum I long to be.

Transition

Cyndy Muscatel

Thoughts go back,
feelings ride along.
Memories, collective, cellular,
rise in the mind,
ride in the dreamscape.

Seeing into the mirror,
the reflected face on the pillow,
aged, losing earth's glow.
Her hand reaches out,
touching, matching.
No words out loud
no words formed.
No need.

Closing the eyes,
Becoming one with the black hole.
Swirling chaos not to
be circumnavigated.
Can't go around, must go through
the dark of the Bois,
the blackout side of the journey.

Entering into the light,
unburdened by layers of ego
stripped away, left behind.
Peaceful calm, brilliant center,

The pyramid floats aloft in the inner eye.
The vortex bursts open.
Light trumpets out,
filling the void.

New stars streak, incandescent.
Day is done here,
but all is well.

Universe

Bill Hinthorn

News Item: A theory of astrophysics suggests that the entire universe, including all space and time, is vibrating.

> Does the universe reverberate?
> Do space and time ring truly like a bell?
> Do quakes across the universe
> shake earth and stars and galaxies
> and comets' icy rush across the void?
>
> I lie awake and watch you sleep
> and listen to you breathe,
> and wonder what the dreams
> that gallop through your mind.
> I softly touch your tousled hair.
> While still asleep, you grasp my hand
> and pull my arm around you like a cloak,
> a shield against a clanging universe.
> And then we sleep, in tangled sheets
> soft-silvered by the moon.
>
> A golden dawn displays
> your bright and ready smile,
> your calm and gentle face.
> I watch you move with easy grace,
> with soft but certain tread,
> or see you sit relaxed within a soft blue chair.
> A yellow cat sleeps soundly in your lap

while at your feet the sun paints
golden window squares on tiled floor.

Do space and time ring truly like a bell?
Perhaps. But when you're with me,
space and time are still.

What Will Become Of You Without Me?

Cheryl French

What will become of you? She inquired from her bed.
What will become of you, when I'm dead?
Who will care for you without me?
How will you live and how shall you be?

The window looks misty through my tired old eyes,
And the leaves fall gently as my days' pass.
How I long to hold you for one more day,
Yet I know heaven beckons and I cannot stay.

When you wrap your arms around me in the mysteries of your
 charm,
I long to kiss your salty tears and hold you in my arms.
All the seasons have come and gone like a sonnet in the wind,
Whispering its' familiar song as it beckons me home once again.

A ribbon of rhyme seems to weave together the passage of time,
And yet I feel the presence of God's dear hand in mine.

Oh, the comfort in knowing that you are near,
Feel my heartbeat, my darling dear.
How tender is your gentle touch upon my graying brow,
How soft is your delicate cheek,
Yes, I can feel it now.

What will become of you when I'm gone?
As the night turns to day with the mornings' new dawn.

I was a treasure of beauty in my time,
A tower of strength, a lover sublime.
A statuesque stranger, a deep caring friend,
With secrets and dreams and passions without end.

I have always longed to love you so that you might know,
That my self-assured posture was only for show.
You have seen more of life, much more than I had wanted,
You have struggled with life,
Much more than I had counted.

But as shades of darkness now begin to fall,
When I look back on life and start to recall,
No days were lost, no nights were too brief,
Promises unkept, they escaped like a theft.

Forgive me my darling for not showing you the way,
For I, too, was blinded by lives harsh fray,
But please remember me always when my days are gone,
Remember me, my darling,
Remember me long.

Where Is The Gold?

Shirley Gibson

The old man lay in the casket.
Upon his face he wore a grin.
Some said he was a bastard,
For he left no gold to be found.

Robert searched throughout the house,
Looking even in the basement.
He crept in the attic quiet as a mouse,
There was no gold to be found.

The old man left a will,
Casting Robert without a penny.
It was all to go to Bill.
He didn't tell Bill where the gold was.

Samantha was now eleven.
She was looking at old photos,
And found one of herself at seven.
She held a basket of gold coins.

In the photo of the old man in the casket,
There was a note that said,
"Bury me with this basket."
Now I know where the gold is.

Wife

Anita Knight

Why do I remember my first love?
The boy in school who never looked my way.
And why the gripes and moaning to my friends
about the man I live with every day?
Why am I always cold when he is hot?
Never hungry when he wants to eat,
grouchy 'til he gently rubs my feet,
often nasty more than I am sweet?
Why do I wish I had another life?
One all alone is often what I'd choose,
with time to read, or write, or simply muse.
I say I'm leaving just to light his fuse.
He calms me, tells me just to settle down,
then plans a lovely night out on the town.
Why does he say I'm gorgeous when I'm not,
and bring me flowers to brighten up my days?
Why does his beaming smile start at his eyes
to tease me in a hundred different ways?
Why does he try to give me what I want,
instead of what I think I ought to need?
Could it be he's my white knight on a steed,
who freed me from my past?
Oh, Yes indeed!

Wishes

Anita Knight

I wish I were a harpsichord
In seventeen-seventy-five.
I'd strum along with Mozart,
He'd teach me how to jive.

I wish I were a violin
Stroked by Stradivari.
I'd really love to spend my life
With one so legendary.

I wish I were a bugle.
I'd toot at everyone
To make them wake and find out
That life has just begun.

I wish I were a tambourine.
I'd go out in the street
And jingle, jangle, jingle,
At everyone I'd meet.

But I am just a plain old note,
A part of every song.
As long as I am living,
I'll always hum along.

Writer's Block

Jeri Schmitz

Stark white paper, reams and reams
Stacked atop my wildest dreams
Little balls, a crumpled mess
Erato sleeps upon my desk.

Dried up ink, cracked desert floor
Silenced pen will scratch no more
Caught between a lull and flurry
Why am I in constant hurry?

Voices fading, lights that climb
Overtures play in my mind
Curtains rise, but naught to follow
Stagnant bitter pill to swallow

Myself, on seesaw, up then down
Mostly sitting on the ground
Fleetingly I reach the top
Why can't this be my final stop?

Essays And Memoirs

A Moment in Time

Cyndy Muscatel

It is summer—maybe August. Maybe 1949.

The apartment is hot—the air, stifling in the small bedroom I share with my brother. He is gone to stay overnight at his friend's house so I am alone. I can't sleep.

Monsters, who by day are under a magic spell, begin to wiggle out of their beds in the shadows. They loom at me.

I escape—go out into the living room. Mother is sitting on the brocade davenport, a book in her hand. Her eyes stare out the window. Dad is across the room, playing the piano, his fingers above the keys so as not to disturb the silence. I am quiet, too, but he must hear me. He turns when I come in.

"I need a glass of water, Daddy," I say. "I'm so thirsty."

He smiles at me and gets up from the piano bench. "Go get your sneakers, Cynthia," he says. "And I'll get your water."

I run back to my room, and open the closet door. Daddy comes in with the water. He ties my shoes, tousles my baby curls. "Let's walk to Uncle Sol's," he says.

We live in an apartment complex called Edgewater—New England-style buildings that sprawl along the edge of Seattle's Lake Washington. My aunt and uncle live six blocks away. To walk that far with my dad would be an adventure. To be alone with him is a treasure beyond compare.

Daddy takes my hand, and we tiptoe out of the drowsy apartment, leaving Mother still staring. I wonder what she sees, but I don't linger. I'm anxious to escape with my prize before it is taken from me.

Safely away, we stroll along, me in my summer pajamas, Daddy in his shirtsleeves. We pass the building next to ours. Raised voices blare out an open window. I move closer to Daddy.

Two more blocks and we're past the bus stop. It's got a wooden house, where other monsters lurk. Sometimes when we wait for the bus, the rain drums so loud on the tin roof that I have to put my hands over my ears.

But tonight the sky is clear, a silver-blue as the light leaches away. The twilight paints the street with rose-colored magic so the houses glow in the pipe tobacco-scented air.

I smile and take a little skip, unable to contain my joy.

I am with my dad. He is with me. For this one moment in time, he seems to need no more.

Adventure In Tangiers

Barbara J. Savage

My husband sat in his favorite chair, holding a hot toddy that was a concoction of tea, honey, and whiskey. He blew his nose, and whined about some hot soup. It was snowing outside. I looked out onto all the ice glistening in the garden.

"Wouldn't it be wonderful to be in Spain now, by a pool with the air soft and warm with the smell of flowers? Why don't I make us reservations for two weeks from now for the Costa del Sol?" I suggested.

We landed in Malaga and spent three wonderful days by the pool. Walking by an activity board in the hotel, we saw the advertisement for the day flight to Tangiers in Morocco. We signed up for a departure the next day.

At six in the morning, we were loaded onto a four engine plane. There were mainly tourists from England, singly and in pairs. Married couples had left their children with babysitters at the hotels. We were a happy lot. Everyone was very talkative and friendly.

As we sat on the tarmac, I noticed that the plane's personnel seemed to have a tough time closing the door to the cabin. They pushed and shoved, not being able to close it. All around the door you could see daylight. The crew came and gathered all the pillows and blankets, stuffing them around the openings.

We finally took off. We flew so low over the ocean that the water rippled and I could see the faces of the fishing crews. I also noticed that they looked up at the plane while dodging something. I finally realized that the pillows and blankets were being sucked out to fall on the fisherman below.

We arrived in Tangiers. My husband wasn't too happy about Visa Control taking our passports. We were told they would be returned when we left in the evening, and were taken to a small cafe for a refreshment. Sitting at the back were the officers with our passports scattered over the table. Some of them had fallen on the floor and were left there. This didn't instill confidence that we would see them again.

We toured by foot all day. It must have been ninety-eight degrees and humid. We were tired, sweaty, and hungry. Many of the couples were concerned about their passports. "I wonder if we'll get them back. We'll probably never see them again. Did you see them on the floor of the cafe?" someone said.

The bus was waiting for us at six that evening. We happily sat down in the seats with the air conditioning blowing the first cool air of the day. At the airport, we would have to cash in all Moroccan money since it was prohibited to bring it out of the country.

We arrived at the airport and proceeded to try to cash the money in, but the gentleman would not take it, saying we would need it again if we wanted to dine out that evening.

"We aren't staying here tonight. We're returning to Spain," my husband said.

"Maybe so, maybe no," the official said. The telephone rang. He spoke for some time, then turned to us. "You will not be leaving to return to Malaga tonight. The plane did not return to pick you up. You will leave tomorrow morning."

Two men came into the lounge and started to sweep around us. They asked us to step outside so that they could clean up and then locked the door after us. The gentleman from behind the cash desk bid us all good night, and started to walk away. We were a mob by this time. He was not getting away from us.

"There is someone coming from tourism to help you. A bus will be here shortly and rooms have been booked for the night in Tangiers."

The rooms in Tangiers were some of the worst I have seen in my travels. Cockroaches were everywhere. When we turned on the light in the bathroom, it seemed that the floor was moving. There were also no towels or soap, dashing all hope of having a shower.

I said to my husband, "Let's lay on the bed, and take a nap. Then we will go to dinner."

I dozed lightly, but woke when I felt something walking on me. Roaches streamed all over the bed. As you can imagine, I was hysterical and did my famous dance that my brother always teases me about.

All the while I was screaming, "Oh my God, get them off of me."

In the lobby, all hell was breaking loose. The couples with children were trying to call Spain to explain what had happened and to be reassured that their children would be cared for. The desk would not make calls to Spain.

Two couples with flights out of England the next day were trying to ascertain what time we'd return the next day. We complained about the lack of towels and soap. Some people wanted fresh sheets, but I warned them about getting into bed because the roaches went there, too. Everyone had a complaint and the desk was going crazy.

We had friends who lived in Tangiers who'd suggested we have dinner together if we were to stay late. I asked the concierge to call them for me since the telephone in our room was out of order.

"I will not call them. You are trying to leave to go to another hotel," he said.

"I promise you, they're friends, and we're not trying to leave just because we wanted soap and a towel," my husband tried to explain.

"You are trouble makers. Go elsewhere to make your call."

I don't know why he thought we were trying to leave that oasis of friendliness.

We went to another hotel to use a telephone and called our friends. They took us to a wonderful place that had Moroccan food and the best belly dancing show that we have ever seen. We told them about the hotel. They were shocked, inviting us to stay with them. We declined only because we didn't know what time we'd leave the next day. We wouldn't want to miss the plane again.

We slept in chairs so that the least amount of roaches could get to us. The lights being on all night didn't stop them from coming out in force. At 4:00 AM, someone knocked on the door and told us to get dressed. We had never taken anything off. After twenty-four hours in the same clothes, we felt disgusting.

The lobby was filled with tired, angry, and dirty people. People always speak of the ugly Americans, but we watched as the people from England lost all civility, shouting and yelling imprecations at the people behind the desk. One gentleman, who looked like old British military, threatened war with Morocco, promising never to step foot there again.

Loaded again onto the bus, we arrived at the airport. We were told that we would have to wait. About two hours later, the gentleman from the cash booth arrived, took our money, and returned our passports. That still did not quell this angry group.

We watched a plane come in. It unloaded another group of tourists for the daily tour. We told those coming in about our experiences. One of the newcomers mentioned that the flight crew had stuffed pillows and blankets around the door of the plane.

We boarded, trying to get comfortable. There was a commotion again with the door—the same drill as before. We flew low again and the pillows and blankets were sucked out, raining down on the fisherman below. I could not believe that this happened twice a day. That airline must have had a huge budget for pillows and blankets, not to mention the mess they made on the water every day.

Whenever I fly, I sit by the engines to be aware if anything is going wrong. Not fifteen minutes out of Morocco, I noticed oil or gasoline leaking out of one engine. The motor stopped. I turned to tell my husband, but he was fast asleep, covered with a blanket that he had refused to give up to the flight attendant as an offering to the sea gods.

I watched the next engine do the same thing. Now, thick, black smoke poured out of the two engines on my side. A fellow passenger had seen this and yelled for the attendant.

The younger of the stewards looked out the window and ran up the aisle screaming in Spanish. All the others went with her, babbling and holding each other. No one came back to calm us or tell us what was happening. People on the plane started praying and crying, but the crew remained up front.

One of the older attendants finally did come back and told us to leave our seatbelts on (as if we were dreaming of not leaving them on) and to put our heads down. Of course, we had no pillows to put them down on since they were strewn over the waters between Spain and Morocco. The English gentlemen who threatened war with Morocco now threatened a lawsuit against this shoddy airline if he got back safely.

The attendant did announce that the airport was waiting for us. Fire engines would be there if needed.

I woke my husband who became combative because he thought someone was trying to take his blanket again. I apprised him of the situation.

We landed at Malaga safely, but shaken. The people on the flight were rabid by this time. Everyone was dirty, tired, mean, and threatening lawsuits.

It was an adventure not to be forgotten. We've been back to Morocco many times. Each time we've had a memorable vacation.

A Short Long Day

Eleanor Tyus Johnson

Suddenly the sidewalk was rising up and heading straight for me. I twisted my body to the side to try to avoid it, and then felt its full impact hit my shoulder. I heard a loud "pop" and then a sickly, sucking sound. When I opened my eyes, I was flat on my back staring at the hot mid-day sun.

The city had been embroiled in a heat wave for several days with temperatures well over 100 degrees. Today was just a continuation. Not a breath of air stirred. I was bathed in my own perspiration. It dripped across my forehead into my eyes. Why couldn't I wipe it off?

"Okay, get up," I said to myself", and let's see what the damage is." Nothing happened.

"Get up," I commanded. Again nothing.

Then my left hand moved and wandered across my body towards my right arm. Half way down my arm were two big lumps pointing in the same direction. No elbow.

The hand reached for the two lumps and tried to pull them together, for that's the way an elbow is suppose to be, but it couldn't make them stick. They kept pulling apart. My left hand just held on to them as tightly as it could.

Then I felt a heavy weight across my chest.

A man's voice said, "Don't move."

I tried to turn toward the voice, but nothing happened.

"The paramedics will be here in a minute," the voice continued. When he sat down beside me, I could see him.

Paramedics! Oh no. I don't have time for this. I'm in a hurry.

A woman's soft voice came from the other side, "I picked up your things. I think I got everything you had in your hands. It's all in your purse and I'll hold on to it until the paramedics arrive." She, too, sat on the ground next to me.

I started to panic. *What happened to me? Why can't I move? How did I fall? What's going to happen to me now? Think, think!*

I remembered leaving the house in a hurry with my "things to do today" list in my hand. Being Monday, it meant that the list was longer and would take more time. As I'd turned on the ignition, I'd noticed that the gas meter was on reserve. I remembered thinking, I don't have time for this. I'm in a hurry.

I drove the short distance to the gas station and, after a little maneuvering, got to the right pump. I jumped out of the car with my purse, keys, pen, and note pad in my hands, and headed to the cashier office. As I approached the curb in front of the door, I thought, what is the number of my pump? Without slowing my stride, I turned my head and glanced back to check. The rest was now painfully clear.

"Miss?" a voice spoke to me. "I'm a Paramedic. Are you awake?"

"Yes." I opened my eyes.

"Did you hit your head?" he asked.

"No." I tried to sit up.

"Don't move," he said. "We're going to get you to the hospital as quickly as possible. First, we have to immobilize you on the stretcher and then move you to the ambulance. It may be a little painful, so try to relax as much as possible."

I must have closed my eyes for I have no recollection of them strapping me to the gurney and lifting me into the ambulance. The next thing I remember, the ambulance was speeding down the street with me clutching the two bones of my elbow and thinking, I do not have time for this. I'm in a hurry.

Back In The Saddle Again

Cheryl McFadden

Lately I'd noticed that because of my commitment to a rather casual aerobic routine, i.e. web and channel surfing, and the fact that I am one of the frontrunners of the Baby Boomer generation, my flexibility and strength had dramatically diminished. Something had to be done unless I wanted to face a future filled with prescription drugs and medical procedures. Definitely a scary prospect.

As luck would have it, while performing one of the aforementioned exercises, I happened upon an Internet coupon for a free yoga class at a local gym. I interpreted this serendipitous discovery to be a cosmic nudge, of sorts. Yoga might very possibly return me to that state of vibrant youth and suppleness, and perhaps even improve my mental state, which could definitely stand a tune-up as well.

As I recalled, I really liked yoga when I was young: Downward Facing Dog, Salutation to the Sun, Camel pose … Ah, yes, I remembered them well. Yep, that might be the very thing I needed and it shouldn't be all that difficult to resume the poses (asanas, I think they were called). Sort of like getting back on a bicycle after a long absence. How hard could it be? The decision was made, and with much enthusiasm I headed for the gym.

Following the sweet, woodsy scent of burning incense, I entered through the open doors of the darkened studio. Dim light emanated from rice paper lanterns, casting a warm glow over burnished oak floors. Not a breath of air stirred; only serenity occupied the space. I'd discovered an oasis of tranquility nestled peacefully in the middle of the desert. For the next hour my mind, body and spirit would be brought into alignment. Eagerly I anticipated the reversal of decades of abuse and neglect.

Quietly I removed my shoes and padded softly over to a spot in the back. With a quick snap that echoed through the room like a gun shot, I unfurled my mat and set it on the floor behind several people all seated with eyes closed, legs crossed, and perfectly straight backs. Grunting and groaning, I lowered myself to the floor, settled into a greatly modified version of the Lotus position, and began concentrating on my breath. *Inhale through the nose. Pause. Exhale through the mouth. Repeat! Fill the lungs. Empty the lungs. Release those stress filled thoughts. Just let them go.*

I began drifting with each calming breath, ebbing and flowing on a wave of tinkling chimes. Ah yes, this was going to be the answer. Already I could feel my mind, body and spirit queuing-up. See, just like bike riding. It was all coming back to me.

Suddenly a voice intruded upon my reverie. "Please come to a standing position and assume Mountain Pose," was the gentle directive from a trim woman standing at the front of the room. Our teacher, I assumed. Well, if ever there was a testament to the benefits of yoga, she was certainly it: serene, ageless and incredibly taut.

The other students rose gracefully in unison and stood with feet shoulder-width apart. I, on the other hand, having managed to get into the cross-legged position earlier, was now finding it very difficult to extricate myself from it. The instructor smiled patiently as I unlocked body parts, thrust my butt indelicately into the air, and groaned a few more times before clumsily landing on my feet. It was at this stage that I began to suspect that perhaps the bike-riding analogy was not an accurate one.

For the remainder of the class we did indeed assume many of the poses that I remembered with fondness. However, as much as the spirit was willing, the body had no intention of complying with the ridiculous demands that were suddenly placed upon it. With graceless and ungainly determination, I managed to endure the remainder of the hour before limping my way home.

Within days my sore muscles had recovered. However, the bruises to my ego were still apparent. Getting back into shape wasn't going to be as easy as I'd thought, but still the idea of continuing the slide into decrepitude was terrifying. It was then that I remembered the abandoned bicycle lying dormant out in the garage. This could be the answer and should be much easier. After all, it wasn't like *getting back on a bicycle*—it really was *getting back on a bicycle*.

How hard could it be?

Child of the Storm

Anita Knight

Still in my mother's womb when storm clouds gathered over England in the 1930's, fear of the looming war must have filtered into my psyche, for I can still hear the worried whispers of my parents.

An Italian who came to England penniless at sixteen, my father made good, married and had two children, but never become a citizen. What would happen to him if Italy sided with the Germans in the conflict that seemed inevitable?

But these fears were not discussed with me. As a toddler I heard only about parties they attended with famous people; theatrical productions where they always had front-row-center seats; fox hunting weekends at country mansions, even trips to local pubs. These were stories they loved to tell, and I looked forward to being old enough to go with them someday.

The cloudburst that flooded our life came early in 1940.

When asked what should be done about non-citizen Italians, Prime Minister Winston Churchill declared, "Collar the lot." Thousands of decent, hardworking men were arrested as enemy aliens, and on June 13th, two men came to our home and took my daddy away.

I was just five years old, but remember it as if it were yesterday.

◆　　　◆　　　◆

It was just beginning to get light outside when the sound of the front door knocker woke me.

Something was wrong. I heard Mummy shout at Daddy. She said he should have listened and got his citizenship papers when she told him to. I thought she was more frightened than angry, because her voice was so shaky.

I crept from my bed to the hallway and peered through the banisters. Mummy, her arms wrapped around Daddy, was crying. My big brother, Peter, was on his knees, his hands locked around Daddy's leg.

The banging continued until Daddy disentangled himself and opened the door.

Two huge men I had never seen before stood on the doorstep. They were dressed in black and looked unfriendly.

Peter ran and hid behind the sofa. I'd never seen him look scared before, and that scared me, too. And why was Mummy crying in front of strangers? Yes, something was very wrong. I shivered.

One of the men spoke, "Sorry, sir, but I have orders to pick you up."

That made me feel a bit better, and I almost laughed. How silly. Daddy was big, how could that man pick him up? And why would he want to? I had to see this.

Hanging onto the banister, I crept down the staircase.

Daddy went to Peter and put his arm around him. "Take care of your little sister and your mummy, Peter. You have to be in charge until I get back."

One of the men grabbed Daddy's other hand and put a funny bracelet on his wrist.

"You don't need those." Daddy sounded angry. "I won't give you any trouble."

When I started to cry, Daddy saw me on the stairs.

"Sorry you're awake, bambina, but I'm glad I can say goodbye to you, too." His voice was still strange.

He hugged Peter and then sat down next to Mummy, who had slumped into the corner of the sofa. A lacy hankie over her mouth, she was making strange sounds. Daddy took the hankie from her, and used it to wipe her eyes.

"Cara, be strong, I'll be back soon."

I saw him kiss her right on the mouth. After that he stroked her hair and kissed both of her eyes, but she didn't stop crying.

Daddy came and picked me up. I touched the funny bracelet.

"This is pretty, Daddy," I said.

Tears ran down his cheeks. I reached up and wiped them away.

"Don't cry, Daddy. Daddys aren't supposed to cry."

He hugged me and gave me a big smile.

"You're right, bambina. I won't cry anymore if you promise to be a good girl, and do what Mummy says."

He gave me another squeeze and rubbed noses with me the way I liked.

"Hey." He tickled under my chin. "Eskimo kisses usually make you laugh, but you're crying too, little one. Come on, cheer up."

Daddy still had Mummy's hankie and he wiped the tears from my eyes. I managed a little smile.

"That's better." He kissed my head and whispered, "*Ciao*," then put me down and went over to the men.

"I'm ready," he said.

Without a word, the men tipped their hats to Mummy. With Daddy between them, they went out.

Peter screamed, "No, Daddy, no," and ran after them.

"Peter, come back," Mummy ordered through her sobs. Then she scooped me up to follow my brother to the gate.

We were silent as we watched the three men stride away. When they got to the top of the hill, Daddy turned to wave. Then he turned again, and was gone.

I never saw my father again.

Chocolate Soup For The Soul

Gitta M Gorman

During the 1940's, Sweden experienced severe winter weather with the temperature dipping to minus 40 degrees Celsius. The Second World War raged in countries around us. Fortunately, Sweden defied the odds and adamantly stayed neutral through the war. All wars for that matter. But we, Swedes, were affected anyway. We lived with blackened windows and barbed wire on the streets. Food was rationed.

My family's home, a small apartment in the city of Stockholm, was not only cold, but quite dark. We were only allowed to have a few lamps lit in case of a Nazi bombing campaign.

When my parents were away at work for long hours at the family flower shop, it became my older brother Jan's duty to babysit me. I was seven and he was sixteen.

One evening I remember well.

"*Janne*! I'm cold and hungry," I whimpered. "Is there anything we can eat?"

"I don't know, but I'll look in the kitchen cupboard to see if I can find anything. Come on."

I followed him and watched as he searched.

"Hurrah, I did find something." He looked at me. "But you'll have to go into the living room, and wait until I have cooked something very special for you."

Soon, I could smell the delicious aroma of hot chocolate drifting into the living room.

What's so special about hot chocolate? I wondered. It was war time, but hot chocolate was not that special. Was it? Maybe he was going to serve it with a large scoop of luscious whipping cream? That would be special. But where would he get it?

"You can come into the kitchen now," my brother called.

When I entered the small kitchen, I saw not only the cheery, blue gingham kitchen curtains, but the small, square table laid with a matching table cloth.

He'd even set the table with two large, blue soup bowls and two silver soup spoons. The aroma from the bowls was wonderful. It made my taste buds water.

"Because it's dinner time, I made you a nourishing soup. It's made from cocoa." My brother beamed with pride. "I hope you like it and feel better soon."

I did, immensely. I was in chocolate paradise. The soup not only tasted delicious, it was also as exciting to eat as forbidden fruit.

Of course, our mother scolded him for using the precious box of *Marabou* cocoa, which she had hidden way back in the cupboard. But I learned that my brother loved me very much by daring her.

The memory of the evening of the Chocolate Soup has comforted me time and time again through the years when I have not been able to see my beloved brother. We literally live an ocean apart. I'm here in California. He's in Sweden.

After forty-five years of separation, *Janne* plans to come and visit me here in California. When he arrives, I will ask him if he remembers that he made me chocolate soup during the war so many years ago. Maybe he will, maybe he won't.

But I always will.

Christmas Spirit

Martin S. Goldberg

My first December home from the service, following World War II, found me filling a corner lot with Christmas trees for sale. The area had promise for good returns so long as I could prevent potential customers from walking away without a tree. A tree's value wilted to zero on the day after Christmas.

The decision to become an entrepreneur was ill timed. The weather was brutally cold, trees expensive, and customers, a hard sell, some with temperament disorders.

The closer December 25th approached, the more effort had to be expended to prevent customers from walking off empty handed. But some hard sells were critics who found fault with a litany of complaints ranging from quality of the tree, prices, and my limited knowledge as a tree farmer.

When I failed to make a sale after hard bargaining, I'd give up and tell them to find a tree somewhere else. Somewhere else, conveniently, was a corner lot across the street with more expensive trees and a more reasonable salesman. When they left my lot, it was usually with a smirk, accompanied with a comment, "Too bad, buddy. You had your chance."

I tried to act nonchalant, but the departees knew it upset me to lose the sale.

Oh, I neglected to mention that the guy running the lot on the other corner was a better salesman. I should know—he was my brother. We were partners.

Closing the Heart

Dolores Carruthers

The Bustle in a House
The Morning after Death
Is solemnest of industries
Enacted upon earth—

The Sweeping up the Heart
And Putting Love away
We shall not want to use again
Until Eternity.
                    Emily Dickenson

My heart didn't give notice that it had gone into hiding. There were no fearful flutters in my heart, no sick feeling in my gut to give me pause. I don't remember sweeping it up or putting it away.

On March 7, 1995 I wrote, "It is 24 days since Stephen died. I feel puzzled after I write this. I'm not sure why I'm starting this journal. I may not even keep writing in it. Part of my reasoning is that I don't always remember dates. Isn't that crazy? How will I ever forget? I dreamed of Stephen last night. He was in running shorts and had just come into the house. I hugged him and rested my head on his bare shoulder knowing he was dead. Except his body felt so real to my touch, his skin warm and smooth, that for just a moment, I doubted my knowing. I remember thinking that I wished I'd hugged him more. When I woke up crying I knew the dream was true. My son was dead."

Two days later, on March 9th, I wrote; "Turn off the phone, lock all the doors, close the blinds. Grieving is best done in private. Today as I was driving, I felt a brief flash of awareness about Stephen in the avalanche, hitting the trees, suffocating in the snow. I was horrified by these images, started crying so hard I could barely see the road. A fear that I couldn't survive poured through me. It was so powerful, I wanted to turn around, go home, stay there. Instead I kept driving until I had done all my errands. Even amidst the horror another fear was greater; if I gave in I might fall apart and never be able to pull myself together."

For the first time, a glimmer of what it must have been like for Stephen during those last moments of consciousness, before the oblivion of death, broke through my resistance. From the moment I'd seen him lying on the funeral home stretcher, a large purple bruise in the center of his forehead, I *knew* that's how he died. It wasn't the avalanche, but the blow to his head as he was pushed into the trees that killed him. I hadn't read the autopsy report, because I already knew the cause of death. Now the reality of how he died swept over me like an emotional avalanche.

Was it at this time I began to close my heart? I doubt it was anything so dramatic. I suspect it began the moment I got the phone call or the first time I wanted to join him in death.

A month later, my husband, Bob, and I went to a 40th anniversary party. While neither one of us felt like celebrating, they were close friends. Their eldest son, who had almost died from injuries in a car accident, gave a toast. Toward the end of it, he casually said, "And thankfully we are here, all together."

No sooner did he say 'all together' when the thin veil of outward strength that I had thrown over my vulnerability ripped apart. Our family was not all together. His grateful words would never be said at any of our family gatherings. I had no defense against the unexpected jagged pain his words caused, and knew the silent tears flowing down my cheeks would quickly turn into gut wrenching sobs. After these many months, I'd learned my control was fragile.

Glancing at Bob, I saw him wiping his eyes. We began walking out of the gathering, trying to slip away without disturbing the joyful celebration. Our friends, seeing our tears, came to comfort us and say goodbye. As we drove away, I told Bob I would not attend any more gatherings for a year. He nodded in agreement.

This decision was partly to avoid becoming vulnerable in public again. But my biggest need was to avoid being in the presence of happiness and joy when I felt only despair. A year's moratorium seemed the answer for both. That it would become a way of life after the year didn't occur to me.

The idea for a moratorium came from my experiences as a child observing the mourning rituals in my mother's family. They observed a period of mourning for one year after the death of a loved one. Everyone dressed in black until the first anniversary of death was honored. They didn't attend parties or gatherings, unless they were wakes or funerals of other family members or friend. My first experience with this ritual came after the death of my grandfather. Although I wasn't allowed to attend the funeral, being only seven at the time, the memories of my mother, grandmother, aunts and uncles dressed in black for an entire year made a lasting impression.

Choosing to take a year off from social activities to heal was a conscious decision. Closing my heart was an unconscious process. I didn't decide one day that I would take a year off from suffering and then return to normal, whatever that might be. Even if I'd known closing my heart would shut off love, joy, and happiness, as well as the pain, I doubt I would have done differently. Like an injured animal, I wanted to hide until the wound healed. Suffering left me heavy with fatigue—foggy days, sleepless nights. No part of me was free of it. All I craved was immediate relief.

On May 12th, three months after my world changed, I asked for a dream. I knew how I was doing in my outer world, but felt shut off from my inner world. For years I've studied dreams and asked for their guidance. I know some people believe that dreams are God's forgotten language. Others, like scientists who study dreams, believe they reflect our daily experiences in symbolic language. Whether they come from God, from an inner dream source, or from the days happenings doesn't matter. Sometimes I ask for them, sometimes they appear. Either way I'm grateful, and try to understand their message.

As the dream began, *I was standing in a desert. There was a bank of golden sand, but not a single tree or bush or sign of life, except for a very small stream of water that trickled down the bank. I saw that a long piece of wood, a log perhaps, had almost stopped the flow of water. As I continued to watch, I saw farther down the stream, people stood at various positions on either side and when the log came close they lifted it and threw it out of the stream. The water, though still a trickle, started flowing again.*

Water, in dreams, symbolizes our emotions, moods, and flow of feeling energy. Water also represents our potential to experience many emotions because it can take different shapes and move in countless ways.

My question had been answered. In the dream, the stream was merely a trickle flowing through a lifeless landscape, its emotional energy almost obstructed. I wasn't surprised or frightened that my energy was scarce, or that my inner life was barren, because that's how I felt in the outer world. I saw people helping to free the stream, which I took as a positive sign, but didn't consider the significance that there were no signs of life in the desert beyond its banks.

It wasn't until years later that I understood the lifeless desert was symbolic of a closed heart. Perhaps I was only able to absorb what looked hopeful. Maybe I wasn't ready to recognize that by protecting myself against suffering, I'd eventually become as muted as the stream, as arid as its surroundings, as unable to nurture life. Perhaps sweeping up my heart and putting my love away was a necessary part of survival until I was ready to live again.

Grandma's Death

Shirley Gibson

It was May 1949 when Grandma died. I was almost seven years old. She'd been working in the garden earlier that day.

Growing up, my family consisted of Mom, Dad, Grandma, Grandpa, three younger sisters and Aunt Mary. We lived in a house that was my grandparents. Grandpa purchased the four-room house when he married Grandma. As the family grew, so did the house. Grandpa was good at building and had a shop where he made many things. The last part added was a walk-in pantry and a bathroom. The house was full of family on weekends.

The kitchen had a wood stove that was used to cook the food as well as providing warmth in the winter. From the large picture window behind the table you could see the barn, chicken houses, and granary. The wood table was covered with a vinyl red and white checked pattern tablecloth. Grandfather was at one end, Dad at the other end. Across the table from my sisters and me were Mom and Aunt Mary.

We had just started to eat supper when Aunt Mary said, "Shirley, go check on Grandma. She's been in the bathroom a long time."

As I rounded the table we heard this thump from the bathroom. I froze in my tracks, unsure of what just happened. Aunt Mary, being the closest to the bathroom, jumped up and ran to the door.

"Mom, Mom, are you okay?"

There was no response. My aunt tried the door knob. It was locked.

Aunt Mary was small framed and weighed ninety-nine pounds all of her adult life. She went to the basement below the bathroom and crawled through a transit in the floor. She opened the door from inside, and my Dad and Grandpa carried Grandma out.

I noticed that Grandma's eyes were wide open and rolled back as they carried her past me. She can't be dead because her eyes are open, I thought.

Soon the house was filled with aunts, uncles, and cousins. It was always fun to have our cousins come over and we were laughing until Aunt Mary told us to hush up because this was a sad time. We were sent to our rooms.

The next day I crept down the stairs from my bedroom to see if Aunt Mary was around. She was nowhere to be found so I started to look for Grandma. As I opened the door to the living room I noticed a coffin. At the end, on each side, were dim amber lamps. Long spears of orange gladiolus, berry colored mums, and white azaleas sat in vases nearby.

I slowly walked up to the casket. There was Grandma. She looked like she was sleeping. "Wake up, Grandma." I gently touched her hand.

Her warm brown eyes didn't open. I stood there in the silence, remembering all the things I loved about Grandma. She wore her hair in a bun secured by hairpins. She would let me brush her long wavy hair. I loved watching her iron. She would put the iron on the stove to heat it up, then iron, and then, return it on the stove. I'd sit at her side filling the pages of my coloring book. She would look at my work, giving me that smile of approval.

Just yesterday we sat in the warm afternoon sun by the smoke house. She wasn't feeling well. Aunt Mary thought being in the sun would help. I don't remember what we talked about nor had I known this would be our last conversation. What I did remember was she always said, "Don't worry. It will all turn out in the end."

Now I stood next to the coffin saying good-bye. The tears welled up; my eyes stung. Slowly the tears flowed down my cheeks. No longer would I feel the warmth of her embrace. I felt I'd just lost my best friend.

Greetings to Our Class

Shell Steckel

I am thrilled to hear all the good news that the writing group's book project is about to "fly" … and to think … I knew you guys when!

I am taking off today on a somewhat spiritual and sentimental journey to the Promised Land. I'll be in amazing Israel for two weeks in hopes of locating some remnants of my family who would have survived the Holocaust. I have located my godson who lives in the Northern Territory bordering Lebanon, and will spend some time there. Maybe I will be in time to write a piece for the writers next adventure!

Happy Birth Day

Virginia Cummings

This is your birth day, Cassandra Kimberly Williams, and this is how my day started.

I went to a seminar in the morning while Mom, Dad, Grandma and Uncle Ed went to the San Jose O'Connor Hospital where you were about to be born.

After I arrived at the hospital, we kept up a conversation with Mom while we waited for your arrival. Grandma had to leave so I took her place holding Mom's hand. Dad and Uncle Ed went for a walk and to have a cigarette.

The next thing I knew, the nurses asked me to leave and wait down the hall. The doctor had decided it was time for you to be born. It was September 4, 1992, a Friday about 6:00 PM.

I walked the halls of the hospital. When I came by the nurse's station, I saw on the bulletin board that Baby Williams had been placed in the nursery. You cannot imagine how excited I became. I wanted to say something to someone, but the family was gone and most of the nurses were busy.

Right then I stopped a nurse. "Where are the new babies?" I asked.

"Who are you?" she asked me.

"I am the Williams baby's great grandmother."

She told me to follow her and took me to a room near the nursery. The nurse indicated I needed to wash my hands as she handed me a set of bright yellow cover-ups to put on over my clothes. Then she gave me a yellow cap to cover my hair and I had to wash my hands again. The nurse smiled and let me know I was ready to see our new baby.

I had had four babies of my own, but never went into the nursery. What a beautiful sight, all these tiny little babies. Some of the babies were sleeping and others crying as hard as they could. You, my little one, were just lying there quietly.

The nurse picked you up and gently handed you to me. "I know you want to hold her, right?"

I guess I must have appeared nervous. "It's been so many years since I held a little one," I said.

What a thrill! I never held one of my grandchildren or great grandchildren when they were newly born. You were barely twenty minutes old and here I was holding you. I was the first one to hold you before anyone else, except your mother. I was so excited.

I looked out the glass from the nursery and saw the surprised look on the faces of your dad and your uncle.

Later they asked, "How did you get there so fast?"

I told them, "Just lucky, I guess."

It is a treasured moment I will carry for a lifetime.

Happy Birth Day to you Cassie.

Love,

Gram

In the Right Place
At the Right Time

Else Jacobs

After reading and hearing abut the Mother and Sri Aurobindo, I was interested in visiting their Ashram so I went to India and stayed there from January to May in 1968.

Right away, I wanted to see the Mother, but when I was told that she only saw people on their birthdays, I requested to see her on my half-birthday (I wouldn't be there on my birthday, July 30th). She agreed. Through my eyes, the Mother looked into my soul for a long time. She then asked me what I wanted to do while I was in the Ashram.

"I like to learn and I like to teach," I told her.

So I taught pre-school children in the morning (I have an education degree), and in the afternoon, I learned batik and marbling.

I also got involved with the Auroville Inauguration Planning Committee. They asked me to have my parents send some soil from our home in Norway. During the inauguration, it was placed in the Urn at the center of Auroville.

As the only Norwegian in the Ashram, I was asked by Udar to translate Auroville's Charter, which was written by the Mother in English. She gave it her Blessing, and wrote my name on it. During the Auroville Inauguration Ceremony, the Charter was read in 18 languages. It was broadcast over All-India Radio, and seen by a large audience. Representing Norway and reading the Auroville Charter in Norwegian, was a special honor given to me by the Mother.

To tell the truth, there was so much last minute scrambling around (Chaos!) that no one on the Planning Committee expected the ceremony to go smoothly. But the Mother's guiding hand was tangibly felt the whole time. That day, for anyone who was fortunate enough to be there, will never be forgotten.

I was truly blessed by the Mother to be in the right place at the right time. Including my half birthday darshan. I saw her seven times during my stay in the Ashram: the first time was the spur of the minute balcony darshan. She gave it to a group of Jains who were pilgrimming through South India. The second was in the same place the next day when the Mother yielded to the many Ashramites who complained about missing her impromptu darshan with the Jains. Then I also saw the Mother on February 21st, February 29th, and April 24th.

The last darshan with the Mother was the day before I left the Ashram. She gave me an autographed copy of *The Mother* and said, "Will I see you again?" However, it didn't sound like a question. It was more like, "I will see you again!" A promise she has clearly kept.

Else Jacobs visited Auroville in February, 2008 for its 40th Anniversary Celebration.

Lady At The Mestre Airport

Barbara J. Savage

My friend Ruth had a beautiful female collie named Lady, and indeed that is what she was. She pranced instead of walked. But she was also a nervous dog.

Ruth had often said that she'd like to have Lady mate with our collie, Konig. Our dog was a great baby and very sensitive to anyone hurt or sad. If you pretended to cry, he'd make "woo woo" noises, and tears would come out of his eyes. He was not as clever as Lassie, but so handsome. He had a wonderful personality. We thought mating Lady with him would be a good idea. How wonderful it would be to have another little Konig.

Ruth had been in Rome for four months when she called one day. "Barbara, could you meet me in Mestre with my station wagon so Lady won't be as nervous as she would be in your sports car?"

I agreed to do it even though I hated that big American station wagon. Once I drove it into our driveway and got stuck in the gates. I had to crawl over the seat and out the back window. It sat, blocking the driveway, until my husband came home.

We lived about thirty minutes from Mestre, the airport that served Venice. I arrived at the airport a half hour early. The plane arrived on time. Believe me, this was the only time that I'd ever seen anything on time in Italy. Ruth and I greeted each other, chatting about her trip and how we had missed her in our circle of friends.

She said, "Let's walk to Cargo to get Lady."

Giovanni, in charge of this area, was delightful and resplendent in his clean, ornamented uniform. He had Ruth sign some papers. He flirted with us, charming us with his accent and his northern Italian good looks. When Giovanni opened the gate in front of Lady's box, the dog pushed out and wildly ran cross the airfield.

We chased after her, calling her name. We sprinted across the airfield with planes taking off over our heads. We were so close we could see the pilots looking at us. We threw ourselves into the mosquito-ridden marshes (filled with snakes I found out later). I found myself sinking in water and lost my shoes. I was trying to keep up with Giovanni, Ruth and the dog. Lady got further from us all the time until we couldn't see or hear her.

We finally had to admit defeat and return to the baggage area. This meant we had to cross the airfield again. No one stopped to see what these two mad women and gentleman, completely covered in mud, were doing on the runway. If this had happened in the United States, we would have been arrested, but not before we had spent thirty days under mental observation.

Scratched from the bushes, dirty and bitten by mosquitoes, both Ruth and I were a mess. I had lost my beautiful Italian shoes. Giovanni's handsome uniform was covered with mud. His pants and shoes were sopping wet.

"Senora Ruth, I am so sorry about your dog."

"We don't blame you. We'll wait for a while. Maybe Lady will come back."

We waited three hours, then left our telephone numbers with the baggage man, and went away hoping for the best.

A month went by and Ruth had lost all hope of finding her dog. One evening around six, the phone rang.

"Buona Sera, Signora, here is Giovanni and we have your dog, Laddy," as he pronounced it. I was dressed up since we were meeting friends for dinner that evening.

I called Ruth immediately and told her I'd go with her and meet my friends later at the restaurant.

As we drove to the airport, Ruth was crying with joy. I was glad that I hadn't thought only of myself and waited until the next day. We met Giovanni.

"I am so happy for you, Senora, that we have found her," he said.

There was Lady. It was a sad sight. She was thin, matted, snarling, and needing a bath. She didn't recognize Ruth. Giovanni turned to open the door.

We both said, "No, don't let her out."

The dog climbed over us. We made a flying grapple for her. The baggage man fell on Ruth and I fell in front of the cage, driving the edge of the door into my ribs. I lay on the ground, gasping for air, but I held on to one of Lady's front paws. Ruth had the other. Giovanni tried to put a leash on her, but Lady had gone mad, trying to bite us, all the while barking wildly.

We finally got her into the car with the help of Giovanni, but she growled at us all the way home. I was uncomfortable driving with her acting like this. I also had ruined one beautiful outfit. My stockings were torn, my hair was hanging, not to mention some badly bruised ribs. I certainly wasn't meeting anyone tonight looking like this.

A month went by and Lady became her sweet self again. Who knows what happened to her in all that time she was missing? She still had one paw that was sore and she favored it. She came into heat and Ruth thought that we might see if our collie was interested.

When we brought them together, I must say my dog was a perfect gentleman and just sat there. Lady was very blatant. He finally got the idea and started to mount her. Lady let out a yelp because of her paw and Konig fell to the floor in trauma. He started to make those strange "woo woo" noises and cry. Lady kept nudging him but he put his head in my lap and looked at me, tears coming out of his eyes.

Lady finally recovered but we never did get them to mate. Every time Konig saw Lady he would remember her yelp and come running to me for help. I think he was still a virgin when he died. We loved him so much we didn't care about his shortcomings.

Losing A Friend

Alan Rosenbluth

I lost a friend in the spring of my sophomore year of high school. Carter Manos was fifteen years old when rheumatic heart disease took his life. This disease involves a bacterial infection of the heart muscle, something not understood at the time. Later, penicillin provided an effective, inexpensive way to preserve the lives of many thousands of stricken people.

In 1943, I was in the fifth grade and Carter was my best friend. (While we were close to the same age, I got to start school a year earlier than Carter.) We did a lot of grappling and wrestling but never in anger. Almost every time we got together out-of-doors one of us would provide a push that led to a shove that led to a headlock … and we were at it again. There were times when Carter was stronger and got the best of me, and then on other occasions, I would prevail.

Carter lived on Seminole Avenue between Second and Third less than a block from my home at 717 South Third. To reach my house he crossed Seminole, cut through a neighbor's corner yard, and vaulted the wire fence into my backyard. I envied Carter's ability to approach the chin-high fence, and with hands together, propel his legs parallel to the fence, up and over. I tried this maneuver again and again with no success. Maybe it was psychological or a question of strength or leverage, but I couldn't do it. That fence was another way he could win at least one of our daily competitions. It made me try that much harder when we fought.

We really liked each other, and thrived on the spirit and cyclic nature of our battles. Our clothes and hair were usually covered with leaves, and our corduroy pants, mud encrusted.

One Saturday, to my annoyance, Carter was the stronger wrestler. He got me down on my back with his legs astride my belly and pinned my wrists to the ground close to my ears. I couldn't get him off. He straightened his arms, placing most of his weight on my wrists. Even the trick of bringing a foot around in front of his face didn't work. Carter bent forward each time I tried. In true anger, I could have delivered a severe blow with a knee to the kidney or ribs. But we weren't really fighting.

He serenaded me with a few sing-song taunts, basically letting me know I was defeated and couldn't do anything about it. Our faces were only six inches apart. It was at that moment when Carter, his thinking impaired by the victory, got a bad idea. He decided to spit in my face. His saliva emerged slowly, descending in a thinning strand. It splashed just under my left eye and across my nose.

More than a decade later in college studying for my pharmacy degree, I learned about the body's stress reactions, sometimes called the fight or flight response. When extremely provoked, people under the surging influence of their own adrenaline and related hormones can perform unbelievable physical feats. For example, a man, with no help available, lifted the front of a car to save his dying child trapped underneath.

You recall that we were very good friends, and I believe Carter regretted his unfriendly act even prior to the moist globule making contact with my face. In any case, with an enormous angry thrust of legs and arms, I threw Carter off like a rag doll. He went several feet up and several feet away before he hit the ground with a grunt. He was up and running as I went after him. I was gaining on him when Carter vaulted the fence and escaped.

I was furious and frustrated that I couldn't get my hands on him. "Come back you dad gum yellow coward!" I yelled.

He paused for an instant, but despite the protective barrier between us, ran toward home as fast as he could. I blindly reached down for something to at least throw, and came up with a smooth, rounded stone about two inches across and perhaps half an inch thick—a stone that would be good for skipping on the surface of a lake. Without thinking, I angrily flung it hard at Carter's rapidly retreating back. Astonishingly, it struck him high on the back of his head. He went down, crying. Then with blood on his head, hands, and clothes, he got up and continued running away.

I was frightened and ashamed, but still influenced by the insult and adrenaline. "Well, he didn't have to spit in my face!" I rationalized.

Carter ended up getting four stitches in his head and a tetanus shot. He was bandaged like someone from the movie *Mummy's Tomb* when my parents took me over to his house to apologize. I was surprised that Carter was so friendly, and his parents were most understanding. What a day! There was more to contemplate than just the typical skinned elbows, torn shirt, and muddy corduroy pants.

Carter, who remained a good friend even though we eventually lived several miles apart, grew up a lot bigger and stronger than I did. Once in a junior high intramural track meet, he set a record in the shot put. In the eighth grade, I pictured myself as a shot putter and finished with a third place ribbon far behind the seventh grader that I had once nearly killed. Again he had beaten me, but it was years since we had competed on a daily basis.

After Carter became ill and homebound, I visited him and talked about things of mutual interest—mostly sports, although he could no longer play ball. His movements were subdued, but Carter's spirit and humor remained high, and his courage monumental.

My outlook was that he would recover, even though he was weak and had lost a lot of weight. We were stunned, one day in the dressing room after baseball practice, to learn Carter had died. Dean Patton, Tom Borland, Bob Self, and I went to his house to express sympathy, something I'd never had reason to do before. I distinctly remember Tom towering over Mrs. Manos as he put an arm around her shoulders, and talked to her quietly. This gave me additional reason to admire Tom because as soon as I saw the family, I began to cry so hard that I couldn't even speak, much less offer words of consolation.

Now a long way from those times and places but still close to the emotions, I offer two whimsical thoughts:

1. Under my adrenaline rush on that Saturday in 1943, I now believe I could have easily vaulted the fence, caught my friend, and "thrashed" him, as writers of boy's books used to say; and

2. I would very much like to put on some corduroys and once again wrestle Carter Manos in the backyard at 717 South Third Street. I wouldn't mind getting leaves in my hair or mud on my clothes—or even losing to Carter.

Mid-Solstice Night Dreaming

Cyndy Muscatel

Summer was knocking on the door of June that evening we met for a quick dinner. Although it was almost seven, the sun shone high above the horizon as we entered the restaurant. Holding my right hand was Garrett, my four-year-old grandson. Squeezing my left was Evan, the three-year-old.

"Welcome to Pizza Magic. You guys want a table for three?" The girl at the hostess desk sounded irritated—as if our coming in the door had interrupted her from doing something important.

"No, there'll be six of us. One booster seat, please," I said, trying not to stare at the ring looped between the girl's nostrils. It didn't look clean, which was something I'd rather not know about. If this was how the hostess presented herself to the public, what about the cook hidden away in the kitchen? I began to picture a guy with long hair as greasy as his apron, twirling pizza dough with bacteria-coated fingers.

Evan tugged on my hand. "I don't want a booster seat, Grammy."

"It's not for you—it's for cousin Eli. He's meeting us with his mommy."

I leaned down to retie my running shoe, counting to ten. Had I sounded annoyed? I hoped not. I usually was so calm with the boys, much more than I'd been with my own children. But Garrett and Evan had stayed over last night, and they hadn't listened to a word I said. Today had continued the same way.

Of course, I understood why they were so unruly. There'd been a lot going on in the family these last few months—with today being the topper.

"Cindy, are they going to seat us or should we go somewhere else?"

I looked up. My husband, lines of fatigue around his eyes, loomed over me. I crossed my fingers, hoping he'd have enough patience to get through the next few hours. Patience was his short suit.

"Moe, calm down. The girl said it would be about five minutes for a table. Jennifer and Eli aren't here yet, anyway."

Garrett took Moe's hand. "Daddo, will you take us to see the fountain?"

Moe sighed. "All right, but just for a minute. Come on, Evan. You come, too." He held out his hand. Evan deposited the tattered remnants of his baby blanket into it.

"I'm going to give your blankie to Grammy. She'll take care of it." Moe tossed the blanket to me. Evan's eyes followed its flight as if it were a World Series strike out pitch in the bottom of the ninth.

"Come on, guys. Let's go throw some pennies in the fountain, and make a wish." Moe had his arms around both boys as they walked out the door.

I sat down on a bench near the restaurant's entrance and closed my eyes. It felt good to just rest for a moment. If anyone had told me I'd have four grandchildren by the time I was 56, I wouldn't have believed them. I always thought grandparents were old. I didn't feel old—present time excepted.

"There's Grammy, Eli. I told you she'd be here."

I opened my eyes to see my daughter and third grandson coming in the entrance. I held out my arms to Eli. "Come here, sweetie. Grammy missed you today."

Eli toddled over to me. I picked him up. "How was school? Did you have fun?"

He nodded, pleating the knitted blue and yellow blanket he held. I hugged him close. He wasn't even two yet. It broke my heart that he had to be in daycare from seven in the morning to six at night.

Jennifer sank down next to me. "Oh, my feet," she moaned. She slipped off her high heels, and we both stared at the reddened blisters on her toes.

"How was work? Besides the fact that wearing those gorgeous shoes is killing your feet." I tried for an upbeat, teasing tone.

"It was okay. I mean it's only the second day. I was on the phone and the computer most of the time—you know, getting in contact with the client base."

A part of me, a part I kept carefully buried, wanted to ask if she really thought her divorce was the best thing. I mean, a baby not getting to live with both his parents? Jennifer having to leave him all day to work full-time? Was it really worth it?

I kept these questions to myself. First, I knew objectively that the answer was yes—Jennifer knew what she was doing. Secondly, I knew my anxiety was at the root of the questions. Besides, these days, my mothering job entailed being supportive and keeping my mouth shut. God, it had been so much easier when the kids were young. Then you could just tell them what to do so they'd stay safe.

"I talked to David and Gina," Jennifer said. "Dave said the baby was doing great, and Gina said she was, too."

"I know. The baby came so quickly. We were all sitting there talking with Gina, and eating California Pizza Kitchen take out. Then Gina frowned, and asked the nurse to check her. I swear Quinn was born 15 minutes later."

Eli put his head on my shoulder and his thumb in his mouth. I kissed the top of his head, and looked at Jennifer. She was brushing tears from her eyes.

"What's the matter, honey?" I asked.

"I wanted to be a stay-at-home mom. I just hate being away from Eli."

"Why do you hate being away from Eli, Auntie Jen-Jen?" Garrett asked.

Moe had returned with the boys. He bent down to kiss Eli and then Jennifer. "How was work?" he asked.

"Fine. I just miss being with Eli."

"Why do you miss being with Eli? Why isn't Uncle B having dinner with us?"

Garrett was in the *why and why* asking stage. If the sun was out, he wanted to know why. If the sun was setting, he wanted to know why. "Why did those men crash the airplanes into the buildings?" he'd asked me in September. "Why is our President, Mr. George Bush, an American, talking to us all the time?"

I wanted to ask why a child, not even four-years-old, had to be burdened by these questions. Garrett also asked about Bernard's absence a lot. He'd even asked when Auntie Jen-Jen and Uncle B were going to make up.

"I have to leave Eli because I have to work, sweetie," Jennifer said. Her voice had become that of the attentive auntie, masking her own distress.

"But why?" Garrett asked again.

"Your table's ready." It was our 'gracious and lovely hostess', come to seat us. Thank God for small favors.

Fifteen minutes later, we'd ordered. I'd let the boys get brown Sprite, as we called Coke just between ourselves, and they were happy drinking their forbidden treat. Eli watched them, grinning around his thumb and blanket.

"So, Garrett and Evan, are you guys excited about your new baby sister?" Jennifer asked.

"Yeah, but we wants to see her," Evan said.

"I bet! I want to see her, too. Maybe Grammy will pick up Eli from daycare tomorrow? Then I can go visit at the hospital on my way home from work." Jennifer turned to me.

I nodded assent. What else could I do? Even if I felt I was holding on by a fraying thread, I couldn't refuse. I had to help her out. But I was so tired—tired to the bone. Tired of all the sadness, tired of all the trauma—the struggles into life and out of it. At least Quinn was perfectly healthy, even if the doctor had been worried she could be stillborn. He'd insisted on inducing my daughter-in-law three weeks early. Instead of a July baby, we had a June girl. A little redhead.

I should be feeling elated, I told myself. After all, Quinn had been born just four hours earlier.

I sat up straight. "Oh my goodness. It's Quinn's birth day—her real and only birth day. We have to sing "Happy Birth Day" to her right now!"

Jennifer looked up from handing crayons out to the boys. "You're right, Mom. We need to sing. Ready Garrett and Evan? Ready to sing for your new baby sister?"

Garrett nodded his white-blond head. "Do you think she'll hear us?"

"I'm sure she will." I smiled at him. "Okay, all together now, one, two, three. Happy Birthday to Quinn," I began.

Moe rolled his eyes, but joined in. After we finished singing, I looked around the table. Each of us was smiling. It might have been a dorky thing to do, but it felt just fine.

"I wants my momma." Evan's plaintive drawl broke the spell.

Moe leaned towards me and whispered, "Where did Evan get his southern accent?"

"I don't know, but his drawl gets thicker every day."

"Remember, Evan, Mommy is at the hospital with baby Quinn," Jennifer said.

I reached over to Evan's plate. "You'll get to see her tomorrow, sweetie. Here, let me cut up your pizza for you."

"Grammy, Grammy. I want to ask you something." Garrett tugged at my sleeve.

"Not now, honey. I'm cutting up Evan's pizza."

"But it's important. It's about Grandpa Sid."

Grandpa Sid. My father who had died three weeks earlier. My beloved father.

Earlier in the birthing room, when I stood next to the doctor, and watched Quinn's head emerge from the womb, it reminded me of the evening Dad had died. It felt like the same process, only in reverse. Loving people supported Dad on his final journey out of this life just as we helped Quinn on her journey into it.

I turned to Garrett. "Okay, honey, what do you want to know?"

"Is that what happens?"

"What, sweetie?"

"So when you die you go back to where it all began, and then you start over again?"

I swallowed hard, startled by his succinct description. I felt Jennifer's hand seek out mine. I felt Moe's hand settle on my shoulder.

"That's a very smart idea. A lot of people think it happens just that way," I told Garrett when I could finally speak.

He smiled and his small shoulders relaxed. He picked up his slice of pizza and took a huge bite out of it.

Later that night I dreamed that my father and Quinn were lying on individual sofas in a tunnel. The sofas were hooked together like train cars. Dad's train was faced in one direction, Quinn's in the other. But for three weeks, they sat side by side, and got to know each other very well.

My First Piece of Chocolate

Else Jacobs

I was just a toddler on April 9th, 1940, when the German War Machine rolled into Norway with the purpose of taking over the country. They planned to kill our King and Crown Prince and install their Nazi government.

Norway, like Denmark, was ill prepared for such attacks. The poverty after World War I had left us with hardly any defense. Denmark surrendered after two days as they relied on a non-aggression pact they had with Germany. Norway lasted two months before it fully surrendered after much bravery and resistance from the people.

The Germans advanced quickly in Norway conquering one city after another. In the course of twenty four hours, sixteen thousand soldiers had invaded our small country.

There was a delay in winning Oslo, our capital, as the Germans thought the fjord surrounding the city would be full of mines after the antique guns of Oscarsborg Fortress managed to sink the German cruiser Blucher. The German soldiers had to go ashore further away from Oslo than planned, making an escape of the Royal Family and the government possible.

The gold reserves of the Norwegian Bank, fifty tons in all, were loaded into trucks and brought north to Åndalsnes through Isfjorden to Molde, a harbor town on the North Sea. From there they were shipped in small fishing boats to Tromsø in northern Norway, then on to England and finally to the U.S. This was all told to me by my father. He was one of the many guards seeing to it that the transportation was safe and to look out for any sabotage from the Germans. "It was quite a risky expedition," he said.

The Royal Family and the government chose the same route. German spies found out about it, and bombers were soon on their chase. Both Åndalsnes and Molde were totally destroyed, but the people were able to evacuate. Many of those sought refuge in Isfjorden, my little village that lies between the two towns. Aunt Agnes, who lived in Åndalsnes, came to stay with us. In the meantime, the

Royal Family and the government made it safely to England, even though it was a close call.

There is a well-known photo in Norway of King Haakon and Crown Prince Olav seeking refuge under a big silver birch tree with its new spring leaves, just outside Molde. German bombers flew overhead searching for them. There were no bomb shelters, so they relied on Mother Nature for their protection.

On April 17th, eight days after they had invaded Norway, the Germans reached Åndalsnes, about two hundred miles north of the capital. Åndalsnes was desirable because of its location on the coast, and its railroads, which connected the north and south. Thus, the war had spread to my village.

To the horror of the villagers, the narrow roads of Isfjorden filled with marching soldiers, trucks, jeeps and officers on their motorcycles with sidecars.

All Norwegian vehicles were confiscated. So were radios. I learned later that some people were brave enough to hide their radios. At certain times in the evening they were brought out so that the owner and friends could listen secretly to "The Voice from London", an update of the war by a Norwegian commentator. National celebrations were forbidden, as was the waving of the Norwegian flag.

The sudden invasion into Isfjorden caused chaos. Soldiers pitched tents for their sleeping quarters while building barracks for a more permanent situation during the long cold winter that was bound to come.

The first floor of my parents' house was taken over by officers for their living quarters. My uncle and aunt and their two young children had one small apartment on the second floor, and so did my family. Our basement was turned into a bakery. Some soldiers had experience in baking bread for a whole battalion. Storage sheds were built in our backyard to keep the breads until distribution.

I can only imagine the tension between my parents and their occupiers. Both my father and my uncle were big strong guys that were utterly humiliated by the arrogance of the Germans. But their hands were tied; they couldn't do anything or say anything or we would all be severely punished. I know my parents were very protective of my brother and me. I always felt safe, even the couple of times we had warnings of possible bomb attacks and had to run for safety to the basement where we huddled together in a corner.

The community center in Isfjorden was turned into a camp for Russian POWs who were used to rebuild the harbor and railroad in Åndalsnes. We sometimes walked past the camp and happened to see prisoners in the open area with a tall barbed fence around it. They were allowed a certain amount of time for fresh air.

Once, I saw a woman throw a bouquet of flowers from her garden into the camp. She was immediately arrested and interrogated by officers. She was gone for several days, I remember.

In the wintertime, the Russians shoveled snow off our roads to keep them open for marching soldiers, trucks and cars. Most of the time they were supervised, but when the Nazis were not watching, we would hide a sandwich in the snow bank in front of our house for the POWs. The next day, in the same spot, we'd find a beautifully carved wooden toy for us kids to enjoy. Sometimes it was a bird, a small bowl or a box, all decorated with colorful painted straws. We treasured those gifts. We had so little. These secret activities took place quite often, and we had fun doing it. It was successful in the wintertime because of the darkness.

So many of the stories about the war have been told to me, but quite a few I remember myself. One day a few of us kids were playing a game in the field close to a barrack where some officers lived. All of a sudden, a dozen huge German shepherds came at us. We ran for our lives. When the dogs were close to attacking us, they were called back. We were unhurt, but I have never forgotten that day or the taste of blood in my mouth. I think we were making too much noise, laughing and running around which annoyed the Germans. They wanted an immediate stop to such nonsense, and they got it. We never returned to that area.

At the age of four to five, I started to become more aware of what was going on around me. The sight of German officers in their fancy uniforms, caps and shining tall boots was already as familiar as if it had always been like that. As a child I didn't understand war, and I didn't know any differently. We had to learn to live side-by-side with our occupiers, and as long as we didn't do any harm to them, they treated us fairly.

My brother and I often stood in front of our kitchen window and watched with awe as soldiers marched past our house on the six mile trek each way to Åndalsnes and back. I can still hear officers shouting out orders to keep them in line.

Rationing of food and clothing was strictly enforced. There was, however, a certain advantage to life in the countryside where we had easy access to local farmers for produce and meats. Fishermen went from door-to-door selling their catch of the day. In the summer and fall we picked the plentiful blueberries, blackberries and cranberries in the forest, some for daily consumption and the rest for preserves for the winter.

In the cities many were on the level of starvation. There simply was not enough food, so they had to find ways of stretching their supply. Lucky were those that had family in the country nearby, close enough that they could walk there or use a bicycle, if they had one.

At Christmas time we were so happy that our rationing of food allowed us one banana and one orange per member of the family. I enjoyed shopping with my mother so much at that time of the year. The only grocery store in the village would offer some extra goodies like hazelnuts and licorice, I remember.

In the summer of 1944, my family spent a day at my uncle's farm helping with the haying before the rain came. After returning home, my brother and I ran into the backyard. There sat two of the officers that lived in our house. I must say, they were always friendly to us kids. They liked to practice their Norwegian on us. I noticed they were eating something out of a box.

"Would you like to have a piece of chocolate? It's quite good. We got a package from Germany today," one of them said in Norwegian with a heavy German accent.

My brother and I looked at each other dumbfounded. We didn't know what chocolate was. Being curious little kids we agreed. They looked quite happy. If they were eating it, so could we.

They handed each of us a small square of the dark brown food. We slowly and carefully bit into it. After the first taste of it we agreed that it was good.

"Else," the other officer said, "you remind me of my little daughter back home. She's about your age, and I miss her."

He patted me kindly on the head.

My brother and I thanked the officers and ran into the house to show and tell our parents about the chocolate.

It seemed to me that my parents took the occupation all in stride. To me, they had learned to be neutral. They were neither happy nor sad. As a child, I was sheltered from the worst of it. I now realize so many emotions were locked up inside them. One had to appear strong. A weak person could more easily be attacked.

There's irony in life, but maybe more so in war-time. Even an enemy has somewhat of a kind human nature. Once in a while, we got some favors from our enemies like a fresh loaf of bread or some crackers they had just received from Germany. They had their families far away that they weren't able to see for a very long time. They believed they had a job to do that they had been trained for, and they were being put to the test with a responsibility to their superiors. They believed this war had to be won for Hitler.

But they didn't hesitate to do wrong to the civilians, inconvenience people or even steal. I remember several occasions being harassed as my mother and I walked to the village store.

One thing I learned much later was that the rape of young women was widespread. When I was in school, there were several kids who had been fathered by Germans. These kids were harassed every day by fellow students. Later, the half German kids were gathered together at special schools.

I do not know how my life would have been different if I hadn't experienced the war. Our parents instilled in us honesty and gratitude. We learned right from wrong at an early age, which in turn built strength of character, both mentally and emotionally, I believe. Being surrounded by enemies on a daily basis and never knowing what was going to happen next, was a scary experience. It's like we were constantly watched. But on the other hand, we were grateful to have survived.

World War II was the biggest and most horrible war that was ever fought. Nearly thirty million people were killed. About half of them were civilians.

I remember, May 7th, 1945, when my father put me on his lap and explained to me that we had won the war—that we were free. Did I understand that? Judging from his happy smiling face, I knew it must be something very good. And how would my life change?

In our Independence Day Parade on May 17th, which commemorates Norway's independence from Denmark, I could walk and wave my Norwegian flag. Another thing I remember noticing was that we didn't have to roll down those blackout curtains every night.

But, even after the war was over, we were still poor. Changes came slowly. Roads and railroads were in bad shape. Communications within the country were broken, and it was slow getting the goods we needed.

Nevertheless, we were happy that our occupiers of five years were gone. They left as fast as they could when they learned that they had lost the war.

Night On The Town

Cheryl McFadden

The hubby and I can hardly be described as swingers, no matter how you define that term. Our idea of a lively Saturday night is to drive over to the neighborhood fast food eatery and pick up a couple of burgers and some fries. Neither one of us care to deal with all the hustle and bustle of the desert during tourist season. Therefore we were somewhat reluctant when my stepson, Chris and daughter-in-law, Vonda, called and invited us out to dinner. They suggested one of the popular restaurants located directly in the heart of Sightseer Central.

"You do realize that this is the height of the season, don't you? We'll never get seated on a Saturday night, assuming we're able to find a parking place," I said while secretly suspecting that the four of us would be bellying-up to a table at the burger place before the evening ended.

"Ah, come on, it will be fun, you'll see," Chris replied. "We'll pick you up at six."

As I expected we ran into bumper-to-bumper traffic heading towards downtown Palm Springs, and although I didn't say anything, I sure was thinking, *I told you so.*

Chris pulled his giant SUV into the parking lot and immediately found an empty space. *Sheer luck!* Guided by the sounds of boisterous laughter and city traffic, we clambered out and headed down the narrow alleyway leading to the main entrance. As feared, the restaurant was packed. *I told you so.*

Normally I am not a patient person, especially when it comes to food. The thought of waiting 30–45 minutes to be seated just doesn't do it for me. I'm an eat-and-run kind of gal. "Mickey D's is only a couple of blocks away," I suggested.

Chris smiled at me indulgently then queued up for a table while the three of us settled ourselves on a bench outside. Emerging a few minutes later with some sort of beeping gadget, he joined us and the wait began. My muscles started twitching at the thought of prolonged inactivity.

Another thing that I don't especially care for are crowds, and here we were smack dab in the heart of touristdom at its zenith. Throngs of sandal-wearing, Hawaiian-shirted, camera-carrying, stroller-pushing vacationers jockeyed for positions along the main drag. The scent of chlorine and sun tan lotion wafted in the air. This evening was not boding well. *I told you so.*

While we sat and waited, I felt my consciousness begin to shift. I noticed the softness of the twilight seeping through the village as the sun slid behind the mountains. I felt the gentle caress of whispery breezes against my skin. Across the street, a horse drawn carriage pulled out into traffic, rhythmically clip-clopping down Palm Canyon Drive as lovers snuggled in the back. Giggling children emerged from a nearby ice cream parlor, racing to lick the sticky sweetness as it oozed over its sugar-coned perch. From deep within the restaurant, a pulsating Latin beat intensified until it finally thrust outwards into the evening air. All around toes tapped and bodies swayed to a rhythm that could not be ignored. The city was alive and we felt its heartbeat.

"Our table's ready," Chris announced while removing the flashing beeper from his pocket. It seemed incredible that an hour had passed.

We entered the darkened interior of the popular restaurant and followed the hostess to a table in the back. Almost immediately appetizers appeared before us along with frothy Margaritas. We settled back to enjoy the ambiance and the food, and especially each other's company. This was not a night for eating-and-running.

An hour and a half later we emerged satisfied and content. The sky was filled with stars, our tummies with great food and our hearts with affection. It turned out to be a fun evening after all, and I'm almost certain that as Chris drove away I heard him say, "*I told you so.*"

First published in *The Desert Woman* June/July 2005 issue.

On Clinton Street, That Great Street

Jeri Schmitz

No matter how old I get or how much time passes, I will never forget the early years I spent in Chicago. To most people, childhood is like a hazy part of a dream, but my sepia-colored memories are so much more than that. They are precious and clear, exactly like old photos in a family album.

There is one June, in particular, I remember vividly. The year I turned seven marked the summer I was finally allowed to play outdoors by myself. From then on, most days found me on the sidewalk, at the bottom of a long flight of stairs.

"Virginia, get up here, right this minute. If I have to come down and get you, you'll be sorry." I can still hear Mother's words and they were not idle threats. I was always quick to answer her call.

"Yes, Mama." Up the splintery precipice I trudged, imagining myself a famous mountain climber like I'd seen in *National Geographic*. My base camp, far below our second-story front porch, littered the walkway with pretend Sherpas and floppy pack animals.

"Virginia, watch the baby, would you? I need to go downstairs and help Mrs. Miller. She isn't feeling well today."

Mrs. Miller was our landlady. Whenever my dad or I complained about the old busy-body, my mother was quick to point out her fine qualities. It was at those times Mama would speak loudly to an empty room. "Where would we be without Mrs. Miller's kindness?" Then Daddy's muffled voice would escape from under the bathroom door, "Probably living at the Ritz." And everybody would laugh.

Mama went down to Mrs. Miller's quite often in those halcyon days. Many times I walked the squeaky floors of the dining room pushing Clover in the baby buggy as I cursed the old lady for disturbing my playtime.

"I wish she'd fall and break her neck," I'd whisper to my tiny sister, who was four months old that summer of 1935. I knew my secrets were safe with Clover.

Then came the day Mama stayed downstairs for the longest time. I couldn't get Clover to stop crying no matter how fast I jiggled the buggy. I wasn't allowed to pick her up under any circumstance.

"Can't they hear all this squealing downstairs?" I hollered, trying to out decibel the baby's cries.

I shook the perambulator like you would shake an upside down piggy bank—with both hands—and pictured Clover's brains falling out like pennies.

Finally, Mama came back. She looked funny, like the time Daddy lost his job at the steel mill.

"I've called for an ambulance," she told me as she picked up the baby. "Mrs. Miller is quite ill this time."

Never having seen an ambulance, I wasn't sure what it was, but one look at my mother's face showed me the gravity of the situation.

"I'm going back down." She picked up the baby. "You stay here. Be a good girl, okay?"

"I'll be as good as gold," I promised. When she was out of sight, I whispered, "As long as you take Clover with you, I'll be an angel of God."

Straight to the window I ran to watch over my domain. The view from upstairs cleared the rooftops of the single-story houses and spanned the neighborhood all the way to the railroad yard. For sport, the local teen-agers climbed up and ran along the tops of the stationary boxcars waiting to be hitched together. Watching the boys barely miss the spidery-web telephone wires was my favorite pastime. I can still hear my mother's skinny sister, Aunt Myrtle, saying, "Someday, someone is going to get electrocuted. Then someone will be happy, won't they?"

Waiting for the inevitable electrocution wasn't always my focus when I stood watch over the city streets. There was something about being up so high that filled me with feelings of omnificence. That second-story lifted me up so that I was not only bigger, but wiser. At those times, instead of conquering a gigantic mountain, I could rule the world. It was with this great sense of super-ego that I watched the ambulance approach the corner of 92nd Street and turn on to Clinton. With the clang of the bell, my circulatory system came to a screeching halt. Stricken with instant remorse about wishes for broken necks, I watched two men put Mrs. Miller into the back of the van and I deflated as fast as a shooting balloon. Within minutes, I felt as low as the lowest step in the basement.

Mrs. Miller was away for days, and Mama walked around like a zombie.

When next we saw the ambulance, there were no clanging bells, just a shadow that approached the curb to silently announce … our landlady had returned home. Once again I watched out the window until the white blur disappeared, leaving us to pretend our lives were still the same. But nothing was further from the truth.

All the rest of that summer my mother did not go to Mrs. Miller's … not even once.

"Virgie, go up and ask your mother if she wants to join me for a cup of tea, would you please, dear?"

The old lady sent me on the same senseless daily errand, but Mama's answer remained the same. "Please tell Mrs. Miller that I'm much too busy now, sweetie."

In September we moved to a new neighborhood into one of those lackluster one-story houses, with no view and no landlady. I grew up never knowing why my mom had cooled so toward Mrs. Miller.

That was, until one day in 1977. We were going through old photos, Mama and I, laughing at my late father's black fedora and overcoat.

I joked, "Are you sure he wasn't a member of Al Capone's gang? He certainly looked the part. Oh, see here! Isn't this me playing on the sidewalk in front our old house on Clinton? I remember Mrs. Miller."

My seventy-three-year old mother looked up. "Oh, yes, and here's one of you and Clover in front of St. Vincent's after we moved to Los Angeles. See? That's Father Casey." She changed the subject and the era.

"Mom, why did you ignore Mrs. Miller after she came home from the hospital? You guys had been such good friends."

She looked away to somewhere deep inside herself. After several minutes, she turned toward me.

"I guess I never told you, did I? I still find it difficult to talk about, but you're certainly old enough to know the truth. Besides, Mrs. Miller passed away many years ago."

She returned the photos to the box and leaned back. "Remember that day she took sick and I went to stay with her until the ambulance arrived?"

"Yes, I do. I remember looking out the window and watching the ambulance as it came down the street."

"While we waited, Mrs. Miller became distressed and asked me to call a priest. She was having severe chest pains. It turned out to be her stomach, but that day, she honestly thought she was breathing her last."

My mother stood up and walked over to the fireplace. She picked up a candlestick from the mantle piece and idly twirled it in her hand. "The ambulance and the priest seemed to take forever, but she was compelled to clean her slate. She began to confess her sins to me. Before I could say stop, I heard things I never thought I would ever hear in all my life. I told her God would forgive her and why not just pray with me until the priest arrived. But no, she went on until … I guess she had run out of sins. The sin that hit me the hardest was the way she had earned the money to buy the house we all lived in."

I started laughing—I couldn't help it. I pictured my mother, holding Clover, making it impossible to put her fingers in her ears.

"Please, let me continue, Virginia, this is difficult enough. All the while we lived upstairs and for years before that, Mrs. Miller had been receiving gentlemen callers." The color of my mom's cheeks indicated the struggle she was having with her own confession. "She had been engaging in prostitution right under our living room window. I think you know what I mean."

My poor mother still could barely utter the words she had heard that day so many years before. "From that day forward, I couldn't look Mrs. Miller in the eye and I shuddered every time I thought of all the times I drank out of her teacups. We moved away as soon as we could."

By now, I had collapsed to my knees on the floor, eyes wet. "Oh, Mom, that is hilarious. To me, she was so old. That is the reason we moved to California, isn't it?"

"Don't be silly." She handed me a tissue and I smiled at her *naiveté*. "We moved to California for your asthma."

One More Day

Alan Rosenbluth

It was obviously going to be the last time I would be with my father. His cancer had progressed too far, and there were not many good times left for him. As his medication wore off, pain would return and become intense. The stronger medication I suggested the doctor prescribe eased his pain, but caused him to sleep a great deal. Never-the-less, my father greatly enjoyed the short visit I was able to arrange. Just being together and chatting about family, past good times, work, and some trivial things was enough. I cherished the golden, waning moments. It was a final desperate opportunity to bridge the two thousand miles between us, and somehow bring the margins of our lives together.

A long-time friend once advanced the theory that as we age, our distinctive features become more pronounced. He felt that we don't become different; we become more of what we are. For example, those who complain about incidentals from time to time may, in their later years, find fault with almost everything … in much the same way that individuals known for their kindness become even more considerate over time. I have concluded that this theory is relevant to many of my family and friends. It certainly applied to my father, who occasionally may have appeared a bit gruff and unnecessarily outspoken, but basically was a caring, supportive, loving, and appreciative man. There was an underlying sweetness in his relationships, especially those with children. All these features intensified in his final decade and more so in his final year.

Dad invariably praised Mother's cooking and thanked her warmly for the delicious, well-balanced meals she prepared for him. In later years he was inclined to speak in superlatives. He would say repeatedly and with obvious conviction, how marvelous the food was. More and more often he'd assert that, "This is the best I ever ate!" Similarly, during his illnesses, Dad, despite discomfort or even serious pain, would gently and politely thank hospital nurses and aides for what they did for him. He wasn't attempting to ingratiate himself with them. Rather, his fundamental sweetness and appreciativeness just surfaced more often.

During my last visit, I recall taking my father to the doctor, going to the pharmacy to get the more potent prescription drugs, taking my mother to the grocery store, and visiting with my mother and sisters. The primary goal was to be with my dad. When he slept during the day, I would run several miles under the hot, dry winter sun of the California desert.

As the visit came to an end, I dreaded saying good-bye. I'd be leaving him for the last time. Somehow I got through it. I slept at my sister Myrle's house, and left early the next morning before Dad got up. It was very quiet in the car on the way to the airport. My sisters and I were lost in our own (probably identical) thoughts. My throat became constricted. I couldn't swallow or speak. Pent up tears began to escape. Within moments I was crying helplessly in the back seat.

The sisters stared directly ahead to give me privacy as we drove the ten minutes to the airport. Half way there, my oldest sister, Gloria, attempted to assuage the embarrassment of a middle-aged man crying before his sisters (who were destined to cry for the same reason at a later date). She whispered, "It's all right to lose control of your emotions. Everyone loses control sometimes. We understand."

Gloria was well intentioned, but mistaken. After the sobbing subsided, I explained, "I didn't lose control. It's the most appropriate thing in the world to cry the last time you will ever see your father." They nodded agreement, and nothing more was said. But I ached with the need to stay with my father,

The airline agent grimaced as I approached the check-in counter, making me wonder if he could read the sorrow in my face and posture. "I'm so sorry," he said in an unusually consoling tone, "Your flight's been cancelled. Equipment problem. All the other flights are booked, and we can't get you out until tomorrow morning. Can I help in any way?"

He was pleased at how well I took the bad news, and was probably amazed to receive my courteous, friendly response at being forced to miss a flight and connections. You should know that at several pivotal times in my life, I have been extraordinarily lucky. On this lucky occasion, I won an extra final day with my father. I hurried to him!

When I arrived, Dad was resting, fully clothed, atop the covers of his bed. We were enormously glad to see each other again. I kicked off my shoes, crawled onto the bed, and propped my head on a large upright pillow beside him. There we were, identically posed: hands clasped behind our heads, legs crossed at the ankles. Then I put my arm around his shoulders. From that position I could see that he was gazing at a cluster of photographs high on the wall. The largest was a delightful portrait of my sons, Kirby and Brady, at ages of four and two. It was a dazzling picture: brilliant dimpled smiles, flashing blue (Kirby) and brown (Brady) eyes, carefully brushed hair, and immaculate outfits.

He gestured to the picture and grinned at me, love in his eyes. He said, "You could just...." Without finding the words, his hands showed me that he wanted to touch and perhaps pinch those beaming faces. I realized he spent considerable time contemplating that picture before falling asleep, upon waking, and during the day. I'm glad my boys gave their grandfather moments of pleasure during his daily routine, and comfort during the difficult times.

That evening before he went to sleep, my father looked at me. "Sonny, are you still my little boy?" he asked.

"Yes, Daddy, I'm still your little boy," I answered.

"Good," he said.

Early the following morning, grateful for one more day with my father and accepting the inevitable, I flew home to my wife and smiling children. There were no tears on the way to the airport.

One Moment in Time

Anita Knight

The winds of change blow constantly, whether we feel them or not.

Think about yesterday. Did everything remain the same, or did some unexpected crop up. Maybe a new idea popped into your consciousness. Perhaps an existing problem was solved.

Most of us are guilty of trying to orchestrate our lives, but if we can learn to let go—let whatever greater power we believe in take over—we can make better use of our precious time.

Right now, take a deep breath. Look around. Notice the sound of water as it runs from a stream, a fountain, a faucet, a sprinkler. Focus on a silvery cobweb magically attached from wall to flower, wonder at the work of the tiny spider. Pray that she catches something to make her work worthwhile. Smell the flowers. Dwell on what miracle gives each its own powerful aroma. Think about how the bee decides which tiny speck of pollen to make into honey.

Enjoy the here and now, without worrying about what might have been or what might happen. It doesn't matter. Somebody's life changed radically in the few seconds it took you to read this. It may be your turn next.

Whatever comes, know it is meant to be.

And know that it too shall pass.

Pam's Room

Dory Rose

The large bedroom window was open wide to bring in the warm wind off the lake. The tree in front was plentiful with large green leaves. The robins were chirping. Pam couldn't turn her head, but she would know it was a July summer day.

Otto, the dog, slept under her bed. His paws were crossed, holding his brown and black spaniel face. The two cats, Bianca and Buddy, were curled up at the end of the bed.

I walked in as Pam opened her eyes.

The TV showed Oprah's program, but there was no sound. The room was silent except for the repetitive bubbling of the oxygen machine on the right side of the bed. The hospital tray on the other side held a paper cup with a melted Popsicle. Pam's frail hand grasped a small pump that released morphine when needed,

"Good afternoon. Did I wake you?" The hospice nurse reminded me never to ask how she felt. Keep the conversation positive.

Pam stretched her small frame. The cats jumped off the bed, and scampered out the door, their nap interrupted.

I washed out a soapy washrag from the bathroom. Pam took the cloth and wiped her face and hands with great effort.

"Nice, thanks." She smiled. "It feels nice."

I put a fresh root beer Popsicle in her hand. This had been her favorite flavor since she was five. She took a lick, and put it the cup with the other melted Popsicle.

"I'll finish it later, I promise." Her eyes closed.

The morphine took over.

Pole In Chimney

Barbara J. Savage

We had been living in our villa in Italy for six months when I decided to try the fireplace in the dining room. Christmas was coming and all I could think of was how festive the house would look with the added pleasure of a roaring fire.

We opened the flue and piled dry branches into the log holder. As the fire increased, so did the smoke which rolled into the house. The air took on the appearance of a London fog. We coughed and choked, dragged the branches out, getting burned in the process.

"Do you really want a fireplace?" my husband asked as I put salve on one of his burns. "Couldn't we do without it, since you know that everything here turns into a disaster?"

I was still upset about the explosion of the boiler, and not having the washer and dryer connected. I wanted something to work. "It's there to be used. I won't be disappointed in this," I said.

I took myself down to see Rene, the owner of the villa. I listened to all the words about how my appearance made his day happy.

He said, "How beautiful you look today, *amore*. Let me hold your hands to feel how my heart pounds." He held my hands to his chest so that I could feel his excitement.

If I had been single, I most certainly would have been interested in how his heart pounded. I digress.

I think he felt that since I'd been through the previous disasters, I wouldn't ask for anything else. He didn't know the female mind.

"Rene, I want the fireplace checked. I tried to light it this morning and all the smoke backed in."

"Did you have the flue open?"

"The flue was open and we looked up the chimney. It's solid black. Could you please send a chimney sweep to clean it in the next few days? I don't want to wait for weeks since I would like to put it on for Christmas."

He promised to send someone. With many kisses I went on my way.

Three weeks later, the door knocker was being pounded. I opened the door and there stood two men with a long slim stick. They introduced themselves as Giovanni and Giuseppe.

"Rene sent us to clean out the chimney."

I looked at them. "Are you chimney sweeps? Do you have experience at this?"

They assured me that they knew what to do. Why did I believe this was going to be different than all the other times? But you must, now and then, have faith.

Giovanni stuck his head up into the chimney, using a stick trying to dislodge what was stuck. Nothing budged. They went up to the roof, discussed and gestured in Italian for an hour. It seemed that the fireplace had not been cleaned in the ten years the villa had been empty. Bird nests and leaves were packed solid by rain over all that time.

Finally, they agreed that they would be back *domani.* I immediately grumbled that I would never see them again. I spoke with myself, agreeing that maybe it was best that there would be no fire. I could picture the calamity that would most likely occur.

My husband was happy that they'd left. He felt disaster lurked in every corner of Italy since something was always going wrong or blowing up.

The next morning, we were having breakfast on the patio when I heard someone knocking on the door. It was Giovanni and Giuseppe with two other men.

"Buon Giorno, Senora. Today we will work again to open the fireplace."

I could not believe that they'd actually returned as promised. They proceeded up to the roof. One jumped down into the chimney onto the stopped up material as the others held him, just in case things let go. He pushed with the stick, but only small nests came down the shaft. I watched as they stomped and dug, but nothing much seemed to be happening.

Giovanni, who seemed to be the boss, said, "Senora, we are going to get another piece of equipment and will be back shortly."

Again, I became pushy." I want the chimney cleaned as soon as possible. Are you really coming back?"

Giovanni looked hurt. "Senora, we would not lie to you. We will be back in twenty minutes."

To my amazement, after only twenty minutes, I heard Giovanni's voice. I looked outside. They now had a telephone pole.

"What will you do with this?" I asked.

"We are going to use it as a battering ram to free the chimney," Giovanni said.

"What a great idea." It was at this point I realized I was becoming as "mad" as they were.

They went to the roof with the pole. We heard some mighty banging for over an hour, but nothing moved except for small nests falling into the living room. Suddenly there was total silence. Then I heard some heavy cursing.

"What's happening and why have you stopped?" I called.

"The telephone pole is stuck, Senora, and we can't get it loose. It is caught on one of the cleats," Giovanni yelled back.

They did all they could to get it free, but nothing worked. They decided to set it on fire and burn it down that way.

"Are you crazy? It's a thick pole and it could cause a fire in the chimney."

They shrugged their shoulders and said that they could not think of anything else to do. I was furious, since now I had a telephone pole sticking out of the chimney. Was this going to be a permanent feature, this ugly architectural addition? A blemish on my beautiful villa!

My husband came outside since he'd heard the word fire and my anxious voice.

He shook his head, looked at the pole, muttered under his breath, "I told you so," and went back into the house.

The telephone pole became a beacon. Friends would often give directions, "Look for the house with the telephone pole sticking out of the chimney." We did not appreciate this distinction.

On Christmas Day we had a party. Everyone admired the fireplace since we had banked it with logs and greens. Like so many other things in Italy, it was beautiful to look at but it didn't work.

My husband felt I'd finally ceased trying to get things done. He couldn't have been more mistaken. "Perhaps we could saw the pole to the top of the chimney and no one could see it? The fireplace wouldn't work, but at least I wouldn't have a pole sticking out of the chimney. I'm going to speak to Rene about this," I told him.

Hope springs eternal in a woman's breast, and I kept "fighting the good fight." I loved living there. It was always a challenge, but even when Italy won and I didn't, my love remained for Italia, *La Bel Paese!*

September 11th 2001

Mary Burton Olson M.D.

September 11, 2001 dawned as every summer day in Rancho Mirage, bright, sunny, no wind. My husband, Bob, read the morning paper. Our daughter, Julie, and her husband, Mark, slept in our casita. I activated the computer. My attention was riveted by a picture of an airplane crashing into a building.

"Bob, was there a plane crash last night? Have you read about one in the paper?"

"No, why do you ask?"

"Come here and look at this," I said, not recognizing live news on the computer.

We turned on the TV and heard the announcer proclaim facts and speculations. At first, we thought it an accident. When the second plane hit the World Trade Center, we knew it was deliberate. Buildings collapsed. A third plane hit the Pentagon and a fourth crashed in the Pennsylvania countryside. Terrorists had struck. Déjà vu, Pearl Harbor repeated.

Julie and Mark were living with us that summer. We woke them with the news. Immediately alert and horrified into complete silence, they isolated themselves for the entire day in the casita. Glued to the big screen TV, they feared for the lives of friends possibly trapped in a collapsed edifice. They previously lived at Lincoln Center in New York City. Mark worked for American Express in an office across the street from the World Trade Center. Julie worked for Price Waterhouse-Coopers on Wall Street. She banked at the World Trade Center.

Bob and I watched the events unfold on the living room TV. Tears rolled down our cheeks as we learned of the people trapped in the skyscrapers and of the firefighters overcome by smoke. We smelled smoke, inhaled dust and experienced that queasy feeling in one's stomach associated with fear.

We spoke by phone to Mark's parents in New York and other family members and friends, sharing shock, anger and disgust. Over the next few days, Julie and Mark learned three of their friends died on 9/11, two in the World Trade Center and one on United Flight 93.

Our nation, the land of the free and the home of the brave, was consumed by grief. Unlike acts of God, such as earthquakes and tsunamis, this was an act of men, an act of war making our world a more dangerous place.

As Pearl Harbor brought us into World War II, 9/11 brought us to the Global War on Terror, our freedom at stake, twice. The first time, three evil dictators tried to grab it; in the second, a group of evil terrorists went for the jugular.

History repeats itself. There are evil people in the world. They are jealous individuals who seek to steal our liberty and justice, high standard of living, and powers of democracy that work for most of the people most of the time.

We won World War II, eliminated the threats of Hitler, Mussolini, and Tojo. The Allies established world peace. Everybody celebrated VE day and VJ day. I remember revelers driving through the streets singing, yelling and honking horns. Americans put closure to the war and although we had to fight later wars, our soil, until September 11, 2001 was never again invaded.

After the Korean War, America engaged in the Cold War with its terrifying threats of nuclear holocaust. When Ronald Reagan ended the Cold War, complacency shrouded us in a false sense of security. We didn't take warnings seriously—the first World Trade Center bombing, the blowing up of the Khobar towers, or the attack on the Cole. We should have seen these as threats to our freedom and acted. Had we done so, 9/11 might be remembered simply as a beautiful summer day, not one of death and destruction.

The world is not a kind and gentle place. It is ruled by brute force. It always has been and always will be. Wars will forever be with us. Therefore, we must never shirk from protecting our freedoms. Until we win the War on Terror, we will never put closure on 9/11, never end the vigils at airports, our coasts and border crossings, Hoover Dam, and our nuclear power plants. People who lead a life of hiding from terrorists are not free.

The War on Terror is more difficult than World War II. Victory is elusive even with our spectacular advances in technology. We are armed with superior planes, ships, and weapons, allowing for battles involving far fewer troops. The media and its high powered technology bring us censored news, falsified accounts, and editorials pandered as news. It's misleading, divisive and unpatriotic.

We don't know where our enemies hide, in what country they live, or how to eliminate suicide bombers or control the development and spread of weapons of mass destruction.

I cried at the brutality and sadness in the movie, *United 93*. I am so proud of those brave Americans who lost their lives, but not before mortally wounding the plane to prevent it from flying into our nation's capital. It would have killed hundreds or thousands of people, including our elected government officials. The story of United 93's passengers deserves to be told. I need to be reminded of 9/11 so I never again become complacent and give in to media propaganda. I must always vote for whatever leads to permanent preservation of America's freedom.

The Ice Cream Cone

Dory Rose

"Grandma, can we go to Ben and Jerry's after my piano lesson? I worked so hard on Chopin. I need a treat, please?"

Rachel looked at me with her light blue eyes and smiled, showing her toothless front teeth. I melted.

"Okay, I'll take you, but remember whenever you get an ice cream cone, you spill it and you start to cry."

Rachel squeezed my hand. "I'll be very careful, Gram, I promise."

She was born neat. She never wore a bib. Rachel hated to soil herself. She never spilled. At the rare moment that she spilled milk, she would cry. She potty trained herself early, as she hated wearing diapers. It was a mystery how Rachel got this way. Her parents were slobs. Drawers were left open, towels left on the floor, clothes weren't hung up, dishes were left in the sink. Her dad was one of four boys, and he was used to living in a mess. He and my daughter were a perfect match. How did this delicate blonde blue-eyed little girl become a neat-nik?

I knew we were in for a battle. Again I tried to convince her,

"Rachel, we can get a candy bar or popcorn at the drug store. If you get ice cream on this hot day, it will melt and drip all over your new tee shirt."

We opened the glass door to Ben and Jerry's where we saw customers licking huge ice cream cones. Rachel inspected every tub of ice cream. She ran back and forth, frustrated by all the choices. Finally she stopped at chocolate swirl and pointed.

"I want that one and put on lots of sprinkles, and two scoops. Nuts, too, please!"

I had to stop and interfere. "Two scoops will melt and spill, Rachel."

The young man behind the counter just shrugged his shoulders, and continued to shape the cone generously. He poured the sprinkles and nuts on. Rachel jumped up and down with happy anticipation. She grabbed the huge double deck cone, and the first scoop fell. Then the second scoop plopped on the floor.

Rachel started to sob, tears pouring down her pink cheeks.

I rolled my eyes and was so tempted to say, "I told you so." But what's a grandma to do?

"That's okay, Rachel, don't cry. We'll get another cone."

The Essence of Alice

Eric H. Spitz

I was about to see Alice again after forty years. I had called her when a friend told me she was living on the Cape near me. I left my name on her machine and she called me back that night.

"Hello, Eric, how nice to hear from you." Her voice sounded tired, but familiar.

It reminded me of the day I came to Philadelphia to stay with her family for my sophomore year at Friends School. She was a senior and I fell in love with her the moment I saw her. Pretty, if not beautiful, she'd been outgoing, always friendly and full of fun.

I remembered Sunday mornings. The boys in the family played touch football in the large front yard. Jack, her older brother, was the quarterback. He lived at home while studying to be a doctor at the University of Pennsylvania. I admired him for his good looks, confidence and friendship.

One Sunday, I leaped and caught a pass from him in full stride, hoping to catch Alice's eye. She was cutting up vegetables in the kitchen preparing lunch. I tossed the ball back to Jack, and jogged casually inside. She didn't look up as I approached her, sweat dripping. Barefoot, she wore only a halter and shorts. I could see the down on her sensuous bare legs, a tantalizing bit of thigh. Her long auburn hair caressed her bare shoulders. My virgin crotch stirred but settled back on command.

"Can I help?" I asked.

"Go fetch the scrapple from the icebox and put it in a pan."

I nudged closer pretending to look at the vegetables. Her head turned suddenly and she pushed me away.

"Oh, Eric, you reek."

Words forever inscribed in my fragile ego. I rushed to the bathroom to soap my underarms.

That spring, Alice was given a small part in the school musical. She asked me to help her with lines. We spent many nights together in the attic going over them.

Some late afternoons before supper, Alice would take a half-hour to kindly offer me dancing lessons. She demonstrated the Lindy, her lithe body moving gracefully to a jitterbug record. She would take my hand and move me back and forth to the rhythms. Then came the precious moments of slow-dancing, her dear head nestled on my eager shoulder, her warmth pressing educationally.

Too soon it was June. I was leaving for New York to be with my parents. She would be off to college before I got back. My suitcase packed, I stopped by her room to say goodbye.

"Take care, old boy." She gave my arm a quick squeeze and resumed her reading. As I picked up my suitcase, she looked up again and gave me that teasing smile I would always remember.

Arriving at the Sheraton after so many years, I saw a small woman sitting on a bench. Her glasses hung from a string around her neck. Her hair was closely cropped and pure white. She was wearing open sandals and her frail legs were bare. I would not have recognized her except for the penetrating deep blue eyes.

"Is it you, Eric?" She rose with some difficulty. I held her closely as never before.

We talked for two hours over drinks. She told me about her brother Jack, his suicide, her depression and shock treatments, her painful divorce and her grown children.

"I can't believe it. Jack was always so confident. Everyone looked up to him."

"He had problems we never knew about. He seemed like a man's man to the world, but underneath he was very fragile." She wiped away her tears and regarded me carefully. "The only thing I remember about you, Eric, is your big brown eyes."

"For me it was a wonderful year in my life. I thought you were the perfect girl. Do you remember our rehearsals for *Iolanthe* in the attic?"

"No, but I do recall after the show your telling me I was overacting."

I'd forgotten that.

We promised to stay in touch. Driving home, my fantasies took me to the large field that separated the commuter station from Alice's house where we threw the football around.

She is standing in her cheerleader's outfit. The white sweater outlines the perfection of her youthful breasts. She's wearing bobby socks. Her blue eyes are welcoming me and her arms reach for me. I am no longer an insecure, skinny tenth grader. I have become a handsome successful businessman, actor and singer. I bury myself in her arms and kiss her passionately.

Some days after our reunion I called Alice again and got her voice mail. I said I'd call again.

I never did.

The Great Leo

Ralph Spencer

God created men and women born under the astrological sign of Leo to be great natural leaders, visionaries, charismatic, popular and brilliant. A Leo stands out from the also-rans born under other astrological signs. When Leos enter the world, the spotlight of the universe shines on their heads and shoulders with mega-watt power.

I am a Leo! Born in the oppressive heat of a New York City summer day, great expectations fell upon me.

As a preschooler, my father who had experimental recording equipment—an old-fashioned wire record—encouraged me to make up stories with dialogue. These would be recorded.

In first grade, the class put on a play for parents and other students. Actually the play was completely narrated by one person with the others acting out the narration. I was the narrator.

In sixth grade, there was a city-wide Christmas program in Nashville, Tennessee where my family had moved. I was chosen to read the biblical Christmas story.

In high school, I gravitated to public speaking. Teamed up with a brilliant Jewish student, Andy Silver, we became a fantastic debate duo in Tennessee Interscholastic Debate.

In college, I became part of the university's radio station, getting my own show in my junior year.

And when I chose a career, I found myself going to Theological School and studying for the Christian ministry. I have been expected to write and deliver a 3500 word essay, called a sermon, every Sunday morning for more than forty years.

Add to this my life-long passion to be a magician. I have developed and performed an hour long magic show with my stage name Dr. Magic.

Need I say more? Leo's are the divinely appointed center-pieces of humanity!

BUT…. (and there is always a "but") … underneath the bravado, behind the façade of the self-assured extrovert, there is an insecure, faltering and too often failing soul. There is a person aware of his or her clay feet, filled with human weaknesses that appear at times to be wider than the Pacific Ocean, deeper than the Grand Canyon.

My father had to run around the room with the microphone to capture my make-believe story. I failed to stay put in one place as my father told me to do. As a four year old, excited by being recorded, I couldn't stand still as I acted out my fantasy.

On the night of the performance as narrator, I forgot half of the play and over ten characters never made it on stage.

My parents gently told me that at the city-wide Christmas show I read the part about the shepherds leaving their flocks to the manger too fast.

Andy and I didn't win the big debate in Tennessee and so we were only number three instead of number one.

All too often I put the needle down wrong on the record I was airing on WGRE 91.7 FM. I would announce one song and a different tune would come out.

My inside hope to be a golden-tongued preacher like Billy Graham or Robert Schuller never materialized. Over the many years I served as minister, I had to accept the reality that I was an ordinary journeyman preacher like countless of my colleagues struggling with self-doubts and ordinary human passions.

And only my wife experiences the angst I go through prior to a magic show. Knowing all the possible places to screw up, I am a true basket case.

Perhaps, a Leo is really no different than a Gemini or a Capricorn—a person who has good and bad hair days, a person who loves, cares, serves others and pursues personal desires, wants and passions. Likely God created humans pretty much the same—a wonderful conglomeration of conflicting feelings, emotions, hopes, dreams, and loves. As hard as it is for a Leo to say, I have come to the point where I know that's all right.

The Miss That Became A Hit

Gitta M Gorman

Stockholm, Sweden, 1944.

Boom! Boom! Bang!

I woke up terrified from the horrific noise. The five story building shook as if it had been hit by an earthquake. The blackened windows of our apartment rattled.

It had all been so peaceful when I had gone to sleep. My mother had been in the kitchen. I could tell from the awful smell that she was roasting roasted dry yellow peas again to sneak into the coffee beans, her clever way of stretching the rationed coffee. Food, gasoline, and all luxury items were controlled by coupons because of World War II.

Also, the smells from my father's oil paints and turpentine had drifted into my bedroom as I'd closed my eyes. If my father had been working in our flower shop, he would have arranged the blue, red, and purple anemones in front of him into a vase. Now, due to lack of customers, he transformed the picture in his mind into an oil painting. His way of therapy.

Now my bed rocked.

I heard my father lose his balance, and there was the sound of paints and brushes hitting the floor.

He rushed into my bedroom, and came to my bed to hold me.

My mother screamed from the kitchen. "What was that? What happened?" Then she rushed to join us.

Father tried to calm both of us down, but the expression in his brown eyes betrayed him. He was terrified. When he found his voice, he said, "I know what it is. It sounded just like that in Berlin when I was growing up." My father had lived there during World War I.

Mother looked at him, horrified. "A bomb? But Sweden is not in the war. We are a neutral country."

I started to cry. I was only eight-years-old.

278

"You two stay here," my father commanded. "I'll have to go to the flower shop to make sure the display windows haven't been shattered by the blast. People are quick to steal money when it's so scarce to come by."

"You'd better go." My mother held me tight. "I left the money we made today in the cash register because it wasn't very much. Who can afford the luxury of buying flowers during war time?" She sighed deeply.

No answer. He had already left.

A few hours later, *Pappa* came back with a happy grin on his face. He cradled a bottle of *Akvavit* in each arm like they were babies.

"Our flower shop is intact."

"Thank God," my mother said. "But where did you get the *Akvavit?*"

"I did what a lot of other people did. The windows of *Systembolaget* (the Government Controlled Liquor Store) were all shattered. There were a lot of people there helping themselves to all the liquor bottles they could carry."

My mother frowned. "Including you."

"You know how expensive liquor is, plus you're only permitted one liter per month these days. So I took two. Not a big deal really." He sounded embarrassed.

My mother shrugged her shoulders. "What can I say?"

"Get two schnapps glasses on the table in the kitchen. Let's drink some of this to calm our nerves. You, little one, will just have to go to bed." He hugged me. "Don't be afraid. The bomb must have been dropped by mistake."

The next day, we heard on the radio that the bombs had missed their target, the important ship lock *Hammarbyslussen* between *Lake Mälaren* and the *Baltic*. They detonated in the east end of *Eriksdalslunden,* a park close to our residential area.

No casualties, no damages, just a big crater. The Swedes were shocked. Who did it? Nobody knew. The incident was hushed down. Sweden remained a neutral country.

Years later, it was determined that Russian war planes dropped the bombs by mistake. One block of the residential area close to *Eriksdalslunden* is now named *Den Ryska Smällen* (The Russian Bang).

The ship lock *Hammarbyslussen* has not changed since 1944, but the crater did. What did the Swedes do with it?

"How about building some swimming pools?" they asked themselves. "No excavation needed for this project."

The miss in 1944 became a hit in 1950 when *Eriksdalsbadet* opened for the first time for the recreation and enjoyment of the residents of Stockholm. *Eriks-*

dalsbadet was rebuilt in 1999 and now boasts five indoor swimming pools and five outdoor swimming pools to accommodate swimmers of all ages.

Nowadays, few people know about or remember the dark night in 1944 when the bombs fell. But I do. I have my father's oil painting, *The Anemones*, signed by him in 1944 hanging on a wall in my living room.

It's worth more to me than the most famous oil painting in the world.

The Umbrella

Else Jacobs

Early one morning I was having breakfast on my kitchen patio and happened to look up at my umbrella. I noticed it had some holes in it and seemed worn and faded. I had enjoyed it for a long time.

One part of me said, *"I certainly need a new umbrella, but I'll be soon leaving for Seattle where I plan to spend four months. Maybe I should wait till I return?"*

Another part of me said, *"But I'm having company, in a couple of weeks. My nephew from Norway is stopping over for a few days on a business trip. It would be nice to spruce up my patio a bit!"*

I pondered on this for a while, but since I don't like shopping, I just dropped the whole idea, thinking, *"If it's meant to be, it will be."*

A few days later I stopped off at one of the nearby markets to pick up a few things for supper. While waiting in line at the cashier's, I noticed I was standing under a nice umbrella.

"Nine feet wide," the advertisement said.

I looked at the price tag which was practically right in front of my face. Yes, the price was right! "This is it. I want this umbrella."

At this moment I noticed a gentleman standing next to me. I never saw him walk toward me. It was almost like he had dropped down from the umbrella and landed beside me.

He smiled, "Isn't that a nice umbrella. I need a new one. They have them in all kinds of colors."

"Yes, I know, but I'm getting this red one," I said as if that was the only one in the store.

"I want a blue one, that's my color. Let's both buy one, and I'll take yours home. I have a truck. Do you live nearby?"

"Yes, on Golf Club Drive."

"And I live in Canyon Country Club. My name is Bill."

"Hi, I'm Else."

During our purchase I found out that the umbrellas had been put on the floor that very day.

We chatted for a while. I learned that he was a "snowbird" and spends his summers in Washington, south of Seattle. I shared my plans of spending four months in Seattle since my son and his family live there. "I like Seattle very much," I said.

He was just beaming. I could almost hear him thinking, *"what a co-incidence and what fun!"*

When I saw the small box the umbrella came in, I said: "I can easily get mine in my car."

No, that was out of the question! He handed me his business card with his name, phone numbers and addresses. "Retired veterinarian. Hobbies: Flying airplanes and horseback riding."

"I'll follow you home and bring the umbrella on to your patio."

"Ok," I agreed. I couldn't easily get out of this without being rude.

"I'm single," he seemed proud to announce, "and I guess you are too." He probably had been searching for a ring on my finger.

After arriving at my patio, he quickly picked up the old umbrella and took it to the trash area. Quite professionally, he unpacked the new one and placed it into the umbrella hole in my white table. Then he opened it.

"Yes, it looks great," we both agreed.

"Else, I'd like to take you out for lunch, maybe on Sunday. You seem like good company. I'll give you a call."

I felt safe in giving him my number. He seemed like a decent guy. I thanked him very much for the help. "Good-bye and see you later."

Sunday morning arrived. I went for an early walk, followed by breakfast, listened to some music and did a few chores around the house. I couldn't help but wonder about my lunch date.

At about eleven o'clock I started getting hungry for lunch, made myself a sandwich and enjoyed eating it.

Having just swallowed the last bite, the phone rang. Yes, it was he.

"How about lunch?" he asked.

"I got so hungry I just finished my lunch."

"Oh," he said, "well, I had a late and long breakfast with some old classmates of mine that are in town."

"So when can I see you?" he asked.

I was not the slightest interested in seeing him. He seemed too needy for company.

"How about next Sunday?" I suggested.

"Oh, I can't wait that long! Can't I see you before then?"

"Well, you see, Bill, I'm pretty busy and still working."

We chatted a little, said goodbye, and that was the end of the "relationship." I never heard any more from him.

He certainly was looking for a woman. I was not looking for a man. But he was instrumental in my quick purchase and delivery, for which I am grateful. I believe that people come into our lives for a certain purpose and may disappear just as quickly.

Epilogue:

I have a single Norwegian friend who lives in the Cathedral Canyon Country Club. I told her this story and gave her a suggestion:

"If you ever see an elderly gentleman sitting alone under a blue umbrella, tell him you have a friend that has a red one."

Time and Space

Mary Burton Olson M.D.

June 2, 2006, Kelsey, our only grandchild, celebrated her first birthday. Nothing could deter us from her party. I thought of holding her soft body in the night sky, and singing *Twinkle, Twinkle Little Star* to her.

My husband, Bob, drove his planned itinerary. Zion and Bryce National Parks were first stops between home, Rancho Mirage, and Kelsey's domain, Denver, Colorado.

We had to extend our necks way back to see the tops of Zion's majestic peaks meet the clouds. Their multicolored sedimentary strata, some perpendicular and others horizontal, reminded me of The Grand Canyon. I thought of the millions of years required for formation. Crashing tectonic plates, earthquakes, volcanoes, and erosions combined to reshape and reorient mountains.

In both parks. we photographed the shapes, colors, and light reflections of rock formations. At Bryce, bright reds predominated. I recalled similar iron pigments at Sedona. We would have stayed longer, but couldn't be late for the birthday party.

We drove through Utah's breath-taking scenery to reach the familiar ski mountains of Colorado, and finally Kelsey's home on San Juan Range Road in Littleton. Our moods had taken on spirituality appropriate to the miracle of Kelsey, a perfect little person complete with 25,000 genes, a fourth of which were mine. All were ancient having been carried out of Africa over 50,000 years ago and handed down from generation to generation.

Kelsey delighted us with smiles, coos and attempts to walk along the couch no handed. Bright colored helium filled balloons floated above her as she played away her waking hours. Two days of entertaining Kelsey (or she us) were perfect.

We headed home taking a southern route. At Santé Fe, we visited a historical museum displaying memorabilia of the past three centuries, a time so short compared to the ages of mountains and Kelsey's genes. Native Americans of Santé Fe are related to Kelsey through African ancestors who lived 500 centuries ago. The forefathers of American Indians took an eastern route through Asia and across the Bering Straight, and Kelsey's a western road to Europe.

The Painted Desert and Petrified Forest presented us with more thoughts of antiquity. We photographed Indian petroglyphs, drawings on rocks etched out a thousand years ago, and the tree stones of the Petrified Forest, 50–250 million years old. The beauty of the reds, yellows and browns of iron, the blues and greens of copper, the black of manganese and carbon and the whites of quartz inspired us to buy two pieces.

We accidentally found and visited Meteor Crater, near Flagstaff, Arizona, and learned it was created by the impact of a meteorite 50,000 years ago. It measures 1.2 kilometers in diameter and is 200 meters deep. It reminded us of the dinosaur extinction 66 million years ago by a much bigger meteorite striking the Yucatan Peninsula in Mexico.

Home with our memories, pictures and petrified wood, we realized the trip had not ended, but merely begun. Our curiosity, fueled by our trip, led us to read *The Blue Planet* by Brian J. Skinner, Stephen C. Porter, and Daniel B. Botkin. We also viewed 56 astronomy lectures on CD by Dr. Alec Filippenko, and read *Krakatoa* by Simon Winchester.

In *The Blue Planet,* we learned the details of earth's formation through the explosion of a massive star about five billion years ago. This event is referred to as a super nova. It ejected gaseous materials that coalesced to form our solar system, its sun, planets, and moons. We were taught about protons and electrons interacting as in a nuclear bomb to fuse hydrogen atoms into helium. This is the source of energy in our sun.

Carbon, oxygen and nitrogen are formed in fusion reactions at other phases in the lives of stars. Heavy minerals, like those found in petrified wood, are only created in super nova explosions. All earth's minerals are more than five billion years old, even those in our bodies, yours and mine, and baby Kelsey's.

In astronomy lectures, we studied the energy of our sun and other stars. We learned how far away solar bodies are from us and each other, and about the lengthy life cycles of the hundreds of billions of stars in our galaxy. We learned of mass and energy and reviewed Einstein's famous formula. We garnered other laws of physics explaining the formation of our universe. We're only half way through the course. I look forward to what I'll learn in the second half.

On Aug. 27th, 1883, Krakatoa, an island volcano in Indonesia, exploded. It eliminated an island, killed nearly 40,000 people and affected the entire earth. It spewed gases that circled our planet three times, clouded the skies for months and caused temperatures to fall.

Energy operating throughout time and space is what life's all about, yours, mine and Kelsey's. At her second birthday party, I will point to the sky and sing *Twinkle, Twinkle Little Star, Now I Know What You Are.*

Too Short, Too Sweet

Eleanor Tyus Johnson

"You, two, come here!"

It was my mother's voice with her "right now" sound in it. My sister and I immediately began to move towards her voice.

"Miss Brown will be here in an hour. You are starting piano lessons today."

PIANO LESSONS! She hadn't said anything about this. Not a clue. Well, maybe there had been a clue.

Last month we'd all gone to a recital for Miss Brown's students. My mother's friend's daughter was performing and had invited us to attend. Betty played okay, but I couldn't figure out the song she was playing. She kept running her fingers up and down the keys like she was exercising them or something. Everyone clapped a lot when she finished. She seemed to have liked what she'd done and kept smiling and smiling. Miss Brown seemed pleased for she, too, just smiled and smiled.

I wasn't sure that I liked what my mother was saying. Yes, I had thought that one day I would like to learn to play the piano when I was older … maybe twelve, but not at nine.

"Better clean up a bit," my mother continued, as she stepped back to look at the piano she was dusting.

It was a big, black Story & Clark upright that had stood against the north wall of our living room since before I was born. We had played with it since we were large enough to sit on the bench and touch the pedals. It was an ideal attention-holder with lots of buttons, levers, pedals, and all kinds of movable gadgets. Rectangular boxes filled with punched paper rolls sat nearby. A single roll could be pushed into a box-like compartment above the piano keys. Then all you had to do was push a button, move the pedals alternately with your feet and you would have music. Another button would make the keys go up and down as if they were being played. *The World Is Waiting For The Sunrise* and *Tea For Two* brought me hours of pleasure as well as healthy exercise.

"If we take lessons from Miss Brown, will we have to play in a recital on a stage in front of everybody?" I asked.

"In time, I suppose. But you're getting ahead of yourself. That's way down the road. Years away," my mother said.

"How many?"

"Several. You've got to learn to read music and play it. Then you've got to strengthen your fingers and technique so you will be able to play runs smoothly and effortlessly," Mother said.

She said it would be several years before I'd have to play in a concert. So what am I doing sitting on this stage less than two years after my first lesson? And why am I having difficulty breathing every time I look out at that big auditorium with all of those people looking at me? And why is my little lace hanky a damp ball and my hands still so wet?

All of Miss Brown's piano students are sitting in two rows at the side of the stage. We are to keep our eyes on Miss Brown and when she points to you and smiles, its doomsday, your turn.

My mother and sister are seated out there somewhere. After a few months, Miss Brown and my mother had agreed that my sister's talents must lie in another direction and she was allowed to quit her lessons. They also agreed that I had potential so I was encouraged to continue.

I can't panic now. I've got to do this. Let's see … The hardest part is those runs at the end. I've practiced them hundreds of times. I'll go over them again in my mind … 1—2—3—4 Good. Once more … 1—2—3—4. I know them. I'll try one more time. 1—2 … Miss Brown is pointing at me. My turn!

I try to smile, as directed, rise, and walk to the piano in the center of the stage. I sit in front of it and stare at the row of black and white keys as if I've never seen them before in life. Start! *I tell myself and place my damp hands on the keys.* Remember the runs. I think as I play the opening introduction. You have to keep them smooth … and no hesitation.

I begin the main melody. It builds smoothly and begins to resolve. Then my fingers begin racing up the keyboard. The runs … I'm playing them and I'm doing it fast and smoothly … no hesitation. Great! *Now a few closing chords following the runs … Slow it down … The last note … I'm through. That wasn't so bad.*

I smile, rise, and walk back to my seat. Miss Brown is looking at me a little odd, and she isn't smiling. I played all of the runs swiftly and smoothly. Surely she is pleased. I take a deep breath and sit down. Why isn't she smiling? Then it hit me. The melody of my composition is repeated for the last time just before the hard runs on the last page. I had played the introduction and only the last page of my selection. *What an idiot! No wonder she isn't smiling. I've ruined the recital.*

Then a thought passed through my mind and a smile touched the corner of my lips. *Maybe this performance would convince Miss Brown and my mother that my talents must lie in another direction.*

Writing Aerobics

- • Act Your Age •
- • The Night Sky •
- • Regrets •

Act Your Age

◆

A 14 Minute Writing Exercise, May 16, 2007

Dolores Carruthers

"Act your age," she said, smiling thinly to cover the insult.

"And if I did would that make you love me?" her daughter asked.

"What a ridiculous question," her mother snapped. "Acting your age has nothing to do with love. It's behavior that I'm talking about."

"Why do I have the feeling that they're related? That if I act my age, what am I now 40," a pause, "if I act my age then you'll act like a loving mother?"

Silence filled the space between them, eyes looking everywhere except at each other. The many battles between mother-daughter had caused a chasm larger than acting one's age could fill.

"Oh for heaven's sake," her mother muttered. "You know I love you. I'm just not one to go around telling you. If you acted your age, you'd know that. Instead you act like a child whining for her mommy's attention."

The daughter, eyes hot with hurt, looked directly at her mother. "I could freeze to death on what you call love." she said, and stalked out of the room.

The tears she'd been hoarding until she was out of sight fell quickly. Perhaps her mother did love her. Except, during their fights, her mothers stabbing words injured the daughter's most tender places causing doubts about that love.

Tossing her head to clear away her tears, she continued walking away from the battlefield of their relationship, unaware that there was another wounded left behind.

Judy Cohn

"Act your age," he said. "You can't yell and scream every time you don't get your way."

"I don't want to go to school and that's that."

293

"I don't understand why. You were up all night doing your work. You're certainly well prepared."

"It stinks. It's awful. The class will laugh at me."

"Don't be ridiculous. If they laugh, they'll be laughing with you, not at you. Now hurry up, and finish getting dressed. We'll have breakfast together."

"I'm not hungry. Besides, I gained two pounds this week so I'm not eating breakfast."

"That's some way to start the day. You're the one who's always talking about good nutrition."

"Screw nutrition. I'm going to drink a can of coke and then go back to bed."

"The hell you are, Sandy. Now finish putting on your clothes and get into the damn car. Your students will really be upset if their teacher is late."

Phyllis Costello

"Act your age," my husband ordered.

How does a thirty-five year old act? I wondered. I sure wish you would act your age. You must have been born an old man.

My inner fun-loving child had stepped out at a cast party, after a theatre opening.

Dancing around barefoot had been my way of celebrating.

"Put your shoes on. I think we better go home."

"Yes, Grampa."

"I don't like theatre people. They are immoral and strange."

"What? What did you just say?"

"I said theatre people are immoral and strange. I don't want you associating with them, anymore."

"How can I do theatre, if I don't associate with them?"

"You can't."

I sat stunned and silent. My husband had removed the one pleasure I enjoyed outside my home.

It was the beginning of the end of the marriage.

Shirley Gibson

"Act your age you're not a teenager," my daughter said. I was about to go on a date for the first time since my divorce.

I met Robert at the pet grooming shop. He had his lab in for grooming. I had Fluffy there for a shampoo. We talked about our dogs. After some time we exchanged phone numbers.

Robert called last week asking me out to the country club for a dinner dance. He is six foot tall with a slender built. He gets his tan completely from days of golfing.

"Well how do I look Samantha?"

"Mom, lets work on your hair. It needs a little fluff; some hair spray will keep the style. I'll show you some make up tips also."

I was wearing an emerald green, knee-length sleeveless dress with a matching shawl. My beaded bag swung loosely over my shoulder, picking up the glitter of my necklace and earrings. The dress would flair out slightly when I danced. Inside I felt like a teenager on my first date. I was singing as I swirled around the foyer pretending to dance.

When I opened the door he looked so handsome that my stomach felt like butterflies dancing. I don't know if I will act my age of forty-two, I thought.

Gitta Gorman

"Act your age," my daughter said to me when I was fifty. I was stunned at the way she talked to me, but now I realize she had given me very good advice.

She had seen me looking in the mirror, not pleased with my image. Gray hair was growing in. "Do you think I should have it streaked or colored?" I had asked her.

"No, Mom. Act your age. You're a beautiful fifty-year-old woman. Adding chemicals to your thick wavy hair would only ruin it. They'll ruin its texture little by little. Why not age gracefully?" she added.

"How do I do that?"

"By having positive attitudes, eating healthy and doing your exercise. That will keep you young forever."

Now twenty years later, I do have great looking, silver-gray hair that I'm very proud of.

Have you seen the movie *The Devil Wears Prada*? I think Meryl Streep looked stunning in her grey hair. Maybe she will make it fashionable?

I sure hope so.

Else Jacob

Three-year-old Bobby was making a nuisance of himself at his younger brother's birthday party. He just wanted to do everything his way.

He didn't mind his parents who asked him to sit down at the table to have some cake.

His mother said firmly, "Bobby, act your age!"

"What do you think I'm doing?" he said. "I'm acting like a three-year-old!"

Eleanor Tyus Johnson

"Act your age, Mother!" My daughter was laughing at me.

What age is that? I thought: the age I feel, the age I'd like to be, or the age I am.

Today is so hot that sitting motionless on the patio is strenuous work and sapping my energy. I feel like I should be jumping up and down in the pool, trying to splash all of the water out of it like a seven-year-old. Or maybe I should just swim back and forth counting the laps as they go by ... I think I'll sit at the edge of the pool under the umbrella, and dangle my feet in the water.

The age I'd like to be would find me deep in the lush forests surrounding Lake Michigan. It is always cool there and walking is a favorite pastime. We walk to the store.

We walk to the lake. We walk to the neighbor's farm. A five mile hike is just a stroll, and with good company it is pure pleasure.

The age I am limits my activeness: not as much swimming, less walking and a lot of sitting around. I do have time to read all of the books that I want and my trips to the library have become regular excursions including "lunching out." There is no excuse for not having time to practice my organ. (*My friends say I sound better than ever*). Everyone volunteers to drive me anywhere I need to go, (I *don't think they want me to get near the steering-wheel),* and most household chores are considered too strenuous or too trivial for Great-Gran's time ... Hmmm.

Maybe I'll just have to let my mind do most of my splashing and walking and take my daughter's advice. Act my age.

Anita Knight

Act your age, Mother told me enumerable times. I know she didn't mean for me to suck my thumb at two, wet my pants at four, pick my nose at eight, but these were the things I was probably doing when she uttered those words. What she really wanted was for me to act older and behave as if I were already fully grown.

If she were here today, she would still chide me, for now, at seventy-three, I run around in ratty jeans, often without a bra, for goodness sake, with sunburned skin, and hair that responds to every slight summer breeze as if it were a hurricane.

No, Mom, I guess I never will act my age, for now I am reliving the teenage years I didn't enjoy because of your strict rules. I eat and drink things that aren't good for me, swear when I feel like it, sleep in when I want to, and am generally irresponsible.

Maybe someday I will get the hang of being grown up, but not yet!

Carol Mann

"Act your age," she said, folding the last of her cocktail dresses into a bag bound for the senior center thrift store. They were so pretty she hated to part with them.

"Come on." Harry stuffed his hands into the pockets of his polyester pants. "Let's go down to the Spa Casino. It's Salsa Night."

"Salsa night?" Edith plunked her hands on her hips. She was tired of his outlandish ideas. "I have plenty of salsa and chips in the cupboard." She went back to folding the remnants of younger years.

Harry scratched his high forehead, made higher by gray hair inching backward. "I mean salsa dancing. You know. One, two, cha-cha-cha or whatever they do."

Edith clamped her mouth. The old fool. I ache in every joint and he dodders like a sail trying to catch the wind.

Harry's raised eyebrows crinkled his forehead. He licked his lips. Edith knew the look. He was up to something, like he was about to close a car deal, like he did for forty years. "How about this? We'll ask our grandson George to paint the kitchen."

She stopped folding. The kitchen had not been painted in over twenty years. Harry always argued it was too much fuss and commotion at their age.

"You'd actually do that?" She stood a little straighter. Maybe she could try a little dancing.

"Yep. And something else. I want you to wear one of those pretty dresses."

"Oh, Harry, for Pete's sake, I can't get myself into any of these."

"I remember the red one. You looked like Ava Gardner."

Edith felt her cheeks flush. Maybe a seam could be let out here and there.

Later that evening she and Harry walked into the Spa Casino and, after many questions and directions, found the Salsa Dance Party. Harry was oblivious to the snide remarks of several young people about to join the gyrating bodies on the dance floor.

Edith heard, but she didn't care. She never felt so grand.

Cheryl McFadden

"Joshua, for heaven's sake, act your age. When are you ever going to grow up?"

I overheard a frazzled mother admonish her rambunctious young son, the other day, in the grocery store as she attempted to control him and, at the same time, tend to a squirming baby in the cart. It was obvious that neither child shared her agenda.

I was once that mother, and although I only had one baby, I, too, was overwhelmed by the entire ordeal—anxious to be through with the diapers, the teething and the all-nighters. Later I wanted to hurry him through the terrible twos, the sleepovers, and especially, the teen years. "When will you ever grow up," I often mumbled between clenched teeth.

While sympathizing with the young woman, I suddenly remembered an incident that had taken place in a grocery store nearly 30 years earlier when my son was less than a year old. Brian was fidgeting and fussing in the seat as I grabbed items from the shelves and tossed them into the cart, hoping to set some sort of land speed record and get out of there with a portion of my sanity still intact, when an older woman tentatively approached us.

She reached out and gently touched his wispy blonde curls and brushed his silky cheek, "Hang onto these moments as long as you can—before you know it he'll be grown and gone," she tearfully warned before turning and walking away.

She was right; Brian did grow up—so terribly fast.

Perhaps I should have approached the young woman in the store and warned her, "Don't be in such a hurry—before you know it he'll be grown and gone."

Mary Burton Olson, M.D.

"Act your age," she said to her husband. "You're five years older than I and behaving like a child." She looked away from him.

"With age comes wisdom." Bill drove 30 miles per hour above the speed limit and passed a sporty red convertible.

"You've made my point. You drive like a stupid teenager." She turned her head to look out her window.

She never saw the traffic light turn red. She didn't see the cement mixer stop for it. If she heard the screeching brakes or the sound of impact, she didn't remember it.

Her first memory was that of a chorus of sirens ringing in her semiconscious mind. She opened her eyes and saw through her cracked windshield the oncoming flashing red lights of police cars. She turned her head left. Her heart stopped when she viewed the empty seat next to her and the missing glass on the driver's side of the windshield. She tried to scream, but no sound escaped her paralyzed vocal cords.

A fluttering sensation in her left chest coincided with the touch of a hand grasping her arm. A strange voice instructed her to breathe deeply. She took a deep abdominal breath and scanned the road in front of the Lexus. There beside the open door of a police car, she saw Bill sitting beside a huge red splotch on the cement. Paramedics were bandaging his head.

"He's sitting up and talking. He'll be all right," said her deep breathing coach who unfastened her seat belt. "I guess your husband didn't believe in buckling up."

"I guess not," she said.

When will you act his age? she silently asked Bill.

Ralph Spencer

"Act your age," he said to his 72-year-old father. "Dad, you're not the spring chicken you once were."

"I can't help it," the father responded.

"What do you mean?"

"Twenty-two years ago I made a list of all the things I wanted to do before I died. One by one I've checked them off. This is next on the list."

"Right, for a guy in his twenties," the son retorted.

"I must do it—even if it kills me."

The son said, "Going down in a mini-sub, crawling out of the air lock with scuba equipment to take pictures of sharks up close is **NOT** for you."

"Son, I love you for your concern. But Ma and me talked it over. She's not thrilled about it but I've pestered her so long she's finally relented. I'm going to do it."

"I give up," the son said. "You can do what you jolly well please. But don't expect me to pay the undertaker to put your body back together after the shark's ripped it apart."

The father looked aggrieved. "I'd really like your blessing."

"Can't do it, Dad."

"How about your support?"

"Nope. No way," the son shook his head. He paused. "I've got only one question for you, Dad. Does your $3 million life insurance cover you for this?"

The Night Sky

◆

A 16 Minute Writing Exercise,
November 7, 2007

Judy Cohn

I look up into the night sky and see a figure. It is floating between the stars. It dips and turns as it bounces over the mile high mountains. I'm amazed. I run inside for my binoculars. I peer through the lens. I make out a creature. It's face down with two arms stretched wide and legs trailing through the darkness.

It can't be. It looks human, but it can't be. It twists around and I see a face framed by blonde hair. Its hand reaches up. Fingers open and close. My goodness, it seems to be waving. I wave back. I can't believe I'm doing this. I focus on the face. It's smiling. I adjust my binoculars, look very closely, and let out a scream. It's me. It's me. I'm flying. I'm flying. Wow. My dream has come true.

Virginia Cummings

I looked up into the night sky to see if I could recognize a familiar star formation. My dad, a former sea captain, told me there were signs in the sky that helped them navigator ships before all the techie equipment became available.

I watch the night sky often. I can find the Big and Little Dipper. There are other star formations astrologists use to forecast the future. I have heard that all astrological signs are shown in the stars.

I know from checking the charts that I am a Gemini. The stars were dim when I was born at 8:00 AM in the morning, but that hasn't dimmed my life at all.

By the time I find my birth sign on the star chart and set myself to study the night sky, I am so engrossed in the beauty I usually put my book down and watch with wonder.

I don't know for sure if the stars affect your life and times. I just love resting and watching the stars twinkle. I wonder how far away they are and who, if anyone, keeps the stars in formation. I wonder, too, if anyone in my lifetime will ever travel far enough to touch or see a star up close.

Shirley Gibson

I looked up into the night sky and saw three lights traveling in unison from far off in the distance forming a triangular shape. As I focused more closely, I realized that there were three more sets of lights. They were floating across the night sky as a thief creeping upon its prize. Could that be a plane? As the thought escaped my mind, the lights stopped. Well, that answered my question. It wasn't a plane.

I was sitting in a rocking chair on my uncle's back porch at two in the morning. After sleeping for several hours, I was unable to return to sleep. Enjoying the quietness of the cool night air was something that refreshed me. Looking at the stars gave me a feeling of peace.

This night was turning out to be exciting. I aimed my binoculars towards the mountains. I had used them earlier that day for bird watching. The groups of lights were like children playing a game of hide and seek. The crafts dashed through the night sky then stopped turning off the lights only to reappear somewhere else with them on. All at once in unison, the crafts became a cloudscape of color: red, blue, orange, green. The lights flashed from one color to another. What were they saying? Did the colors mean something?

As I pondered over the lights, they started to move in my direction. I was motionless as they came nearer. Could this be a UFO?

Losing track of time was easy as I was caught up in the show. I can't believe I feel asleep, but when I woke up in the morning, I was in my bed. I don't remember going to bed, just remember them coming closer. The television made no mention of them. Then I searched the newspaper—there was no spotting of any kind. Did I dream all this?

Bill Hinthorn

I look up at the night sky to see Orion, the Hunter, throw his leg over the horizon as he climbs higher in the sky to begin his nightly hunt. I imagine his thirst as he reaches for a drink of cool water from the Little Dipper. But Ursa Major, the Great Bear, the never-to-be-caught prey of Orion, is watchful. They're both condemned to an eternal waltz, of hunter and hunted, through the night sky. Polaris, the North Star, points the way for the Ursa Major toward Orion, but the wary Great Bear never follows its lead, carefully keeping its distance from the Hunter.

Gemini twins, Castor and Pollux, a short distance from Orion and his eternal prey, seem to show an eternal lack of interest in Orion's hunt, but dance the night away across the night sky.

Anita Knight

I look up into the night sky, pleased to live in a spot that gives me such a clear view of the twinkling stars. I feel the presence of those who are no longer with me, and I am peaceful as I speak to them.

I tell my mother what is going on in my life. I thank her for guiding me and being there through thick and thin. I let my dad know how sorry I am that I didn't tell him I loved him often enough, and wish he were still here to remind me how important it is to laugh. I tell my infant son David that I never forget him, although he only lived for six short weeks, and I tell many others who enriched my life how glad I am that they were part of it.

Will I see them again someday? Nobody knows the answer to that, but it's okay. I can see them as often as I want, by raising my head and looking up into the night sky.

Carol Mann

I look into the night sky at the Big Dipper. I want it to scoop me up and transport me away.

I shake off my foolishness. No one can scoop away the problem that confronts me. No one can change things. I want to find my son.

When I entered the Cedar Pines Home for Unwed Mothers fifty years ago, I felt trapped. At sixteen, I was too young to have a baby. My life was ruined. I didn't know how to take care of a child. But I could feel the love grow in my heart. This was *my* baby, *my* child.

"You will give the child up. It will be placed in a good home." My father glared at me. My mother nodded her head, an automaton.

My parents were shamed by my actions and embarrassed in the community. My younger brother stopped talking to me. An older sister called me stupid. Extended family shunned us. Friends turned their heads.

At Cedar Pines, I found myself with other frightened, lonely girls. When my time came, I gave up my son. He was whisked away. His father never saw him. He didn't care.

Today at my computer, I look for a 50 year old man—my son, Robert. Bobby.

Big Dipper, if you could put me back in time, give me back the years, how grateful I would be to know my little boy.

I can only hope he wants to know me.

Cheryl McFadden

I looked up into the night sky waiting for the meteor shower to begin. It was 1:00 a.m.—way past my bed time and it was too cold to be outside in bare feet and light-weight pajamas, but the astronomers had promised a once-in-a-lifetime celestial show. So there I stood, whining and freezing, along with my best friend Chris, the self-proclaimed cruise director in my life, always nudging and prodding me to be "spontaneous." This was entirely her idea; I was just the grumpy passenger who came along for the ride.

"Come on, Chris, let's go in, it's late and there's not a meteor in sight," I complained as I hopped back and forth from foot to foot in a feeble attempt to keep warm.

"Just wait, it's gonna be spectacular," she gushed with her usual enthusiasm.

"Right now sleep would be spectacular," I grumbled.

I continued fidgeting for what seemed like an eternity, when suddenly a streak of white light sped across the sky, followed by another, and yet another. Dozens of meteors slashed through the blackness before disappearing into the inky void.

The magnificent display continued for more than an hour while far below two infinitesimal specs on a blue planet looked up in awe, completely unaware of time and cold feet.

Mary Burton Olson, M.D.

I looked up into the night sky. Darkness and cold enveloped me, no moon, not one star, a twinkle-less night. Had the universe taken on the gloom that filled my world since my daughter Julie died in an automobile accident?

Who said the world is fair? I'd like to tell him a thing or two, like the story of how little Julie won her battles against Tetrology of Fallot and Down syndrome. At age five, surgery corrected the four defects in her heart. The will to live and the desire for a healthy heart, like everyone else had, carried her through.

Her desire to be like others grew as she did. She wanted to live in a group home, to attend a regular high school, go to movies and sports events and to have a job and a boyfriend. She accomplished these things with the dedicated help of the many staff members at Frazier.

Later, she wanted to get married like her sisters had, have a fairy tale wedding and live with her husband, independent of the group home. She and the man she loved, Robert, convinced family, clergy, group home staff and social workers that two intellectually compromised people could handle marriage and home making. They worked tirelessly over five years to be allowed to make their dream come true.

Unlike most other brides, she had no anxieties. Julie smiled with a face full of happiness and a heart full of love. Her wedding was exquisite. Nobody ever imagined the fate that would befall her exactly one year from her wedding day.

My thoughts blew in the wind that starless night. In total darkness, I could only hear the Palm fronds sway. I felt proud that Julie accomplished all her goals but sad that she and Robert didn't have more time together.

Suddenly the wind blew the clouds away and the moon and twinkling stars popped out. The moon glowed from around the smiling face of a beautiful bride. I recognized every Down syndrome feature in that face and thought how much I love Julie and what she contributed to my life. I have learned from Julie to make the best of everything that comes my way.

Dawn Huntley Spitz

I look up into the night sky and there it is! I would not have believed it possible but it is clearly streaking—no, quietly passing, overhead. What a funny name it has—Sputnik!

If I had known the implications of that new heavenly body, I would have awakened my two young children to see it.

"Look, Pam! Look, Kim! That's a satellite. It will make history as the beginning of the space age. Because of that little bright spot, America will soon have people orbiting the earth in spacecraft. And one day we will see a man walk on the moon."

Then I consider other implications. Will there be a space war? Will we pollute the space around us as we have the earth? And if we do pollute the earth and its environs, will there be any place out there that we can live?

Suddenly, I wish I could be Sputnik—that I could travel far above the earth's surface in high orbit. What would I see? What could I learn?

In a few minutes, Sputnik flies out of sight and I am once again left with the night sky—beautiful, mysterious and studded with stationary stars.

Regrets

◆

A 12 Minute Writing Exercise, Jan. 11, 2008

Judy Cohn

"Your regrets are accepted." Susan read the note over and over. How did he mean that? She wondered. Was he being sarcastic, or did he truly understand why she wouldn't be there?

It had taken her a long time to come to this decision. She hadn't slept well since receiving the invitation last month. At first she was furious at him for sending it. After all that happened, how could he even consider inviting her? True their relationship had changed from acrimony to polite friendship. They'd had some casual dinners together, and took in a movie once in a while. He treated her better as an ex-husband than when they were married. But she still harbored feelings for him, so when the invitation arrived she didn't want to believe it.

He wants me to come to his wedding? Forget about it.

Phyllis Costello

Regrets tie us to the past. They serve no purpose other than to remind us of failure and wrong decisions.

Regrets released, free us to move forward in life without the dead past pulling us down. Learn from past mistakes and decisions, and move on. Otherwise, they are useless.

Every move I made has brought me to the present time and place, and I am delighted to be here.

Life is change. Life is moving forward. Look forward. Create your future.

If you put on the brakes with regrets, life steps in and creates some changes. They are not the kind we choose—illness, divorce, accidents—etc—.

I prefer to love it all without regret and tap-dance thru life.

Virginia Cummings

Regrets are backsliding on intention. We plan, and then use forgetfulness as an easy excuse for not following through with projects, we set for ourselves.

If I hated myself, the one thing I do not like is to have to say, "I forgot."

I regret I didn't take more notes to remind me of places I visited, and folks I befriended. My address book is sadly neglected and unfortunately, it will stay that way.

I have heard there are many ways to help keep the memory working. Vitamins and herbs may help, and being physically active is a good plan.

Mostly though, the articles I have read tell you to keep playing bridge or do crossword puzzles. My choice is cribbage. If I miscount my cards, my opponent husband, is ready to take my points.

I would like to have a better memory and I really regret my poor name recognition syndrome. Friends and neighbors are important to me and apologies flow easily.

I work on remembering. My intention is good. Still the easiest way to give in to the Master Clue that I have slipped is to say, "Hi, I'm Virginia and what's your name?"

Eric H Spitz

Regrets are usually a useless exercise. Sadly, most of us have them and they stay with us for varying lengths of time depending on the severity of the experience or non-experience.

We understand that having regrets serves no positive purpose. Does maturity help us to cast them off? Can we resolve them by taking action now?

One of my regrets is that I never availed myself of an opportunity to spend a summer in summer stock. I had just graduated from Brown and was awaiting the dreaded letter from my draft board shortly after the Korean War. I decided to go home and spend the last weeks or months with my parents in New Rochelle, N.Y.

Likely, I would have been a set-painter or a tree on stage. At best, a part of the ensemble in a musical. I had very little experience acting or singing, save a few small parts in college and high school.

But I might have gained valuable experience working with professional directors and musicians. I might have even gotten a date with a cute, aspiring actress who wanted to experiment with a younger, wide-eyed, frustrated boy-man. I could conceivably have met a fine singing teacher who could have brought out the hidden tenor voice I only found in my fifties. Maybe I could have become another Domingo, that world acclaimed tenor who had so many ladies falling at his feet.

Who am I kidding with this regret?

Shirley Gibson

Regrets are part of all of us. There has been a time in all our lives when we look back and wish we had made a different choice. As long as we don't dwell on them they can prove a playground of choices.

The one regret that comes to mind is when I was about to graduate from high school. I had planned on going to New York to become a fashion model. As my senior year came closer to graduation, my mother checked out a place for me to stay in New York. I would stay at the Barbarason hotel for women.

I would spend many hours dreaming about how my new life away from the farm would be. No more milking the cows, working hours in the vegetable garden, and no more summers spent canning. I was off to New York, a city full of glamour and excitement. I had gone to modeling school in Cincinnati, Ohio in my junior year. I had a photo folio. I would take the train from Cincinnati to New York. I had a girlfriend who was also going with me. I dreamed of my modeling career taking me into movies, leading me to Hollywood. I would find an acting group and take acting lessons. The sky was the limit.

Just before graduating from High School my mother passed away along with my dreams of ever following my career and leaving the farm. I was the oldest. It became my responsibility to take care of my Dad, who had a handicap from a farming accident. There were also three younger sisters who needed me.

I would, from time-to-time, wonder how my life would have been different if only I would have pursued my dreams. Instead I got married and had children. I felt through the years, that being a mother was one of my greatest experiences—no regrets. Perhaps if I had followed my career dream I may have missed out on being a mother.

Years later, being single again, I had an opportunity to move to California. This time I knew it was the right opportunity—with no regrets.

Bill Hinthorn

Regrets are, apparently, a part of everyday life, although I think they're mostly minor regrets. Yes, there's things like the house I sold when the market was down and didn't make the profit I should have, but that and most other things I classify under crying over spilled milk. I probably have more regrets about things I didn't realize—the friend I could have helped, except I didn't know she needed help;

the kind word not said; the failure to take time to understand needs of friends, etc. All the rest I put in the spilled milk category.

The holiday season came and went this year while I was apparently on some other planet. I wouldn't have noticed except for the commercialism and barrage of advertising. I'm not a particularly religious person, but I do regret the constant demand, particularly at the holidays, that we buy things and the relentless effort to part us from our money. But I suppose advertising is here to stay. As much as I regret it, I may as well get used to it. There's an old rhyme that's been around for many years (I don't know who wrote it), and probably says it best:

> *"The codfish lays a thousand eggs, the helpful hen but one;*
> *But the codfish doesn't cackle to tell you what she's done.*
> *And so we scorn the codfish coy, while the helpful hen we prize,*
> *Which indicates to thoughtful minds, it pays to advertise."*

Eleanor Tyus Johnson

Regrets are ideas and opportunities that are not considered important enough to pursue. Then, at a later time, they reoccur as a "maybe I shoulda." I have always believed that when a person makes a choice or decision he makes the best one that he can make at that particular time. There can be no regrets. You did what *you* had to do.

Shortly after childbirth, I couldn't fasten the waistbands on my skirts and pants. Since I knew it would be temporary, I decided to live with it. I took two inches of elastic, sewed a button at one end and made a buttonhole at the other. I did the same thing with a hook and eye combination, stitched all the edges, and "voila", I had *extenders* for the waist-bands of my clothes. My family and friends saw them and asked me to make some for them. I did. Soon I was getting calls from strangers.

Why not put them on the market? I thought. This was 1946 and I had a very young baby. I just didn't have time to do it. I decided I would wait. In 1980 a product called the "EXTENDER" hit the market. It was designed for men and women and was to be used to extend waistbands, necklines and bra connections. Regrets?

I had the opportunity to live on the beach in a charming two-bedroom, two-bath house. When I walked out the front gate I would be in the sand. If I walked a few more feet, I would be in the Pacific Ocean. I had lived there about three years when the owner became ill and wanted to sell the house to me at an unbelievable price. I hadn't decided if I was going to remain in California or return to Chicago, my home, so I hesitated. Regrets?

These two incidents may challenge my belief, but not refute it. Who can say that being a millionaire would have made my life happier or more satisfying? Can you?

Anita Knight

Regrets … are a waste of time and energy. If you allow them into your head they create a tangled web that precludes clear thinking. The 'what ifs' and 'shouldas' don't do anything except get your brain going around in circles, as you try to recreate what you regret when it is already too late.

Just let it all go, unless you store the information for future use, in which case you might do everything right from now on.

Or you might not …

Carol Mann

Dear Carol,

You know, regrets are useless burdens. Whatever happened, happened. Sometimes I just get sick and tired of the mind tapes you play. Yah-da-dah, yah-da-dah.

Do I have your attention? Do you want an example? I'll give you a few. How would you like to keep listening to these replays?

There's the time you were nine years old, and you were supposed to sing a solo in church. Yes, that's right. You choked. Your mother got mad. End of story. When you grew up, you sang leading roles in musicals. You got over it, evidently.

Then there's the time you and your sister had a knockdown, drag out fight over who was going to dry the dishes. You didn't talk to each other for days. Now, you laugh together all the time. I'd say you've learned to value that relationship.

The one that really lights up the marquee is that first marriage. You should have bailed the first year. Your instinct was right. So maybe you waited 10 years too long, but eventually you got the job done. And you're better off.

I have a simple request. Will you please stay in the present? The *now*? It's much more interesting, with many more possibilities than that antique trunk of regrets you dig into. Time to move on.

Love,

Your Conscience

Cheryl McFadden

In my case, the few regrets that I have are the result of things that I didn't do rather than things that I have done. Strangely enough, one of my biggest regrets is that I didn't *ride the canoe* when I had a chance to.

My best friend Chris and I had traveled to Canada with our teen-aged sons, some 15 years ago (a torturously long road trip with or without teenagers in tow), our goal being to see Lake Louise, one of the most spectacular places on earth in my estimation. Shortly after arriving, Chris suggested renting a canoe.

"Sounds like too much work to me, the three of you go ahead," I suggested blithely.

In actuality, it wasn't the rowing that I objected to, but rather the cost. Having already spent quite a bit of money on our 5000 mile odyssey, I was feeling a definite poverty-consciousness and decided to forego what I thought was an unnecessary extravagance. Watching Chris and the two boys glide across the icy blue waters surrounded by snow capped mountains, while alp horns serenaded their journey, I immediately regretted my decision. It may have been only a canoe ride to them but it was a major regret for me.

I have since adopted the personal slogan, *Remember to Ride the Canoe* whenever I am tempted by something I secretly want to do.

Cyndy Muscatel

Regrets are something I dwelled on when I turned 50ish. I think it was my midlife crisis.

I read an article that said women who had given up a career for raising a family regretted that they hadn't followed their muse. Those who'd had the career looked around and saw they'd missed out on having children. No one was happy.

There comes a time, I think, when you realize you can't have it all. The Road not Taken is closed to you, and no matter how wonderful your road as been, you yearn for that grass across the fence that now appears so green. It's a stage like the Terrible Twos, but you grow out of it. You have to go through the rocky valley detour before getting to the other side. It's when you get stuck in the murky mire that you're in trouble. Often people take out their resentment on others. A spouse and family are convenient for that: "I could been a contender. He didn't let me." "No one appreciated how hard I worked."

Regrets produce resentment, and maybe the impetus for change. Dwelling on regrets is non-productive—Creating a new life for yourself is.

Somehow, at 62, I've reached a new stage: *Play with the cards you've been dealt.*

What is is. Seize what you have got and ENJOY each day.

Mary Burton Olson, M.D.

My regrets are regrettable. I regret I have no regrets, instead, only fleeting memories of past regrets and today's regret of having to write this aerobic exercise.

When in my teens, I regretted being 5'10" tall. I towered over every fellow in my high school. Instead of spending time with a boyfriend, I read *War and Peace*, did extra credit algebra problems, practiced the tenses of Latin verbs and after school dissected animals including an earthworm, a starfish, a cat and a dog-fish shark under the tutelage of my biology teacher. I regretted that excelling in every class made me unpopular with my peers. When an adult, I celebrated being tall and academically successful.

I've regretted romances, deaths, and nasty things that have happened to me, but un-regrettably I have gone the way of the optimist who finds a pony at the bottom of every manure pile. I've stunk like a feed lot for awhile, yet in the end I have come out with a pony and a smell like the bouquet of roses around the neck of a winning race horse, no regrets.

I don't regret anything for long. When things look regrettable, I just keep going like the pink rabbit in the battery commercial. I'll write and write and rewrite until blood pours out of my forehead. Eventually I'll get published. No regrets.

Dory Rose

I was hired by the art curator at General Mills to help select art works. After a week of working, I knew that I was really hired to hang picture and measure frames. I was an experienced docent at two art museums so the tour department seemed like a good choice for my talent. I left the art department.

I was given a script, a blue uniform, a tie designed with a big G and a badge with a big G. I was told where to park, where to enter, where to eat. My boss explained that it was important to explain to the guests that there was never a Betty Crocker. She was invented by a public relations firm to describe the perfect housewife who stayed home and baked using General Mills flour. She ate Wheaties and Cheerios.

After an extensive training to ensure my devotion to the company, I was assigned daily tours. I showed them the new kitchens, the offices lined with art, and then they saw a film extolling the virtues of the company. Every Wednesday we were introduced to a new product. At lunchtime we were to eat together to share tour stories.

I thought I followed the rules. One day my boss asked me why I didn't eat lunch with the others. I told her I like to read during lunch hour. She noticed that sometimes I didn't attend the Wednesday meetings. I decided I better follow the rules.

After a few of months, I felt very secure in my role. One day I was guiding a group of school children. I reminded them that there was no Betty Crocker.

"There isn't a Betty Crocker. It is a fantasy, like Santa Claus," I said.

The next day, I was called into my superior's office.

"You are fired."

I didn't argue. I regretted that I didn't punch her in the nose. I was the best tour guide they ever had. I didn't regret a thing. General Mills wasn't for me.

Alan Rosenbluth

Regrets are … wonderful, delightful, comforting, helpful, and enjoyable things…. to be FROM. Just as my Dad was apt to say that, "A hospital is a good place to be FROM."

A regret, to be useful, is something to be anticipated along with options and alternatives in making important decisions, large and small. Will I regret taking this path? What outcomes are apt to make me happy with my choice? What will make me regret it?

On the other hand, what elements will bring happiness (if it turns out as planned)? It is probably more important to concentrate somewhat more on the positive outcomes of the decision in question.

That is, don't over react and be primarily influenced by fear and concern about bad things that might occur. Give much more weight to the joyous, positive possibilities (and your gut instincts) about crucial decisions.

Jeri Schmitz

Regrets are a huge part of my life, which means I often have to say, "I'm sorry." Phrases like, "I won't be able to come", "I have a terrible cold" and "promise you'll ask me next time" seem to roll off my tongue with little feeling. I regret having to say this, but it is true. Since I was twenty-years-old, I have suffered from severe social anxiety disorder.

Not being able to attend parties, weddings, plays, meet the teacher nights at school, sporting events and concerts has been an affliction I compare to leprosy. Except that instead of everyone shunning me, I am the one that avoids human contact.

Of course, when I was twenty there was no name for this malady. I only learned it this past decade, on TV, during a commercial for a pharmaceutical. I perked up when I heard the perfect description of myself followed by the newest cure-all available at the drugstore. I rushed as fast as I could to a new doctor, chosen out of the yellow pages. My own doctor just wouldn't have understood.

The doctor asked, "Have you always been this way?"

"No," I answered truthfully, "as teenager I was the belle of the ball. It was after I got married that I just couldn't mix well in a crowd." I thought back. It happened so suddenly I surprised myself one summer day when I found myself telling my very close friend I could not be in her wedding.

"You're kidding, aren't you?" Janette had recoiled a few feet until my dining room wall caught her and held her up. Right away I regretted that I was responsible for the look on her face.

"No, I am not kidding—I just can't leave the kids for a whole day." I didn't know what else to say. That spur of the moment reply became my standard response for the next fifteen years. When the kids were grown, I switched from one lame excuse to another like, "I am so busy, I have to work at home every day, you know."

Over the years, regrets tapered off, but only because invitations stopped coming. Today my reclusive nature has rendered me a lonely old woman, the stereotypical "witch at the end of the block".

You are probably wondering if the medicine helped. I regret having to say this, but I haven't tried it yet.

Dawn Huntley Spitz

Regrets are non-productive. They do nothing for us but create negative energy, which prevents us from moving on.

Of course, we all have times in our lives when we wish we had done something differently. I have moments when I cringe at my remembered behavior or decisions. But then I remind myself that I was acting within the confines of my experience—influenced by pressures, beliefs, and emotions of my life at the time. The past has led to the point where I am now. I am satisfied with that. How can I be sure that other choices might not have led to a less favorable outcome?

If there is anything to be learned from regrets, it is forgiveness—of others certainly, but especially of ourselves. When we can truly forgive and love ourselves, then hopefully we will no longer live in a way to cause regrets.

Kay Virgiel

Regrets are a lack of following through to buy some shares of *Google* when it was first offered for sale to the public. Details of where it could be purchased were unclear. No brokers' names were mentioned in the public offering. Where was Charles Schwab when I needed him?

I called a bank manager, two CPA's, and finally a local broker on the last day of the public offer. The price had been quoted in the paper as $104.50 per share. The final sale was $20.00 less. Only $84.50!! It seemed a deal. The broker told me a customer had decided against going through with the purchase, which pushed my buttons to do the same. I missed my chance to be a contender! When the *Google Earth* signature flashes across the television screen, I am reminded that I, too, could have been a proud participant. My latest look at the paper informs me *Google* now sells around $476 per share.

Meet the Authors

Cyndy Muscatel is a teacher, mentor, published author, and journalist. She began the Creative Writing Class eight years ago at Mizell Senior Center in Palm Springs, California, to offer the study of craft. A tribute to her skill, participants re-enrolled with each new session. Over the years, a bond of trust and support has inspired her students to keep reaching higher. Ms. Muscatel lives in Rancho Mirage, California, with her husband and their Havanese, Bogey.

The authors, from many parts of the country and world, are full or part time residents of the Coachella Valley in southern California, in and near Palm Springs. They are people from diverse walks of life with one thing in common: the desire to write.

Dolores Carruthers	Judy Cohn
Phyllis Costello	Virginia Cummings
Janet Davidson	Cheryl French
Shirley Gibson	Martin S. Goldberg
Gitta Gorman	Bill Hinthorn
Else Jacobs	Eleanor Johnson
Anita Knight	Carol Mann
Cyndy Muscatel	Cheryl McFadden
Mary Burton Olson, M.D.	Jeanne Packer
Dory Rose	Alan Rosenbluth
Barbara Savage	Jeri Schmitz
Ralph Spencer	Dawn Spitz
Eric H. Spitz	Shell Steckel

Kay Virgiel

Dolores Carruthers, a retired psychotherapist, has written several short stories and started a memoir about an event that changed her life; the death of her son. She and her husband, Bob, recently relocated to Palm Desert from Upstate New York. Their three children and spouses have thoughtfully provided them with a wonderful grandson, and two lovely granddaughters. The Road Taken symbolizes her belief that during our lifetime we travel many different roads, some our choice, some handed to us by fate.

Judy Cohn, a New Jersey native, was an elementary school teacher. Now retired, she and her husband live in Rancho Mirage, California. They have a son, daughter and five grandchildren. An avid sports fan, Judy also enjoys music, art, reading, playing golf and traveling. She writes short fiction, memoirs, and poetry. The Road Taken has led Judy to the joy of writing.

Phyllis Costello is a former hypnotherapist and spiritual advisor who moved to the Coachella Valley and began writing humorous, award-winning fiction about outrageous seniors. When not writing, this mother of four grown children and a grandchild, enjoys her family. Other passions include gourmet cooking, gardening, painting, schmoozing with friends, reading, movies, and, playing with her Bengal cat. To Phyllis, The Road Taken represents a creative and fulfilling life that stretches endlessly.

Virginia Cummings joined the Creative Writing Class with a goal to record stories about herself and family. Her careers as fashion designer, engineer, insurance broker, and now as Great-Grandmother help to inspire stories for her daily writing. Virginia has expanded her tales to short stories. Her entries in The Road Taken show a passion for writing and devotion to putting words on paper.

Janet Davidson began writing short stories and poetry at the age of eleven. She has had several award-winning short stories and poems published. She has written, produced and acted in puppet plays. One of her dramatic one-act plays has been presented several times in Little Theater. A retail manager for over twenty years, Janet gleaned story nuggets conversing with the public and staff members. She has three children, eight grandchildren and four great-grandchildren. The Road Taken is one Janet chose to be her own woman and pursue her dreams.

Cheryl French has been a poet all her life. Her first works were broadcast on radio in 1969. She has been a desert dweller for over 30 years. The Road Taken is her personal journey through life, embracing choices, which determine one's final destination.

Shirley Gibson spent many years doing accounting, bookkeeping and being an office manager, but now is an artist, writer, stain glass maker, bridge player, and likes to write children stories. Shirley writes of magical, mystical times that were once part of childhood dreams, daydreams long forgotten. Her fiction storytelling will tickle the imagination like a magic carpet ride to other worlds, realms and dimensions. The Road Taken is about the people she has met along her chosen path in life with all the twists and turns that help her grow and learn.

Martin S. Goldberg, a semi-retired trial attorney, has completed one book, and is working on two more. Married to Donna for 45 years, he is a member of the Palm Springs Writers Guild, the Distinguished Flying Cross society, the Friars Club, and serves as an Arbitrator deciding medical malpractice claims. His Road Taken is leading him to finding another agent who isn't averse to working with a World War II vintage senior.

Gitta M Gorman was born and educated in Stockholm, Sweden. She worked as an executive secretary for IBM Svenska AB until she retired in 1990 and moved to Palm Springs, California. To learn the writing craft and to share her early memories, she enrolled in Cyndy Muscatel's writing workshop. Gitta's memoir pieces represent for her, The Road Taken. Gitta is a member of the Palm Springs Writers Guild, and an award wining amateur photographer. She is working on a novel.

Bill Hinthorn's first poem was published when he was eight years old and in the third grade. Now a retired engineering designer, he has taken classes in Creative Writing as well as an on-line writing course from UCLA. In the past few years he has published both poetry and short stories, winning a few awards in both categories. His contributions to The Road Taken reflect decades of personal experiences, friendships and observations. It is only a partial journey, however. The road continues.

Else Jacobs is a Native Norwegian who taught elementary school in Norway before moving to the United States to work at the Golden Door as a fitness instructor. She later studied Yoga in India, T'ai Chi and Chigong in China and has taught these disciplines for several years in the Coachella Valley and Europe. A massage therapist and certified reflexologist, she has two sons and three grandchildren. "In the past, I've experienced some resistance in writing about myself, but now I've taken the road of creative writing to bring forth the many interesting experiences life has given me," she says.

Eleanor Tyus Johnson, the middle child of three girls, spent most of her first sixty years in a school setting as a student, teacher and guidance counselor. During these years, she also assumed the roles of wife, mother, aunt, grandmother, great-grandmother, musician, choreographer, nuclear scientist, and statistical analyst. Writing has always been a fun skill for this senior. The Road Taken is the fulfillment of a long time dream.

Anita Knight raised four sons, traveled, sold real estate, and thought it was time to retire before enrolling in Cyndy Muscatel's Creative Writing class and stepping onto The Road Taken.

Her screenplay, Off Your Rocker, won first prize in a Palm Springs Writer's Guild contest, and her short story, The Catch, was published in Writer's Journal Magazine. Anita has completed a novel, two screenplays, several novellas and short stories, as well as a book of poems. She writes daily at the remote Piute Mountain home she shares with three miniature horses, three cats, and three dogs.

Carol Mann has worked in both public education and theater. A published author of fiction, poetry, and nonfiction, she especially enjoys writing short stories. She is a member of the Palm Springs Writers Guild and serves on the board of the National League of American Pen Women, Palm Springs Branch. Leisure time is spent with a good book or a good friend or sampling her husbands handmade chocolate truffles. The Road Taken symbolizes her journey as a writer in progress.

Cheryl McFadden is a member of the Palm Springs Writers Guild and has had several stories published in The Desert Woman. After being employed for 35 years with a prominent securities firm, she took early retirement and began searching for a new career. She soon discovered the author hiding within and leading to The Road Taken. She has one son living in Northern California and a stepson nearby in the desert. The stepson has graciously given her two grandchildren and a great grandchild; the son is still working on that.

Cyndy Muscatel is a journalist and has published many short stories. A former English teacher, she now teaches writing and literature to adults. Besides writing, her passions include her husband, grandchildren, and children, reading, walking, and enjoying the outdoors. The Road Taken symbolizes her continuing quest for knowledge and wisdom, and the expression of what she has learned.

Mary Burton Olson, M.D. collected stories in her pre-retirement days, while living her roles of wife, mother, medical oncologist, and creative cook. In retirement, she embarked on a new road, the avenue of creative writing. Cyndy Muscatels class has given her the tools and the confidence to pursue the craft. Mary has written a whimsical set of stories about food, memoirs for family, and is working on a novel about hereditary breast cancer.

Dory Rose, a Minnesota native, wife and mother of four, has been a devoted docent at the two major museums in Minneapolis. She taught art history classes for the Community Adult Education system, has lectured on Modern Art, and has led tours to art museums worldwide. She also published articles on understanding art. At eight years old, she published an article in a national school magazine. Her writing career continues with stories specializing in humor and surprise twists. Being a part of The Road Taken is a highlight of her time in Palm Springs.

Alan Rosenbluth is a pharmacy professor emeritus and senior softball player who also enjoys yoga and Tai Chi. He lives with his wife, Gwen, in Morgantown, West Virginia. His creative writing journey began in 1991 with a book of stories for his 40th year high school reunion. Six more self-published books of fact and fiction include two devoted to his two grandsons. Taking this road was inevitable, but greatly enhanced by writing classes and workshops.

Barbara J. Savage grew up in Boston, but for many years lived and traveled through Europe and the Middle East. She presently resides in Rancho Mirage with her husband and her toy poodle, Jacques. Her colorful family and great adventures in her travels are the subjects of her humorous stories.

Jeri Schmitz's stories and poems are often tinged with snippets of real life about growing up in Los Angeles, and her teen years in Orange County. Always happiest with pen in hand, her three children counted on her for the absolute best absentee excuse notes in school, while her husband utilized her exper-tise in creating health tip brochures for his medical practice. Honing her writing skills for the past six years, The Road Taken provides an excellent opportunity to showcase life back when the living was easy. Now residing in the Southern California desert, Jeri is employed by a credit reporting information company where her collection letters are becoming legend.

Ralph Spencer, a dual citizen of Canada and the United States, is an ordained minister in the United Church of Canada. Married to Linda Benson, together they have 5 children and four grandchildren. When he turned 60, he took up the sport of golf and plays with gusto, if not accuracy. Writing both prose and fiction has been a life long passion.

Eric H. Spitz, a retired businessman living in Rancho Mirage, California, has written two novels: The Earth Moved about a community dealing with an earth-altering event and Different Animals, which concerns the rehabilitation of prisoners by training service dogs. A graduate of Brown University, Eric has been a long-time performer on both the east and west coasts, playing leading roles in The Sound of Music, South Pacific, Cabaret, and Guys and Dolls. A former softball player, an avid golfer and tennis player, he is grateful for his experience in The Road Taken, which has inspired him to refine his writing skills.

Dawn Huntley Spitz was a member of a professional duo in New York called, The Headliners, for which she created the original material. She is the president of the Palm Springs Writers Guild and a member of the Pen Women. She won the title of Ms. Senior America of Southern California in 2007 as well as the Top Talent Award. She is a singer and former teacher with a degree in music from Skidmore where her poem Where Lilies Grow is set in bronze in a college memorial garden. The Road Taken is the fulfillment of a dream of cooperative creativity and friendship.

Kay Virgiel, former bookstore owner, is a mother of three. Her world travels have led her to the wonders of the Taj Mahal, Topaki Palace, the Van Gogh Museum, the Hermitage, and other inspiring sights. The Road Traveled has been instrumental in her life. A desire to write entertaining fiction is the result.

The End

978-0-595-49916-8
0-595-49916-3

Printed in the United States
120125LV00003B/52-75/P